HOW AUTHORS' MINDS MAKE STORIES

This book explores how the creations of great authors result from the same operations as our everyday counterfactual and hypothetical imaginations, which cognitive scientists refer to as "simulations." Drawing on detailed literary analyses as well as recent research in neuroscience and related fields, Patrick Colm Hogan develops a rigorous theory of the principles governing simulation that goes beyond existing frameworks. He examines the functions and mechanisms of narrative imagination, especially the role of theory of mind, and relates this analysis to narrative universals. In the course of this theoretical discussion, Hogan explores works by Austen, Faulkner, Shakespeare, Racine, Brecht, Kafka, and Calvino. He pays particular attention to the principles and parameters defining an author's narrative idiolect, examining the cognitive and emotional continuities that span an individual author's body of work.

Patrick Colm Hogan is a professor in the Department of English and the programs in Cognitive Science, Comparative Literature and Cultural Studies, and India Studies at the University of Connecticut. He is the author of fifteen books, including *The Mind and Its Stories* and *What Literature Teaches Us about Emotion*, and the editor of *The Cambridge Encyclopedia of the Language Sciences*.

How Authors' Minds Make Stories

PATRICK COLM HOGAN

University of Connecticut

CAMBRIDGE
UNIVERSITY PRESS

32 Avenue of the Americas, New York NY 10013-2473, USA

Cambridge University Press is part of the University of Cambridge.

It furthers the University's mission by disseminating knowledge in the pursuit of education, learning and research at the highest international levels of excellence.

www.cambridge.org
Information on this title: www.cambridge.org/9781107475892

© Patrick Colm Hogan 2013

First published 2013
First paperback edition 2014

A catalogue record for this publication is available from the British Library

Library of Congress Cataloguing in Publication data
Hogan, Patrick Colm.
How authors' minds make stories / Patrick Colm Hogan, University of Connecticut.
pages cm
Includes bibliographical references and index.
ISBN 978-1-107-03440-2 (hardback)
1. Authorship – Psychological aspects.   2. Creation (Literary, artistic, etc.) – Psychological aspects.   3. Creative ability – Psychological aspects.
4. Cognitive science.   I. Title.
PN171.P83H64   2013
808.02019–dc23   2012044091

ISBN 978-1-107-03440-2 Hardback
ISBN 978-1-107-47589-2 Paperback

For Keith and David

Contents

Acknowledgments

An earlier version of part of Chapter 2 was published as "Characters and Their Plots," in *Characters in Fictional Worlds*, ed. Jens Eder, Fotis Jannidis, and Ralf Schneider, *Revisionen* vol. 3 (Berlin: De Gruyter, 2010): 134–154 (www.degruyter.com). An earlier version of part of Chapter 3 appeared as "Narrative Universals, Heroic Tragi-Comedy, and Shakespeare's Political Ambivalence," in *College Literature* 33.1 (2006): 34–66. An earlier version of part of Chapter 4 was presented at the conference on Entrenchment and Plasticity at the University of California, Santa Barbara, April 2011. I am grateful to Vera Tobin for arranging the talk and to the participants – particularly Kay Young – for their comments and questions. Marie-Laure Ryan and Jan-Noël Thon provided challenging comments on an earlier version of part of Chapter 6. Two anonymous readers for Cambridge University Press provided valuable comments and suggestions. Thanks are due to Alison Auch of PETT Fox, Inc., for her careful copyediting of the manuscript and to Robert Swanson for preparing the index. The University of Connecticut Research Foundation generously supported the preparation of the index. I am particularly grateful to Adina Berk for taking interest in the manuscript, finding such able referees, and shepherding the book through the initial stages, and to Eve Mayer for ably and patiently completing the work begun by Adina.

Introduction

From the Universal to the Particular

Readers of Rabindranath Tagore's *My Reminiscences* may recall the importance of the blue manuscript book the author received as a young boy. With the encouragement of his older brother, he wrote and wrote in the book. That practice in written self-expression was the seed from which Tagore's later poetry grew.

In his short story "Exercise-Book," Tagore seems to take up some of this personal history. Uma, the main character, also writes feverishly in a notebook. Indeed, the notebook serves as the major outlet for this character's feelings and thoughts, just as it did for young Rabindranath. But there is a difference. This hero is a girl. Rather than being celebrated by her older brother, she is married off at the age of nine (in keeping with Bengali customs at the time). In her in-laws' home, she is forbidden her notebook. Needless to say, she will never become a great poet.

The story recalls Virginia Woolf's parable of Shakespeare's sister.[1] For our purposes, however, the feminist themes, although deeply important, are secondary. They are secondary for the simple reason that they are the product of something else – the way authors produce particular stories.

To consider this issue more carefully, we need to back up for a moment. Any study of literary narrative may be concerned with a number of different levels of generality. Thus a narrative theorist might be concerned with cross-cultural patterns – narrative universals that cover a wide range of works in different times and places. Alternatively, he or she might wish to focus on more culturally and historically specific patterns. More narrowly still, a theorist might be concerned with the works of one author or a single text.

Much previous work in cognitive theory of narrative has been concerned with general principles, cross-cultural or cultural. It has rarely focused on the particularity of authors or the particularization of individual texts. This is not to say that theorists have not analyzed unique literary works. They have done so extensively. Indeed, the main work of narrative literary analysts, cognitive or otherwise, commonly involves drawing on narratological theory to explicate particular texts. But that is a matter of *criticism*. To say that cognitive *theory* of narrative has tended to ignore particularity is to say something else. It is to say that there has been relatively little theorization of what makes narratives particular, how they come to be specified.

For example, *The Mind and Its Stories* and *Affective Narratology* set out general principles governing literary universals. They isolate broad patterns of genre structure. Moreover, the second book takes up those patterns to interpret individual works. Neither work, however, devotes much attention to the ways in which individual works come about. In keeping with this, they both discuss the structure of romantic tragicomedy. *Affective Narratology* examines a Sanskrit play, *Abhijñānaśākuntalam*, in terms of this structure, but it has little to say about how the author, Kālidāsa, came to produce that work. Put differently, both books isolate some cognitive structures that are very general – narrative prototypes. It is clear that those narrative prototypes play an important role in the production of many particular narratives. It is also clear, however, that specific narratives are not simply the reproduction of the prototypes.[2] For example, *Romeo and Juliet* is not the same as *Abhijñānaśākuntalam*, even though they are both romantic works. If the prototype is nearly the same across cultures, why are the individual works so different? Moreover, why are works by an individual author often recognizable as sharing features distinct from those that either occur cross-culturally or are found elsewhere in the author's historical period or culture?

Here we may return to Tagore. Readers of "Exercise-Book" are likely to feel that the story is very characteristic of its author. Moreover, it is different from other stories of familial separation, both those within Tagore's traditions and those from elsewhere. Even by placing Tagore's story in the context of his memoir, we begin to get some sense of what is going on in the particularization of this work. Tagore had emotionally important experiences of writing as a child. When he composed a story and reflected on his position as a writer, some of those memories were "primed."[3] In other words, some of those memories were partially activated but not necessarily made the object of focal attention. Primed memories help orient our self-conscious processes, pointing our thought and action in certain directions, affecting our inferences and judgments of likelihood, coloring our emotional responses, and so on. The memories in this case involved a child developing capacities as an author through practice with a notebook and through the encouragement of an older sibling.

We cannot precisely reconstruct what happened in Tagore's development of "Exercise-Book." We can, however, infer that there are two key elements in this development. One is the broad, cross-cultural prototype that provides the basic narrative organization of the story. This is the prototype of familial separation and reunion[4] – although here it is in its tragic version of familial separation and unfulfilled longing for reunion. This prototype is combined with the notebook and brother memories to produce the kernel of a story. The prototype subjects the autobiographical memory to a change. Now, the budding writer is separated from his brother. In Bengali families at Tagore's time, such familial separation would not occur normally for boys; however, it did occur normally for girls. Specifically, girls were married at a young age and, once married, were sent to live with their in-laws. This early separation was also a recurring concern in Tagore's stories. Thus this topic was regularly primed for Tagore and available for contributing to the formation of any new story.

When these elements are combined, the result is that Tagore must reimagine his own childhood experiences with a systematic alteration. The alteration is that the writer is now a girl rather than a boy. As he follows out his imagination of this single change, embedded in a familial separation narrative, he finds that the results are devastating. Uma (the girl in the story) will not grow up to be Tagore; society simply does not allow it.

Needless to say, these few observations do not constitute a general account of the generation of particular stories – far from it. They do, however, begin to suggest the rudiments of such an account. Most importantly, they point toward simulation as a central component of particularization. Simulation is our ordinary cognitive process of following out counterfactual or hypothetical trajectories of actions and events in imagination.[5] It is what allows us to get some idea of what it might be like to, say, ask the boss for a raise, before actually doing it. The operation of simulation in literature, first stressed by Oatley ("Why"; see also *Passionate* 171–181), has at least one highly significant consequence. Insofar as literary particularization is a function of simulation, it is continuous with our ordinary cognitive processes of counterfactual thinking. Imagining what Hamlet will do in his meeting with Ophelia is, then, directly comparable to imagining what one's boss will do when one asks for a raise. Thus it is open to the same descriptive precision and the same explanatory rigor. On the one hand, this means that our understanding of counterfactual simulation will contribute to our understanding of literary production. On the other hand, there is a wealth of detail available in literary works, an extensive elaboration or development of simulation that is rarely to be found in ordinary life. This suggests that literature is likely to provide a vast new body of data to enrich and complicate our understanding of quotidian simulation as well. The focus of this book is on literature. In the course of investigating literature, however, it also develops an account of simulation that should be broadly applicable. In other words, the conclusions of the following analyses are only partially confined to authors of literary narratives.

At the same time, not all the conclusions in the following pages are generalizable. What authors do in making stories must be continuous with what we do in ordinary life. But there are differences. Smith's conjectures on the responses of his department head to some request simply do not call for the same plenary, communally shared attention as Shakespeare's *Hamlet*. Both are products of simulation and thus share some features, but they differ significantly as well.

Thus the following analyses, if successful, should contribute to our understanding of simulation generally. As such, they not only draw on, but are part of cognitive research programs in this area. At the same time, they should also contribute to our understanding of the distinctive sorts of simulation that guide literary creation. This too is part of cognitive research, but now in the area of verbal art. This is, presumably, just what a cognitive theory of narrative should do. On the one hand, it should build on and advance our understanding of the structure and operation of the human mind as developed in cognitive science. On the other hand, it should build on and advance our understanding of literary art as developed in narrative theory.

Chapter 1 takes up a fuller account of simulation. It explains simulation's basic principles and explores their evolutionary functions and mechanisms as well as the relationship between simulation and *theory of mind*. (Theory of mind is our capacity to understand other people's mental states – their beliefs, emotions, goals, and so on; see, for example, chapter 3 of Doherty.) The chapter also explores the precise manner in which simulative processes operate. To examine this topic more clearly, it introduces some ideas from neural network theories (or connectionism). These theories model mental processes on brain processes, using a limited architecture of units, connections, and activations that produce changing associative grids. The chapter goes on to argue that an underlying neural network may form the substrate of a system that is more perspicuously described in terms of general rules and representational contents (e.g., images). For example, a grammatical system for plural formation may be manifest in the human brain as sets of neurons, neuronal connections, and activation patterns in circuits of neurons. It may be clearest, however, to express plural formation in terms of a rule operating on a representation (e.g., governing when to add "s"). Recognizing the ultimate intertranslatability of these approaches allows us to shift as needed between, roughly, associative and rule-based accounts of simulation.[6]

It is important to stress here that the distinction between neural-network and rule-based approaches is a matter of general explanatory architecture. It is not a matter of specific theories. The following analyses do not presuppose any particular connectionist or rule-based theories (or theories that combine connectionist networks and rules). Rather, they take up the two broad forms of cognitive architecture used for explanation. Indeed, the rule-based account does not even require that we think of authors as following rules (although, for ease of exposition, subsequent chapters will sometimes adopt this idiom). All that is needed is that we think of authors' activities as (roughly) conforming to rules or principles. That is why the two architectures are ultimately compatible. The underlying architecture is the neural network of the brain, but the psychological and social manifestations of that underlying network are regulated patterns best captured in principles.

Because the theory of simulation can be rather abstract, Chapter 1 goes on to develop and illustrate the central ideas of simulation in relation to literary works. Specifically, it presents within this framework detailed analyses of scenes from William Faulkner's *The Sound and the Fury* and Jane Austen's *Emma*. Faulkner's novel is one of the landmarks of interior monologue and thus a major work of psychologically oriented fiction. In this regard, it is particularly apt for study in this context. The choice of Austen may be less obvious. However, recent critical work (prominently that of Lisa Zunshine) has stressed the nuanced ways in which Austen explores people's understanding of one another's mental states – their theory-of-mind capacities. Thus Faulkner seeks to expose the interiority of characters' minds, whereas Austen examines how we understand – and misunderstand – that interiority when it is not exposed.

Chapter 1 examines story particularization through the more basic but potentially unwieldy architecture of neural networks. Chapter 2 turns to the level of rules and related higher-level cognitive structures, such as prototypes. It does this in order to explore what kinds of cognitive elements contribute to story simulation and what the process of such simulation might be. Specifically, this chapter outlines seven cross-culturally recurring story prototypes. It also presents a two-stage account of literary creation. In this account, one complex of rules governs the development of literary texts, specifically the alteration and specification of prior, more general structures (such as narrative prototypes). Another set of rules or processes governs an author's receptive evaluation of those texts – his or her judgment that the text in question is or is not complete and final (i.e., that it does or does not require further development or revision).

Chapter 2 also distinguishes three types of simulated object – event, character, and scene. The narrative prototypes give the outline of events with some very limited constraints on character and scene. Our simulative capacities, in contrast, seem particularly oriented toward imagining personalities and intentions, thus character. Part of the argument of this chapter, then, is that an author's particularization of a narrative prototype is to a considerable degree the result of simulating a character into the event sequence of the narrative prototype. We have already seen a case of this sort where Tagore appears to have imagined himself as a young writer into the family separation sequence. As this case illustrates, the process is a complex one. As soon as the conjunction of character simulation and prototype occurs, there are changes on both sides. In Tagore's case, the separation becomes a marriage and the character becomes a girl.

Again, readers of Tagore would be likely to see "Exercise-Book" as highly typical of him. By the account presented in Chapters 1 and 2, that is not surprising. One author's emotional and episodic memories – thus his or her propensities for character and scene simulations – are likely to differ from those of other authors. Moreover, the precise clusters of development and evaluation rules will not be the same from author to author. Indeed, even the author's narrative prototypes are likely to vary somewhat from the prototypes of other authors. In other words, there is variation across authors' narrative idiolects – the complexes of memories, rules, prototypes, and other cognitive and affective components that contribute to their creation of individual stories. Thus it becomes crucial to examine simulation in relation to the cognitive operations of particular authors. That is the project of Chapters 3 and 4. In keeping with this change, both chapters signal a shift from the more abstract discussions of Chapters 1 and 2 to the more concrete analyses of the remaining chapters. Although all chapters involve both theoretical development and practical, illustrative analysis, the relative proportion changes at this point.

Chapter 3 sets out to isolate some of the distinctive features of Shakespeare's narrative idiolect insofar as this bears on his production of heroic works. This chapter focuses first of all on story structure, as did Chapters 1 and 2; however, it also pays attention to the emotional and thematic issues that are an important part of narrative production. (The two main purposes of storytelling cross-culturally are to engage an audience emotionally and to communicate some general normative points, usually political or ethical.)[7] Indeed, part of this chapter's argument is that Shakespeare's narrative idiolect exhibits significant continuity in thematic and emotional concerns. Specifically,

Shakespeare's heroic plays repeatedly oppose the usual political tendencies of the genre, systematically cultivating ambivalence. That general orientation, then, has consequences for the more particular development and evaluation principles that give rise to his stories.

Chapter 3 focuses on Shakespeare primarily because of his unparalleled stature in world literature as well as his general familiarity. The stature suggests that his work should reveal successful patterns in the production of verbal art. Familiarity also makes his work particularly suitable for introducing and illustrating the basic ideas contained within the remainder of the book. In addition, Shakespeare has been perhaps the central figure in the recent development of historicism. Many readers are likely to see the cognitive approach of this volume as opposed most sharply to new historicism and cultural studies. In fact, this is a false opposition. Ultimately, cognitive and historical/cultural studies require one another. Nonetheless, given the current critical context, it seems particularly apt to introduce cognitive principles in relation to the primary interpretive target of new historicism, thereby conveying the relevance of the former even for texts closely associated with the latter.

Chapter 3 necessarily treats differences among Shakespeare's heroic narratives, even while concentrating on the shared idiolectal features. However, it does not isolate any particular pattern in those differences. Chapter 4 turns to the issue of how one may speak of an author's narrative skills as developing or advancing across a canon of works, as opposed to degenerating or falling into repetition. To explore this topic, the chapter further articulates the idea of a rule in narrative idiolect. Specifically, it presents an account of cognitive operations according to which rules may repeatedly be revised to include variables or parameters. These parameters interact with one another such that the setting of one parameter leads to cascades of changes in other parameters. For example, a character may be understood as a cluster of principles. Changing the sex parameter in one of those principles is likely to have consequences in a range of others – as well as associated principles bearing on, for example, events and scenes. Returning again to Tagore's story, we can see the shift from Tagore to Uma as involving, first of all, a shift in a character parameter from male to female. This leads to a number of other shifts in parameters. For example, the brother stops being unequivocally supportive of the sibling's literary creativity. This is not simply accidental; it is connected with the differing norms that bear on the activities of boys and girls. Moreover, the places where the child spends his or her time change, as does his or her general authority in the household.

To examine these issues more thoroughly, Chapter 4 takes up Jean Racine's secular tragedies, which are all partially romantic. As explained in the chapter, Racine is a particularly apt figure for this examination as his writings are strictly segregated from one another in a known chronological sequence. This allows us to isolate changes in his narrative particularization across time. In addition, Racine's work has been seminal for the development of modern critical theory. This is shown not only by Roland Barthes's early work, *On Racine*, but also by Barthes's explanation of the critical importance of "Racine's contemporaneity." Specifically, Barthes explains that at the time of his book, Racine's "work [had] been involved in every critical effort of some importance made in France." He lists "sociological ... psychoanalytical ... biographical ... [and] phenomenological" schools, concluding that Racine is the only "French author ... to have made all the new languages of the century converge upon himself" (viii).

The sorts of simulation examined up to this point are largely a matter of character simulation within a prototypical event sequence. This is appropriate, as it seems to be the key manner in which stories are particularized. There are, however, other elements that enter into the specification of plots. The importance of theme suggests that one such element is argument. Authors are sometimes guided in their imagination of a story by what are in effect patterns of reasoning. Indeed, there are suggestions of this in all the authors considered thus far, although it may not be the most prominent feature in any of these cases. Such reasoning is most often integrated with narrative prototypes and character simulations. Nonetheless, it is important to consider particularization through argument separately.

Authors' use of ideas in simulation is not confined to abstract sequences of reasoning in the service of thematic goals. Authors often take up another sort of ideational process in simulation as well, and not necessarily for thematic ends. This is modeling. A model may come in the form of a precursor text (as in Joyce's use of *The Odyssey* in *Ulysses*). It may be found in characters and events shared by a tradition, as when an Indian author imagines two human lovers on the basis of the paradigmatic spiritual lovers, Kṛṣṇa and Rādhā. It may be found in a broader metaphor, as when an author makes a character blind to express some lack of insight. In each case, what we have is not a logical argument but rather some sort of analogy – an analogy that may or may not be used self-consciously. A model may contribute to the communication of themes (in the manner of an argument). However, it may also enhance the emotional effects of the work, orient the simulation of character, or guide the development of events.

Chapter 5 takes up these two modes of particularization. It begins by discussing how, cognitively, the simulation of a work may be guided by an argument. It then examines Bertolt Brecht's "teaching piece," *Die Maßnahme* (*The*

Measures Taken), "one of Brecht's greatest achievements" (43), "his first real masterpiece," according to Martin Esslin. The chapter considers what Brecht's argument is in this play and how it shaped his particularization of the story – or, rather, how initial ideas interacted with narrative prototypes and other factors to produce a simultaneous particularization of the story and of the argument. Brecht is an obvious choice for this analysis given his teaching project in this and other plays. Moreover, *Die Maßnahme* is framed as a criminal investigation, and its embedded narrative is sacrificial in structure. This adds two other genres to those examined in the course of this book, following the heroic (in Shakespeare) and romantic (in Racine) – thus four of the seven recurring cross-cultural prototypes (as isolated in *Affective Narratology*).[8]

Chapter 5 goes on to consider the operation of cognitive models (or metaphors) in guiding simulation. It first treats this process in general and then examines Kafka's *Die Verwandlung* (*The Metamorphosis*), also a sacrificial structure. It may seem that Kafka's novella is entirely straightforward in this regard, drawing on a single, simple model – Gregor is an insect. In fact, this case is interesting precisely because there are several levels of modeling that interact with one another in the process of simulation to produce the final story. An awareness of these models helps clarify the complex operation of modeling in the specification of stories. At the same time, it helps reveal nuances of this particular work that may not otherwise be apparent.

The remaining chapters continue the focus on individual narratives. Now, however, they turn to discourse. The standard distinction between story and discourse is between what is told in the narrative (the story) and how it is told (the discourse). The story is the events, characters, and scenes as they may be supposed to exist "really" in the narrative. Discourse is divided into two components. One concerns the facts of the story world – what is reported, when it is reported, and how it is reported. This is called *plot*. Plot varies the selection, construal, and organization of story information. For example, in a detective narrative, readers commonly learn about the crime first and only learn about the motive for the crime at the end. Thus the plot begins with the crime and ends with the motive. The story, however, begins with the motive and proceeds from there to the crime. The second component of discourse does not concern what the reader is told, but (roughly) who does the telling. For example, in the case of a criminal trial, different witnesses may be tellers of more or less the same story events. Moreover, their narratives will be embedded in an encompassing narrative – for example, a juror's recollection of the trial. This part of discourse is called *narration*.

Chapter 6 and the Afterword concern the ways in which authors particularize narratives through emplotment (the formation of plot) and narrative

voice. Discourse is most widely treated in prose fiction. Emplotment, however, is clearly an important feature of drama as well. In order to consider that
somewhat underexamined mode, Chapter 6 takes up a play, *Hamlet*. It considers the ways in which the selection and ordering of story information serve
to particularize the work and how this particularization serves emotional and
thematic purposes. It also considers the ways in which emplotment manifests
recurring principles of an author's narrative idiolect.

The other aspect of discourse, narration, is highly diverse and complex.
Theorists devote entire books to a single aspect of narration, and it is not
possible to give anything approaching a full treatment of this topic in a book
devoted primarily to the story component of narrative. The Afterword takes
up some selected topics in the particularization of narration, stressing the
simulation of narrative voice. A central argument is that narrational simulation involves exactly the same processes as story simulation but with different
initial prototypes. A prototypical scene of storytelling is not the same as a
prototypical romance, but the imaginative processes are the same in both
cases.

The simulation of narrative voice is, in fact, general and applies to academic
discourse as much as it applies to fiction. The main difference is that the simulation of a narrative voice in academic discourse is commonly concealed. In
acknowledgment of this, the Afterword takes up the issue of narration not
only at the level of argument but also at the level of narration itself, presenting the analysis through a series of different voices. These voices are drawn
in part from the authors whose works are the topics of this chapter – William
Faulkner and Italo Calvino. Moreover, the specific issue addressed in relation to these authors is how one might treat the artificial quality of narration.
Telling a story commonly involves, for example, concealing key information
until the end. It is, as such, a highly contrived process. Authors may deal with
that contrivance in different ways. The options of naturalizing or explaining
the artifice versus flaunting it are neatly exemplified by Faulkner's *Light in
August* and Calvino's *Se una Notte d'Inverno un Viaggiatore*.

Thus, in addition to presenting a general account of narrative simulation,
the different chapters of this book examine patterns found across an author's
works or within an individual narrative in order to isolate the principles that
generate particular stories. In other words, as the title of the book indicates,
they explore some aspects of how authors' minds work. These chapters repeatedly stress that the principles at issue are implicit, thus they are not something
that authors are able to introspect. One result of this is that authors' testimo-
nials are largely irrelevant to the following analyses. It is crucial to emphasize
this at the outset. To be concerned with how authors' minds make stories

is not to be concerned with how authors imagine that their minds work or how they explain creativity when pressed to answer a question in an interview. An author might believe that he or she has been inspired by God (as may have been the case with Harriet Beecher Stowe and *Uncle Tom's Cabin* [see Kazan x]). This hardly means that a cognitive approach to literary particularization – in Stowe's case, often the particularization of a familial separation and reunion prototype – should make reference to divine providence.

The point is not by any means peculiar to authors; it applies across the board. Consider, for example, ordinary speech. As we will discuss in Chapter 1, fluent adult English speakers are very bad at stating the principles that govern English grammar. In their speech, they conform to the principles. But if they seek to formulate those principles on the basis of introspection, they fail. If anything, this failure is more likely in the case of complex activities, such as the writing of plays and novels. In keeping with this, Bargh points out that there is "a deep and fundamental dissociation between conscious awareness and the mental processes responsible for one's behavior; many of the wellsprings of behavior appear to be opaque to conscious access" (560). Indeed, the point even applies to goal pursuit. Bargh cites research showing "that social and interpersonal goals can ... be activated automatically through external means.... The individual then pursues that goal in the subsequent situation, but without consciously intending to or being aware of doing so" (562).

Such failures of introspection are what make cognitive analysis necessary. If the principles of grammar or other human activities were intuitively obvious, there would be no need for cognitive research. Linguistics, psychology, literary theory, and a host of other disciplines would be eliminated as their findings would be self-evident without research. Unfortunately, that is not the case. The following chapters, then, are an attempt to respond to this human deficit in intuitive self-understanding with respect to literary particularization – that is, with respect to how authors' minds make stories.

1

Simulation

Imagining Fictional Worlds in Faulkner and Austen

From Deictic Shift to Simulation

Among cognitively oriented literary critics and theorists, one common way of thinking about the imagination of fictional story worlds is in terms of deictic shift.[1] The general idea of deictic shift is straightforward. Most words have a constant referent (individual object to which they refer, in the case of proper nouns) or extension (set of objects to which they refer, in the case of common nouns). Thus *Barack Obama* refers to one person, regardless of whether Barack Obama says it or Gérard Genette says it. So too *kneecaps* refers to the same set of objects no matter who uses the word. In contrast, some words have different referents depending on the user. If Barack Obama says "I," then he is referring to Barack Obama. But if Genette says "I," he is referring to someone other than Obama. Parallel points hold for "here," "you," "now," and so forth. In fiction, the idea of deictic shift is, superficially, the same. Just as Obama might speak about "here and now" referring to Washington, D.C., in 2012, so too he might shift and refer to Dublin in June 1904 if he is reading *Ulysses.*

There are at least two problems with this view of fiction, however. The first is that it is not clear what, if anything, it would explain, if true. Suppose one's writing or reading fiction involves a deictic shift to the story world. Does that tell us anything about the creation or experience of fiction?

Second, we do not literally engage in a deictic shift to fiction, because we are never actually in the fictional world. Of course, a reader might be fully engaged by the fictional world, so entranced as to in effect fleetingly believe that he or she is in that world.[2] But, in fact, he or she is always in the real world. If Obama begins to read *Ulysses* in Washington in 2012, his "here and now" are still Washington in 2012, not Dublin in 1904. By way of contrast, we might think of David Lewis's possible worlds ontology. Lewis was faced with the problem of what defined the reality of a world. He maintained that reality is indexical – roughly, deictic. The real world is whatever world is the here-and-now world of the speaker. Thus from the world of Obama, the world of *Ulysses* is a possible, but nonactual world. In contrast, for a character in *Ulysses* – say, Leopold Bloom – the world of Obama is a mere nonactual, possible world. (Again, this is according to Lewis's account.) When one reads *Ulysses* in the library, one is, then, encountering a nonactual, possible world. If one deictically shifted to that world, then (in the Lewis account) the world of that library, the world where *Ulysses* is a book, and so on, would simply fade to insubstantiality, a mere wispy possibility.

Of course, one might take deictic shift to mean merely that we interpret a character's "here" as referring to the world of the character, not our world. In other words, we do the same thing that we do when reading a letter (i.e., we take the letter writer's "here" to refer to where he or she was when writing). Indeed, we do the same thing that we do when we understand someone who says, "Come here," and we take him or her to be asking us to come where they are. This is entirely true.[3] But it only restates the problem of what it means for there to be a fictional "here." In other words, it returns us to the problem of what it would explain and how such an explanation would operate.

None of this is to say that deictic shift theory lacks value. In fact, it has considerable value in, for example, isolating types of deixis (see Jeffries and McIntyre 157 and citations). These may guide our attentional orientation in reading texts. In consequence, they may lead us to expand and add nuance to our interpretations. The same point holds for text world theory, with which deictic shift theory is often conjoined. The difficulty is that, even when these two theories are integrated, it is not clear what they tell us as theories (as opposed to how they may guide us heuristically). Jeffries and McIntyre concisely formulate what is at stake: "Conceiving of a text world involves taking up a cognitive position within it. Deictic shift theory specifies how we do this" (161). Again, however, neither point seems true. We do not seem to take up a specifically deictic cognitive position within the "text world." Moreover, if we did, deictic shift theory does not say how we do such a thing; it merely states again that we do it. Indeed, even the precise nature of a text world is not fully clear. As Jeffries and McIntyre note, deictic shift theory "suggests that readers are able to feel involved in a narrative by experiencing vicariously events from a viewpoint other than their own" (158). But that is not an explanation. It is, rather, a statement of what needs to be explained.

A more promising approach to fictional story worlds has been proposed by Keith Oatley. Oatley argues that fiction is a form of simulation ("Why" 101).[4] We know that human minds do engage in simulation. Indeed, we know that people engage in simulation in understanding certain aspects of language (see Matlock). Moreover, there is a long tradition of connecting something like simulation with literary creation and response. Specifically, simulation is closely related to what literary writers refer to as "imagination."[5] Of course, this relation points to a potential problem with the idea of simulation – it is somewhat vague. In consequence, it is difficult to say just how effective it is as an explanatory concept. Clearly, it is important to flesh out the concept of simulation, to define its properties and principles, before we can use it to account for literary production or reception. Before trying to articulate its properties in a rigorous, theoretical manner, however, we should get some intuitive understanding of simulation and why it is appealing in a cognitive context.

One basic principle of cognitive science of literature and the arts is that the human brain operates using the same structures and processes regardless of whether it is addressing literature or life. Of course, it is in principle possible that there is a special set of cognitive and affective structures and processes that apply only to literature (just as there may be neurocognitive elements that are specialized for language). But the default presumption – in keeping with basic principles of simplicity in theory formation – is that the neurocognitive architecture is constant. It seems clear that, however we operationalize the concept (i.e., however we fix it relative to observable phenomena), simulation is something that we do in ordinary life. Perhaps we currently lack a fully adequate explanation, or even a fully adequate description, of simulation. Nonetheless, it is valuable to identify the literary process of imagination with the quotidian process of simulation. This is valuable because it follows the general cognitive scientific principle of understanding specialized, literary operations as cases of broader, quotidian operations. More simply put, we now have only one process to describe and explain (simulation), not two (simulation and literary imagination).

More exactly, in ordinary life, we are continually engaging in rich conjectures about future possibilities. For example, suppose Smith is asked by a publisher to suggest people who might endorse a book. She thinks of various people in the field and then tries to envision how they would react to the book and how they would react to being approached by an editor about endorsing the book. This involves fairly concrete imaginations. For example, she might think that a particular person would find the request odd. In consequence, she may recommend a way of framing the request that fosters a more favorable response. Of course, all simulations are not that complicated. Suppose it is early spring and Jones is going out on a boat. When getting ready to go, he imagines what the weather might be like – that is, he simulates the experience. This simulation leads him to recognize that it may be windy or sunny or both. As a result, he brings a jacket and a hat with a brim.

It seems very likely that this is the same sort of process that occurs in the creation and (in a more limited way) the reception of literary works. As Suzanne Keen notes, citing empirical research, literary authors often view themselves as describing what characters do autonomously (126–127).[6] This seems to be a prime case of simulation, precisely the sort of thing Smith was doing in envisioning how various scholars might respond when approached about endorsing a book. Of course, there are differences as well, but the differences seem to be a matter of detail, vividness, and potential emotional engagement for an audience. The differences do not seem to be a matter of basic principles.

For example, suppose Smith is thinking about trying to cross a river with a wagon – or, to use a more current example, a station wagon. She is likely to envision the possibility that the car will be flooded, turned over, struck by unseen debris, and so on. This is precisely what William Faulkner envisioned in describing the Bundrens' attempt to cross the river in *As I Lay Dying*. In Faulkner's case, the simulation was far more detailed, far more explicit and elaborately developed. If Smith imagines the wagon being overturned, that may be enough to produce an aversive emotional response that will prevent her from trying to pass through the river. In that case, there is no reason for her to dwell on the details and to elaborate on the various contingencies. Faulkner's purpose was to produce an effective story for readers who are not considering whether to cross a river, but who are reading a novel. This is, of course, a difference. However, it is a difference in purpose or motivation, not in the fundamental cognitive processes involved. That identity of processes is, again, the first reason why the idea of fiction as simulation is valuable – it reduces what we have to explain.

Indeed, the parallel goes beyond the sort of causal development just suggested. In describing Smith's decision about the wagon, we noted that she may have an aversive response to the simulation. Alternatively, she may more fully envision a successful passage across the river, with consequent feelings of relief and pride, fostering an inclination to continue forward. In either case, the key point is that the simulation operates emotionally. It is, of course, not only emotional. There are necessarily inferential elements. However, in everyday life, our simulation of possible outcomes is crucially bound up with emotional effects. Simulation has consequences because it engages motivational systems.

Consider again the example of book endorsements. When Smith thinks about the press approaching some important cognitive scientist for an endorsement, she might imagine the scientist responding with irritation at the presumptuousness of the request. This produces an aversive feeling of shame ("How could I be so presumptuous as to ask such a renowned figure?").

At the same time, Smith is likely to imagine the pride she would feel from this person's endorsement of the book. These produce contradictory motivational tendencies. Smith may then try to reconcile the contradictory feelings by formulating a way of framing the request that would be less likely to produce a shame-provoking refusal. We might say that Smith's imagination produces an emotional profile for the complex of possible outcomes. That profile may be more or less strongly aversive or attractive for particular choices. Initially Smith may feel very shy of the distinguished scientist. With a more cautiously worded request for an endorsement and thus a revised imagination of the situation, however, the emotional profile is likely to change. As a result, she may be inclined to carry through with the request rather than refraining from it. In other words, the profile may become more positive toward that action, although it is still ambivalent.

Much the same point holds for the simulations involved in literary creation. These too are designed to produce emotional profiles, with varying degrees of ambivalence related to preferred and dispreferred outcomes.[7] These profiles may have consequences for real-world behavior, most obviously in the case of didactic works that encourage particular ethical or political choices and actions. Nonetheless, in literary works, the emotional engagement of the simulation is commonly an end in itself (even if it is not the only end or goal of the work). Again, this is a difference. But it is a difference within a more encompassing continuity, as both quotidian and literary simulation operate centrally to produce emotional responses in the context of multiple possibilities and preferred outcomes.

It is worth noting that this stress on simulation has some significant theoretical implications. For example, much of the discussion of verbal art has concerned the differences between fiction and nonfiction.[8] The present analysis suggests that, in a cognitive account, the most crucial issue may not be whether a particular narrative is claimed to be true. Rather, the most crucial issue may be the degree to which a given narrative involves simulation that goes beyond experience and logical inference. In other words, the most important opposition may not be fiction/fact, but simulation/report – although, of course, a fictional work will allow greater scope for simulation than a work more or less constrained by claims of truth.

Although the following discussions will not stress the point, it is important to note also that simulation is not confined to the author. Typically, the author chooses to represent one simulation and elaborates on it extensively. The reader, however, must continually engage in the more ordinary, limited simulation of other possible outcomes. In elaborating on the Bundrens' river crossing, Faulkner largely confines his account to what "really happened" in the story world. But the reader must continually be aware – thus must to some degree simulate – other possibilities. For example, the reader must understand that Cash could die when the wagon is overturned. That understanding is consequential for reader response primarily insofar as the reader to some degree simulates Cash's death. That simulation, however limited in time and detail, is what allows the reader to feel relief on discovering that Cash is alive. Indeed, the reader's simulation is presupposed by the author's simulation, for the author incorporates a receptive simulation in anticipating the emotional effect of the work. For example, Faulkner's simulation almost certainly assumed the reader's imagination of Cash's death and relief on learning that Cash is alive.

The Function-Approximating Mechanisms of Simulation

The importance of emotional response simulation is bound up with evolutionary development. Specifically, it seems clear that our capacity for simulation is adaptive.[9] That does not mean that it is perfect. Natural selection operates on mechanisms that approximate functions, not on functions as such. In other words, genetic traits result in certain bodily processes. When there are different traits in a population, one such process may be more likely to lead to reproduction than another. The process is the mechanism; the reasons for the advantage in reproduction constitute the function. For example, certain sorts of perceptual and amygdala-based sensitivity may predispose some people to fear slithering things. That process of fear includes an enhanced inclination to notice, avoid, and escape from slithering things. Since snakes are often deadly, this process should, on the whole, mean that the people with the initial sensitivity are more likely to flee snakes, thus more likely to live, thus more likely to produce offspring. Therefore the function is, roughly, living by avoiding poisonous bites. It is clear, however, that the mechanism (fear of slithering things) leads us to avoid some things that are not deadly (non-poisonous snakes). Thus the mechanism and the function are not identical. However, the mechanism approximates the function adequately. In consequence, it will lead to the spread of the genetic tendency in the population.

It seems clear that simulation approximates an adaptive function. The fact that it is itself a mechanism rather than a function explains why our simulations can fail – indeed, often do fail. The crucial point is simply that having the capacity for simulation confers a reproductive advantage that we would not have if we lacked the ability to simulate. In other words, it is not to say our simulative capacities are the best possible ones or that they succeed in every individual case – just that they succeed often enough to be advantageous.

Conversely, for simulation to have functional consequences in evolution, it must operate through mechanisms. These mechanisms are what we find when we delve into the nature of simulation.

The first property required of simulation is that it be accurate more frequently than chance, as chance is presumably what would govern the benefits and harms of our actions if we lacked simulative capacities. This is straightforward. The difficult part is spelling out how this happens. It is well established that in simulation, many of the same areas of the brain are activated as when we interact with the real world. For example, when we imagine seeing a cup, to some extent our brains behave as if we were actually seeing a cup (see Kosslyn 295, 301, and 325). Moreover, our spatial and temporal relations and actional orientations in simulation are closely related to those that occur in reality. Speaking of a reader's simulation, Zwaan points out, "Ongoing events are more active in the reader's mind than past events, physically close objects are more active than more distant objects," and so on (534–535). Decety and Stevens explain that "simulation of movement ... activates the same cortical and subcortical structures that mediate motor execution" (14–15). Indeed, when simulating a motion, it becomes more difficult to engage in contrary motions (such as moving one's arm in the opposite direction; see Decety and Stevens 5). This parallelism between actual and hypothetical experience is undoubtedly an important factor in the accuracy of our simulations. The mere fact that our imagination of a cup in certain respects mimics our actual experience of a cup presumably makes it much more likely that the simulation is accurate.

Here, then, two questions arise. One concerns differences between simulation and interaction with the real world – that is, perception or action. The other concerns the precise nature of what is activated.

As to the first question, there are fairly clear functional/evolutionary requirements that bear on the difference between simulation and real perception or action. First, we should not confuse our simulations with real current conditions. If we did, we would not be simulating possible future conditions, but hallucinating real current conditions. Second, related to this, our "action readiness" (as Frijda would call it [see 69–71]) must in some way be dissociated from our responses to the simulated scenarios. As cognitive scientists like to say, our simulations take place "off-line." To speak of dissociation may be slightly misleading as it could suggest that our simulations take place in periods of leisure. That may be true, as in the case of potential book endorsers mentioned earlier in the chapter. However, as Decety and Stevens explain, "Simulation of movement precedes and plans for upcoming physical action" (14). Even in a critical situation, one may simulate different scenarios (e.g., if one is in some dangerous situation while driving). In those cases too one needs to dissociate action tendencies from simulation, even if only for a moment as one considers the alternatives ("Should I swerve left or is there a car in that lane?").

At the same time, this dissociation cannot result from the absence of motivational arousal. As already noted, emotional engagement is critical for the evolutionary operation of simulation. If simulation proceeded without emotion system activation, then it could not motivate action in one direction rather than another. That would render it inconsequential. The adaptive function of simulation is no less dependent on emotional response than it is on relative accuracy or temporary dissociation from action. If Jones did not find the imagination of being cold aversive, he would not be motivated to bring a jacket on his boating trip. If Smith did not find some ways of approaching the famous cognitive scientist to be embarrassing, she would not engage in the effort to think of other ways that would not be embarrassing.

It should be clear that all the properties we have been considering are found in literature just as they are found in ordinary simulation. Indeed, they occur with increased intensity. Literature develops the defining characteristics of simulation by enhancing the vividness and detail of our imaginations (a point explored by Scarry). It also extends the dissociation of action from simulation, since we are most often unnaturally immobile when reading or watching a movie or play (as Norman Holland stresses in *Literature*). Finally, it elaborates and intensifies our emotional experiences (as many theorists have indicated – for example, the classical Sanskrit aestheticians, such as Abhinavagupta).[10]

But here a further issue arises. We take enjoyment out of watching painful experiences that produce aversive emotions, such as fear and sorrow. This seems to go against the entire operation of our emotion systems. It makes sense that we would enjoy comedies where we experience pleasurable emotions, such as mirth and empathic love. But why do we enjoy tragedy and melodrama?

This problem is in fact much broader than literary cases. The same issues arise in our response to simulation generally. Indeed, it is crucial to the adaptive function of simulation that it not be confined to pleasurable outcomes. If Jones simply stops simulating the discomfort of a windy period on the boat, then he will not bring a jacket. If one avoids simulating potential dangers while driving, then one may engage in risky behavior. Of course, sometimes this happens, but often it does not happen. Often, we do envision aversive outcomes and thus avoid them.

One possible explanation for this phenomenon may be suggested by research on compassion. When we experience compassion for other people, our reward system is activated (see Kim and colleagues; our reward system is involved in seeking and in pleasure or reward anticipation [see Kupfermann, Kandel, and Iversen 1010]). Our response to our own future selves is in some ways a version of compassion, for we are in a sense empathizing with the emotional responses that we may have at some other time. It is plausible, then, that there is some reward-system activation in all forms of emotionally consequential simulation. Nonetheless, it seems very likely that on the whole, this will be stronger in the case of other people than in the case of ourselves. In other words, in most cases, our reward-system response to other people's suffering will be stronger than any such response to our own simulated suffering – or, more precisely, the reward-system response may be the same, but the countervailing aversive emotions will be stronger with respect to ourselves. (The exceptions here involve strong attachment relations – thus one's spouse, children, parents, and so on.)

Here, of course, we have a difference between literature and much real-world simulation. Certainly, one's real-world simulation involves imagining other people. In the evolutionarily crucial cases, however, it centrally involves simulating oneself as well. This is not the case in fiction – at least not for readers. Thus we would expect the reward-system activations of empathy to be particularly strong in literature (or the aversive emotional response to be less strong than in real life, with its egocentric involvements).

We may summarize many of the preceding points by saying that simulation has adaptive functions only to the degree that it is not the same as fantasy. We may define fantasy as a form of imagining in which one entertains only pleasurable outcomes. This can occur if one simply breaks off the imagination at the point of aversive feeling, as just suggested. But it can also occur if one simply produces happy outcomes. Here we come to another crucial feature of simulation. Our imagination of our own and other people's actions may be guided by our own wishes or by something else. It is crucial that we are able to imagine actions and outcomes consistent with our wishes. These are what yield our preferences. We would never have goals if we did not imagine happiness conditions, feel joy in considering them, and envision ways of pursuing them. However, this remains at the level of fantasy. When we begin to make concrete *plans* – plotting algorithmic sequences of actions that will lead from our current state to the desired state – we need to be able to distinguish between what is possible and what is not possible, what is dangerous and what is not dangerous, and so on.[11] This is the function of simulation, as opposed to fantasy.

In these cases too there are properties that simulation must have if it is to operate adaptively. Specifically, it will do so only if it is not guided simply by our wishes (even though the final goal state is defined by those wishes). In other words, it has to be guided, in some sense, by the objects or conditions one is considering. This is precisely the sort of thing that we find among authors who say that they are reporting what their characters do autonomously rather than simply making up what their characters do (see Keen 126–127) – or, alternatively, among readers who say that an author has made a mistake in judging what a character would do.[12]

In short, simulation involves a response to imagined scenarios that is directly parallel to our response to comparable real scenarios, sharing emotional engagement or motivation system arousal. However, it dissociates that arousal from actional outcomes. The emotional response is in part a matter of the ordinary emotions (e.g., fear in the face of danger). However, it is also affected by the engagement of reward systems, which produce pleasure in imagining even aversive outcomes, perhaps primarily through compassion. This is not to say that all imaginations are the same in terms of pleasure and aversion. Fantasy involves imagining solely pleasurable outcomes and is crucial for defining goals and motivating goal pursuit. In contrast, simulation is constrained by real-world principles, such as the propensities and inclinations of other agents. Such constrained imagination of how people will act or conditions will develop is, of course, imperfect. However, it is accurate enough to make simulation more reliable than chance (thus far more reliable than fantasy) and therefore adaptive.

Levels, Means, Processes, and Topics of Simulation

We may now turn to the second question introduced at the beginning of the previous section, the question about what is activated in simulation. To consider this issue more clearly, it is useful to consider some simple cases of simulation. Suppose Doe imagines having a coffee in a coffeehouse. This may be a quick, spontaneous imagination, the purpose of which is simply to determine if she wants a ceramic or paper cup. If she simulates those choices, then she has certain standard versions of a cup in mind. Thus she is guided by a prototype. Alternatively, the imagination of ceramic and paper cups could be embedded in a larger simulation of going to a coffee shop. Doe envisions entering and walking toward the counter, placing herself in line behind anyone else who is waiting, telling the waitperson what she wants, paying, and waiting to take the coffee away. In this way, Doe's simulation is guided by a script or standard set of actions and expectations in specific social circumstances (here, a coffee shop). (For a fuller discussion of prototypes, see Rosch and citations; on scripts, see Schank and citations.)

These two examples suggest that one important set of guides for simulation comprises the various structures of semantic memory. When we simulate objects, we tend to follow prototypes. When we simulate actions, we often follow scripts – at least if the actions are limited and routine enough to be covered by scripts. The same point applies to circumstances. In referring the "the counter" at the coffeehouse, I indicated that I had in mind a prototype for the coffee shop itself, or even in mentioning that Doe enters. (In contrast with, say, an outdoor coffee stand.) In addition to material conditions (objects, places, etc.) and trajectories of action, we also rely on semantic structures in simulations of people. For instance, Doe might envision various things a waitperson might say or do if she asks certain questions ("What do you think of adding double whipped cream to a Grande Mocha Frappuccino?"). These would be different from what she might imagine her cardiologist saying in response to the same questions.

Note that the coffee-buying simulation is organized by reference to goal pursuit. That is, it unfolds in relation to Doe's aim of getting coffee. However, it is not a fantasy, guided solely by Doe's desires. For example, it involves the possibility of a line. This may be an important factor if Doe is deciding whether she has time to stop for coffee.

This simulation of a possible line may seem to indicate a potential difficulty with the preceding account of simulation in terms of semantic structures. The possibility of a line is not precisely part of what we refer to as the script for getting coffee. However, that is not a problem because, in a standard cognitive account of semantic memory, the structures at issue include not only "dictionary," or meaning information, but also "encyclopedia" information – thus, for example, probabilistic features. In this way, the likelihood of a line can easily be part of semantic memory for coffeehouses and for getting coffee.

This does, however, point us toward another issue. We do not learn about lines by learning the *meaning* of "coffeehouse." Rather, we learn about lines by having experiences in particular coffeehouses (or in establishments with a similar structure, such as fast-food outlets or ice-cream parlors). This is important because it indicates that even the general structures by which we generate simulations derive ultimately from episodic (that is, particular) memories. Indeed, not only the probabilistic inflections of scripts, but scripts, as well as prototypes, themselves presumably derive from episodic memories. (On "semantic memory" as "the residue of many episodes," see Baddeley "What" 11.) Thus my prototype for a coffeehouse – including the length of the line waiting to order – will be slightly different from that of anyone else. This is because that prototype derives from a particular set of memories of coffeehouses, memories that necessarily differ somewhat from those of other people (even though the process of averaging across cases to produce the prototype will make our prototypes much more similar than the original experiences).[13]

These references to episodic memories help us understand how we simulate not only general or unfamiliar circumstances, trajectories of action, and people but also particular circumstances, trajectories of action, and people. (The latter is obviously a key concern in determining how we make particular stories.) To a great extent, particularizing simulations rely on particular, episodic memories. When Buckland simulates how his wife will respond when he asks her something, he does not rely on general information about, say, college professors (assuming she is a college professor). Rather, he relies primarily on memories that involve her relating to similar issues in similar circumstances. For example, if he sees that she is working on an essay, he may envision a negative response to a suggestion of going out for coffee; this simulation is likely to be based on past experiences. Conversely, if he sees that she is correcting student papers, then he may be likely to simulate a more positive reaction, if she has wished to go out for coffee when correcting papers in the past.[14]

Thus we may distinguish two levels of simulation – general and particular. These are associated with distinct, although interrelated means of simulation – semantic and episodic memory. Of course, semantic and episodic elements are not fully segregated. In any complex simulation, real or literary, we make use of both. Perhaps even more important, both are integrated with emotional memory. Emotional memories are implicit memories that revive the relevant emotions when they are activated (see LeDoux *Emotional*). Thus an emotional memory of a frightening event will, when stirred, give rise to fear.

The most obvious process through which semantic and episodic memories operate is direct induction (explicit or implicit). In similar situations in the past, Jones has done q, thus we expect him to do q now. However, simulation may also be driven by models. Suppose Jones is an important cognitive scientist. Suppose, further, that Smith does not know Jones well and that her prototype for important cognitive scientists does not really tell her anything about their likely response to requests for endorsements. Moreover, Smith happens to have had relevant but contradictory experiences with two or three individual professors with different degrees of importance in different disciplines. Smith may use these individual professors as models to generate simulations of how Jones may react to her request. The difference between direct induction and modeling is perhaps more clearly consequential when the models are semantic rather than episodic. For example, a racist writer might draw on the semantic prototype for an animal to model his or her simulation of someone from a racial out-group.

Finally, we may distinguish three topics of simulation – material conditions, action trajectories, and agents (usually persons). The material conditions tend to be the simplest, since induction is fairly straightforward for these – at least in most cases of simulation in ordinary life or in literature. The action trajectories tend to be set in their broad outlines by motivational goals (e.g., wanting coffee), whereas sub-sequences are often driven by scripts or prototypical expectations, themselves derived from episodic memories (e.g., regarding lines at a coffee shop). This means that our imagination of persons is often the most complex and most significant topic of simulation. This is not always the case, but typically our most difficult and consequential simulations involve locating particular people in conditions and trajectories, then focusing on their responses. Thus, in a wide range of our simulations, it is likely that our greatest interest will be in the thoughts, feelings, and behavior of the people involved, and that we will gauge the development and specification of the action trajectory by reference to those people. Put simply, the causal motor for the trajectory of actions is not, so to speak, the actions themselves but rather the predispositions and active motivations of the persons engaged in the actions. To see this, one need only contrast human action with impersonal events of nature, such as an apple falling from a tree.

In keeping with this, cognitive scientists have particularly stressed simulation in relation to theory of mind, our ability to understand other people's thoughts, interests, feelings, and so forth. Initially, there were two opposed views on the nature of theory of mind. One group argued that theory of mind is truly theory-like. Thus it was thought to involve inference based on theoretical premises. For another group, it involved a more spontaneous process of imagining oneself in the position of the other person – thus simulating his or her attitudes, thoughts, or experiences.[15] Now it is commonly recognized that both inference and simulation are important for understanding other people's minds (see, for example, Doherty 48). My preference is for a two-stage model in which we begin with spontaneous simulation but then may modulate or suppress such simulation by reference to inferential processes. Such inferential processes would not occur automatically. Rather, they would have to be triggered by some sort of task conflict – contradictory simulations, an inability to simulate, caution in a particular case due to the delicacy of the situation (e.g., the gravity of possible errors), or other factors.[16] For example, as we will discuss in Chapter 2, one such factor is out-group categorization of the target, which is to say, the person we would have been simulating.

Here as elsewhere, literature is fundamentally the same.[17] Specifically, particular literary narratives are complex simulations produced by semantic and episodic memory. Either sort of memory may be used directly (as when a character derives from a person in real life) or as a model. Indeed, the use of modeling may be particularly widespread in literary simulation. Moreover, we find the same topics. The material conditions are the scene. Persons appear as characters. Finally, action trajectories appear as the story structure.

Indeed, in literature too, persons – thus, characters – seem to play the central role in guiding the particularization of a story. In principle, any component could be stressed. It seems, however, to be most commonly the case that the action trajectory is defined by broad narrative prototypes. These yield the fantasy structure of the story, thus the main goals (such as romantic union). They also set out the standard obstacles or inhibitions that frustrate goal achievement (and produce emotional intensification).[18] Prototypes are to some extent particularized by the material conditions (including the cultural conditions) in which they come to be located. For example, there will be differences between a romantic comedy placed among poor immigrants in New York in the twentieth century and among the ruling elite in India in the fourth century. However, part of the argument of Chapter 2 will be that an even more emotionally and causally consequential element of narrative particularization involves the nature of the characters.

Particularizing simulation should not be understood simply as the insertion of material conditions and characters into a prototype, however. There are variants of prototypes. There are separable narrative motifs (e.g., the quest) that may be added to different prototypes. Prototypes may be combined, either in whole (as when a heroic plot incorporates a romantic plot) or in part (as when the communal sin and punishment sequence from the sacrificial narrative becomes part of the heroic plot).[19] Moreover, authors are never confined to prototypes. They can range beyond them to other patterns of events and other causal sequences.

A Theoretical Note on Rules and Networks

Clearly, the integration of all these elements into a coherent, particular simulation is a tremendously complex process. We have a sense now of what goes into simulation, what properties simulation has, and how those bear on literature. We are, however, far from having an algorithmic account of how the integration of various contributory materials might proceed. In cognitive science, there are two common ways of formulating algorithms for cognitive processes. The first is a matter of rules and rule interaction. The second is a matter of neural networks.

Neural networks are most often simplified versions of brain operation. They comprise neuron-like units and connections among these units. Sequences of connections among units define circuits. Each unit has some level of activation. When that level of activation reaches a certain threshold, then the unit fires. The activation of the firing unit is then sent along the connection to the next unit in the circuit. Connections may be excitatory or inhibitory. If the connection is excitatory, then the recipient unit receives some degree of excitation. If it reaches the firing threshold, then it fires too. If the connection is inhibitory, then the recipient unit loses activation. Any given unit will receive inputs from many afferent (or incoming) units and convey output to many efferent (or outgoing, thus recipient) units. Finally, connections between units may differ in strength. Thus some connections may be weak, and others may be strong. A weak connection will produce less effect on a recipient unit than will a strong connection. For example, if unit A fires and has a strong connection to unit B, then the activation added to B may be, say, 1; in consequence, the firing of A may lead to the firing of B. In contrast, if the connection from A to B is weak, then the activation added to B may be only .5. Then unit B may require activation from other afferent units before it reaches threshold and fires.

The advantage of a neural network is that it roughly follows the operation of the human brain. In this way, every cognitive operation must ultimately be understood in terms of something along the lines of a neural network. Moreover, conceiving of mental operations in terms of neural networks fosters recognition of the ways in which those operations involve multiple processes that may be parallel, interactive, or cyclical – not merely singular and serial. Nonetheless, neural networks are often more complex than the phenomena we are seeking to explain. In this way, they tend to give rise to Bonini's paradox, whereby the explanation is less comprehensible than the initial enigma (see Dawson 49). This is why rules are valuable. Generally, we can approximate the processes of neural-network activation by abstracting some rules. Rules have the advantage of being readily comprehensible and much easier to apply. Their disadvantage is that they tend to misrepresent the processes involved as more regularized, simple (e.g., serial), and clear-cut than they are. For the most part, the discussions in the following pages will develop descriptive and explanatory principles in terms of rules rather than neural networks. However, it is important to have some sense of the general operation of network architecture, just as it is important to have a sense of the relation of both to the empirically isolated properties of the human brain.

First, to illustrate the difference between rules and neural networks, we might take a simple performance task. Linguists sometimes test children's language capacities with made-up words, such as *blit*, *gerb*, and *nooch*. In a test of this sort, a researcher might take something, explain that it is a *nooch*, and then give three of them to the child and keep one for himself or herself. Then he or she may ask the child to complete a sentence such as, "I have one nooch, but you have three ..." The child enthusiastically responds "Nooches!" correctly adding *əz* – not *s* or simply *z* (as he or she would if the word were *blit* or *gerb*). In neural-network terms, the input *nooch* and some input along the lines of "plural" interact in a complex network. For example, *nooch* may activate a set of words including, for example, *know*, *loot*, *bunch* – thus words similar to *nooch*. *Plural* may activate some set of units linked to word endings particularly (although it may also activate internal vowel units, perhaps producing an occasional response of *neech* as the plural of *nooch*, as in *goose/geese*). Thus it would add activation to, say, *bunch*, *lunch*, and *pooch*. It would also activate the regular plural markers, *s*, *z*, and *əz*. The activation of *lunch*, *bunch*, and *pooch* would, in turn, further activate *əz* (the plural of lunch, etc.), which would inhibit activation of *s* and *z* (since words that pluralize with *əz* do not pluralize with *s* or *z*). The result of these (and other) interacting activation circuits would be *nooches* (or, perhaps once in a while, the error *neech*).[20]

Such a neural-network account is obviously very complex. Indeed, it would be even more complex than this indicates, since we left out a number of factors, such as connection strengths (e.g., the connection between *nooch* and *pooch* may be stronger than that between *nooch* and *lunch*). In contrast, a rule-based account would simply say the following: The child accesses the rule, "Form regular plurals by adding *əz* to sibilants, *z* to voiced nonsibilants, and *s* to unvoiced nonsibilants."

Again, in the following pages, we will generally treat literary particularization in terms of rules; the complexity of neural networks only increases with more complex processes of simulation. There are, however, cases for which neural networks are in some ways more transparent than rules. This is in part because our understanding of rule operation tends to presuppose serial and localized processing, which is to say, cognitive operation that treats one aspect of a problem at a time, proceeding in a clearly defined series of steps. In contrast, network operation is parallel and distributed, which is to say, it takes up different aspects of a problem and treats them simultaneously (that is, in parallel). There are cases, such as probabilistic processes, where the latter are likely to be more intuitive and illuminating. For example, I might have begun this sentence with either "for example" (as I did) or "for instance."

Presumably both received activation, but the former received more. It seems unlikely that we could formulate a convincing rule to explain how I did use one but might have used the other. In a case such as this, a network account would be more illuminating, as it is more clearly probabilistic and involves partial activations of alternatives. Even in these cases, however, we are likely to treat some aspects of the analysis in terms of rules or related generalizations. For instance, we might formulate a rule such as "vary the use of 'for example' and 'for instance'" to explain the shift in the current sentence. Thus we are likely to use "hybrid" accounts (as it is usually put), part network based and part rule based.

In the following sections, we will consider two brief examples of simulation in terms of neural networks, or parallel distributed processing (PDP) systems, partially hybridized with rule-like generalizations. This should help clarify how the complex processes of simulation may be understood more algorithmically. The first example, drawn from William Faulkner's *The Sound and the Fury*, considers the use of a model for particularizing some limited aspects of the story. The second example is drawn from Jane Austen's *Emma*. It treats theory of mind simulation within the story world of the novel.

The Resurrection of Quentin Compson

The final chapters of *The Sound and the Fury* take up, among other things, the characters of Quentin Compson and her uncle, Jason. Quentin is the illegitimate daughter of Caddy Compson. She is living with her grandmother and uncle, and her uncle rigorously keeps her away from her mother. Caddy is sending money for Quentin, which Jason steals in keeping with his generally cruel treatment of the girl. Quentin herself is rebellious and somewhat wild. At this point in the story, Quentin seems to be pregnant. This is signaled by her great need for money and her unwillingness to explain that need. In a neural-network account of Faulkner's simulation, this is unsurprising. There is presumably a strong associative connection between Quentin and Caddy, a strong connection between Caddy and premarital pregnancy, and a strong connection between wild behavior and pregnancy, making pregnancy an obvious narrative possibility for Quentin.

Once she becomes pregnant, two clear simulative possibilities arise, both based in obvious ways on other (past) cases, thus episodic memories (biographical or literary): having the child or having an abortion. In a PDP account, there should be strong connections with both. Moreover, there should be connections between having the child and suffering familial cruelty. Because there is already cruelty from Jason toward Quentin, this idea (or unit) of "suffering familial cruelty" should receive particular activation.[21] This should occur at two levels: in the author's simulation of future possibilities for Quentin and in the author's simulation of Quentin's simulation of future possibilities. (It should also occur at the author's tacit simulation of the reader's simulations of both.) In more rule-like terms, then, we could say that the author would expect Jason to be cruel if he discovers the pregnancy, and the author would envision that Quentin has the same expectation. The latter simulation would be strongly aversive for Quentin. Thus one would expect her emotional response to incline toward an abortion. The abortion would, of course, be connected with the acquisition of money as well as some sort of escape from Jason's supervision, perhaps along with travel to another city where she would not be recognized. The difficulty – indeed, near impossibility – of an abortion in these circumstances is likely to activate a further possibility at each level (i.e., for Quentin, for the author, and for the reader). That further possibility is suicide. (We do not need to spell all this out in connectionist terms, since it is fairly straightforward.)

The options thus far are fairly schematic. Most basically, Faulkner needs to choose which option he will have Caddy follow and how he will develop that option so as to further particularize it. It is obvious that some circumstances have direct, causal impact on this specification. For example, because the events take place in 1928, Quentin can escape in a car. Had the story taken place in 1828, that would not have been possible. For our purposes, however, a potentially more interesting impact comes from features of the circumstances that cannot have a direct, causal impact but nonetheless guide the particularization of the narrative. Specifically, at least some of Faulkner's choices in this case are bound up with a model derived from his specification of the circumstances of the events.

Faulkner locates the culminating events of the story on Easter Sunday. This temporal determination has the effect of partially activating or priming a number of religious stories relating to Jesus's resurrection. In particular, it is likely to prime the story of how Jesus's tomb was discovered to be empty on the morning of Easter Sunday and of the appearance of an angel. It would prime this story first of all for Faulkner, but also for many of Faulkner's readers. This priming would in turn send activation to various possible elements of Faulkner's ongoing simulation of his own novel. In the context of Quentin's dilemma it is likely to activate her disappearance and the discovery of her absence. It may also activate the idea that she could be dead. This is particularly likely because there is already some activation of the possibility for suicide, an activation enhanced by the fact that Quentin shares the name of a relative who did commit suicide earlier in the book. At the same time, the model of Easter would be likely to activate unexpected, continuing life, since the mourners going to Jesus's tomb expect to find a corpse but instead find that Jesus is again alive.

This is all precisely what we do find in the novel. In other words, it seems clear that the biblical account of the resurrection has in part guided Faulkner's particularization of the somewhat schematic story about a young woman pregnant out of wedlock.[22] We can get some sense of how particular elements arose by considering how the biblical story would activate the girl's escape, then the manner of her escape and its discovery, then some incidentals bearing on that escape.

It is Easter morning and Jason has demanded that Quentin be brought down to breakfast. This is fitting in a network account as the general conditions of family life at that time and place would activate such a demand for an absent family member. Ordinary scripts activate knocking at Quentin's door and calling to her. When she does not answer, Mrs. Compson (Quentin's grandmother) begins to worry that she has committed suicide. This is consistent with her melodramatic imagination, but it is plausible from the perspective of the reader as well, because the possibility of suicide has been partially activated by association with the illegitimate pregnancy.

When they enter the room, it is, of course, empty – like Jesus's tomb on the first Easter. Indeed, it is very much like a tomb, not in its appearance, but in its emotional resonances. The description of the room is suffused with the despair that has pervaded Quentin's life until that morning. The "hopeless efforts to feminize it" remind us of her separation from her mother and the emotional distance of her family. The link with "anonymity" and "assignation houses" suggests her relations with men that led to the (apparent) pregnancy. The only qualification of its "hopeless" (Faulkner *The Sound and the Fury* 219) quality comes from the blossoming tree at Quentin's window, the tree that allowed her to escape.

In all these cases, we see the ways in which the various precedent developments in the story converge to activate particular associations, leading to further specifications. We have already noted the ways in which the story and the biblical model both suggest an anticipation of death and the discovery of an empty room in addition to the overall emotional tone of the room. Other details result from such convergences as well. The soiled undergarment (pointed out by the narrator) is something we would expect in a teenager's room. But of the many things that could be named in the room, it appears in part because it is given additional activation by the biblical story of Jesus's tomb, with "the linen clothes lying" there (John 20:5, in the King James version). The tree is a prototypical means of escape down a window, but it is

further activated by its association with the cross, often referred to as a tree
(see, for example, The Acts of the Apostles 5:30, 10:39, and 13:29). In keeping
with Christian tradition, the blossoms change the tree or cross from an image
of death to a symbol of the rebirth that follows crucifixion, the blossoms having no literal connection with the escape.

   PDP networks may operate, so to speak, privately or publicly. In other
words, they may be solely a matter of the author's particularization of the
story, or they may, at least potentially, also bear on the simulations engaged in
by the reader. If they are of the former sort, then we would generally say that
they are relevant to biographical criticism and the psychology of creativity.
However, we would probably not say that they are relevant to interpretation.
In contrast, publicly available network connections are generally important
for interpretation as well. Thus they have potential bearing on the emotional
resonances and thematic implications of the work.

   The model of Jesus's resurrection is clearly publicly available and therefore interpretively and responsively relevant to the work. Of course, it is not
entirely evident how we should interpret the connection here. Clearly, there
is some degree of irony. I myself, however, find it difficult to view the irony
as entirely – or even primarily – at the expense of Quentin. Rather, there is
something both sympathetic and elevating in this assimilation of a young
girl, unmarried and pregnant, to Jesus. Moreover, in its biblical version, this
story centrally involves Mary Magdalene, which tends to forge further network links – links connecting her promiscuity with Quentin's and thus perhaps extending her spiritual elevation to Quentin as well. In keeping with
this, when the reader comes to this section of Faulkner's novel, he or she
may form new associations between Quentin on the one hand, and Jesus
and Mary Magdalene on the other, as well as new emotional responses to
Quentin. It seems that both might at least lead us to question the negative
view critics often take of Quentin (e.g., Bleikasten's idea that she is "Caddy's
debased copy" 75).

Simulating Minds: Elements of Emma Woodhouse's Neural Network

The advantage of the Faulkner example is that it concerns a real, human
mind – that of Faulkner. But the disadvantage is the same. We can infer that
Faulkner's simulation of a particular scene was guided by particular network
associations. Faulkner's mind, however, existed beyond the text itself – the
text on which we are basing our inferences. In contrast, we might draw examples from a mind within a literary work. This has the advantage that we do not
have to worry about an inaccessible, extratextual person. But its disadvantage

is the same. It concerns a fiction, which may not be the best illustration of the way real human minds work.

The obvious response to the second dilemma is to choose an author who is particularly admired for his or her representation of the human mind, in whatever aspect we are considering. Jane Austen has been celebrated in recent years for giving us uniquely perceptive and nuanced representations of theory of mind inference. The point seems accurate, even if particular claims are sometimes exaggerated.[23] In this way, she provides an excellent resource for illustrating theory of mind simulation. Moreover, she does this in a way that highlights the value of analysis in terms of parallel and distributed processing.

Emma Woodhouse has the notion that she is an expert matchmaker. Part of being a good matchmaker is, presumably, having a good sense of what people actually want. Thus part of being a good matchmaker is having good theory of mind skills – or at least, knowing the limits of one's theory of mind skills. Emma makes perfectly comprehensible errors in her simulation of other people's thoughts and preferences. However, she lacks adequate self-criticism, thus adequate modulation of spontaneous simulations. As a result, she acts on her mind-reading errors.

For much of the novel, Emma is particularly concerned with forming a match for her friend, Harriet Smith. Emma begins by dissuading Harriet from marrying Robert Martin, a humble but admirable man who clearly would be a good husband for Harriet. In his place, Emma fosters Harriet's interest in the shallow social climber, Mr. Elton. Harriet is bitterly disappointed when it is revealed that Elton has no interest in her whatsoever. One might have hoped that Emma would desist from matchmaking after this fiasco, but she does not.

Here, we may consider two dialogues that nicely illustrate the operation of theory of mind simulation. The first is particularly revealing because it results in a stark misunderstanding between Emma and Harriet. There is an apparently eligible young man who has recently joined the circle of Emma's and Harriet's acquaintances, Mr. Frank Churchill. Emma begins to imagine that he and Harriet would make a good match. The feeling is only enhanced when Harriet has a misadventure in which she is (unreasonably) frightened by some Gypsies. Mr. Churchill happens on the place and escorts her away from the importunate group. The misunderstanding between Emma and Harriet occurs in the following chapter.

Harriet has kept a series of remembrances from Mr. Elton. She now brings them to Emma in order to burn them. This obviously gives a high degree of activation to ideas of Mr. Elton – for Emma, for Harriet, and for the reader.

The recent appearance of Frank Churchill may give him some degree of activation as well, although that is less certain. To assure that he is well in mind for the reader, Austen ends the ceremony of burning with Emma thinking of Frank Churchill and his possible alliance with Harriet. In the story world, this thought precedes the first dialogue by many days. In the narration, however, it precedes that dialogue by only sentences. Because of this proximity, Frank is highly activated for the reader, as is Mr. Elton.

The conversation begins by Emma mentioning marriage. Harriet declares, "I shall never marry." Given the events in the novel to this point, it is easy to simulate Emma's simulation of Harriet. Roughly, there are two possibilities. One, the less likely, is that this is a resolution on Harriet's part. Earlier in the novel, Emma had made such a resolution for herself. This is important because she wavered briefly in that resolution only in favor of Frank Churchill. She subsequently changed her mind on Frank, thus making way for Harriet. However, it is important that this presumably weak connection nonetheless gives some activation to the idea of Frank Churchill in relation to a vow of celibacy.

The other way of understanding Harriet's declaration is as an expectation, presumably an expectation expressing despair. Clearly, the idea of Harriet despairing over marriage would activate most directly the idea of Mr. Elton. This is true for both Emma and for the reader (since we have just read about Harriet's mementos of Mr. Elton).

Showing surprising good sense, Emma actually asks if the reason is Mr. Elton. Harriet declares that it surely is not, going on to explain that the man in question is "so superior to Mr. Elton!" (712). This suggests that Harriet's declaration may indeed proceed from despair. However, it proceeds from despair over someone other than Mr. Elton.

Emma's neural network (simulated by Austen and by the reader) presumably has already activated ideas of Frank Churchill in connection with her hopes for Harriet and also in connection with her own resolution and brief wavering about marriage. Moreover, there is presumably a limited range of men who are likely to receive any activation as potential suitors. Conversely, ideas about a number of men (and women) would be inhibited in the neural network rather than primed. For example, it would take quite a bit of activation for Emma to wonder if Harriet is perhaps referring to Mr. Woodhouse (Emma's father) or to a married man, such as Mr. Weston (Frank's father). Of course, the reader and Emma are both likely to connect Harriet with the idea of Robert Martin. Thus memories of Martin are likely to have some activation as well. The reader may briefly wonder if – or hope that – Harriet has come to her senses and realized that she should have married the estimable Martin.

She then might see him as unattainable because of her previous rejection of him. This is not a likely result in Emma's neural network, however, since "superior" for Emma is inseparable from class standing. Thus, however admirable Martin may be, and however petty Mr. Elton might be, Emma could not consider Martin superior to Elton. Indeed, the activation of superiority undoubtedly inhibits the activation of thoughts about Martin, while increasing the activation of thoughts about Frank.

Emma goes on to test her hypothesis about Frank, but indirectly. Specifically, she asks if the man in question is "too greatly [Harriet's] superior in situation" (712). Harriet confesses that this is so. This leads the reader to reject any idea that it is Martin (through the modulation part of the two-part process in theory of mind simulation). Harriet goes on to mention the "gratitude" she owes him. In the context of other activations, this only serves to further activate memories of the episode with the Gypsies, thus further activating thoughts of Frank. She goes on to speak of her "inexpressible obligation," her "wretchedness before" he came, and so on (712).

We may infer that something else enters at this point. Both Emma and Austen's readers are likely to have a prototype of male valor in rescuing damsels in distress. This involves physical intervention at a moment of physical danger. Thus the mention of her rescue by a "noble" figure for whom Harriet feels "wonder" (712) is likely to prime thoughts of a knight in shining armor riding in to slay the dragon. This fits Frank's behavior toward the Gypsies, in whom he struck "terror" (709).

An astute reader will, of course, note that the name Frank Churchill has not in fact been mentioned. However, it has received such a high degree of contextual activation that a more casual reader may be forgiven for thinking that it has been mentioned. This is because it is very difficult for us to recall what has actually been said in a conversation. It is much easier to recall whatever is salient in a conversation, which is to say, whatever is highly activated. Something actually said may have low salience, whereas something not said at all may have very high salience.[24] Indeed, subsequently Harriet and Emma discuss this very conversation. Harriet explains that she never had Frank Churchill in mind at all and that Emma completely misunderstood her. Emma says, "I could almost assert that you had *named* Mr. Frank Churchill" (742). The misunderstanding illustrates very well how theory of mind simulation, as well as memory, operate.

Indeed, the reader's likely misunderstanding is no less illustrative. In this second conversation, Harriet explains that the "service" done by her beloved was not the manly rescue from the Gypsies, but "a much more precious circumstance," specifically, "Mr. Knightley's coming and asking me to dance" when she had been publicly humiliated by Mr. Elton at a ball (742). There were indeed hints of this, which most readers are unlikely to have remarked. The most notable is that Harriet describes her rescue as "a change" from "perfect misery to perfect happiness" in "one moment" (712). This would be an entirely inaccurate account of her experience with Frank and the Gypsies. When Harriet entered Emma's home on Frank's arm, she was "white and frightened" and immediately fainted (708). This is clearly not "perfect happiness." Readers have undoubtedly not forgotten Harriet's entrance. However, this part of the scene has not been primed. As such, the contradiction with her description ("perfect happiness") is unlikely to modulate a reader's spontaneous simulation of Harriet's thoughts. (Of course, readers will differ to some extent in their simulations. Some may have noticed the discrepancy initially. Others may have produced different spontaneous simulations. Something along the preceding lines, however, is likely to be a common response.)

We can also understand how Harriet's misunderstanding of Emma developed. Unexposed to Emma's fancies about a match with Frank, Harriet has no reason to prime Frank initially as a possible romantic option. Moreover, in the context of romance, the incident with the Gypsies would receive little activation in her mind. In other words, there was simply no activation spread from the discussion of marriage to the episode with the Gypsies. Finally, the mention of Mr. Elton would be most likely to prime any incident in which the beloved and Mr. Elton were involved. Thus, given the events at the ball, we would expect Harriet's simulation of Emma to automatically activate Mr. Knightley. There was no impediment or contradiction that would lead her to modify this spontaneous simulation.

Finally, it is important to note that, in expertly representing Emma's and Harriet's simulations, Austen also expertly manipulates our own simulations. I say this in part because I myself was fooled into simulating Harriet's preference for Frank. I did always recognize that this could prove false because I was aware of the nonmention of his name. However, fooling the reader does not show any particular expertise. What shows expertise is Austen's ability to make the conversation and the misunderstanding wholly plausible in retrospect. Moreover, she does this for our spontaneous simulation at the time of the second conversation. We can go back to the initial conversation and ferret out the hints that show Harriet had Knightley in mind all along, but at least my response to Harriet's later explanation – and I suspect that of most readers – is immediate acceptance. We do not need to scrutinize the text to make sense of the apparent change. In part, this is the result of the suspicion (due to the name being unmentioned), but it is in part the result of Austen preparing the reader's neural network. We may not explicitly remember that Harriet's return with Frank was not "perfect happiness." Nonetheless, Austen has connected Harriet's association to Frank with fainting and fright, while linking Harriet's association to Mr. Knightley with dancing, "very complete enjoyment," and "a continual course of smiles" (706). Indeed, it is important that these are emotional connections, probably bound up – through mirroring responses – with our own emotional memory systems.[25] These memories may have been partially activated even during the initial conversation, perhaps producing a mild distrust of Emma's and our own tendency to associate Harriet with Frank. In any case, Harriet's final explanation about her meaning is likely to feel right to a reader because of the activation of these memories during the second conversation. In short, Austen has prepared the reader's neural network in such a way as to make the conclusion plausible for our simulation of both characters (Emma and Harriet) and their situation.

Conclusion

Simulation is a spontaneous process of imagining trajectories of action in relation to circumstances. It is different from fantasy in that it is constrained by presumed facts about the world, prominently including presumed facts about the propensities, capacities, understanding, and other mental and physical properties of the agents involved. As such, the simulation of other minds is a crucial part of such imagination. Spontaneous simulation may be modulated by inferential processes when there is some conflict or difficulty that interrupts spontaneous simulation. Simulation is parallel to direct experience of the real world. However, it is dissociated from direct links to motor systems and thus actional outcomes. At the same time, simulation remains closely interconnected with emotion systems. Indeed, the evolutionary function of simulation is contingent on this emotional link. Simulation allows us to avoid (some) risks and pursue (some) opportunities that we would otherwise have ignored. It does this by allowing us to imagine and respond emotionally to possible events rather than waiting for the real events. The constraints on simulation (as opposed to fantasy) are crucial for this evolutionary function also. It is those constraints that make our simulations more accurate than chance. Nonetheless, the emotional operation of simulation leads us to ask why someone would ever engage in simulation of aversive events. In connection with this, it appears that we experience some reward-system satisfaction as a result of simulation. All these properties are part of simulations both in ordinary life and in literary creation and reception. The primary difference is that literary simulations intensify the developments and specifications found in quotidian simulations. Thus literary simulations tend to be more vivid and detailed, more emotionally compelling, and so on.

Processes of both quotidian and literary simulation may be treated by reference to two mental architectures. The probabilistic, parallel, and distributed nature of simulation is best captured in terms of neural networks (ultimately in terms of the brain). However, this architecture is often too complex to treat perspicuously. Moreover, when followed rigorously, it leaves out the experiential or "phenomenological" component of mental life. This appears to be better captured by rules and related structures. The latter include semantic structures, such as scripts and prototypes, as well as episodic memories and goals or motivations. Ultimately, all rule-level structures are simplifications of underlying neural networks. In some cases, it is valuable to use a hybrid account, with both rules and networks. This will often be the case in discussing literary works, where we need the rules to clarify the complexity of simulation but the networks to add nuance, thus restoring some of that complexity.

Ideally, a simulation-based account of the particularization and development of a literary narrative will also contribute to our interpretation of that narrative and to our emotional and evaluative response. *The Sound and the Fury* and *Emma* provide examples. In the case of the former, a complex literary incident (drawn from the Bible) seems to have served as a model in Faulkner's development of Quentin's escape from her family. Through the associations of a PDP network, a range of elements – including components of this biblical model, events up to that point in the novel, and common social beliefs and practices – converged to produce many details of the scene. Because of its public nature, this model also suggests interpretive and evaluative points. In the case of *Emma*, Austen simulated characters mistakenly simulating the minds of other characters. At the same time, she simulated the reader's simulation of this process at two points. First, she simulated the reader's simulation of the initial misunderstanding between Harriet and Emma. Second, she simulated the reader's simulation of the subsequent discovery and mutual understanding. These complex simulations guided Austen's particularization of the narrative in such a way as to make it very likely the passages would produce the emotional effects she desired.

2

Story Development, Literary Evaluation, and the Place of Character

Having overviewed some basic principles of simulation in neural-network and rule-based architectures, we may now begin to address what contributes to specifically literary simulation. To do this, we need to consider three main components of such simulation. The first component, touched on in Chapter 1, is the complex of previously existing story structures in the mind of the author. The most particular and fundamental of these are exempla, which is to say interrelated sets of episodic memories that constitute particular stories for that author. The most abstract structures are the schemas, scripts, and definitions that apply across exempla or, to put it differently, serve to categorize those exempla. Perhaps the most important structures – and the ones on which we will be focusing – are prototypes, which fall between these extremes. Prototypes are standard cases or, more exactly, "weighted" averages (on the general idea of prototypes, see Rosch). In other words, they are roughly average cases of a category. They are, however, affected by contrasting categories. Thus the prototypical diet food has far fewer calories than the actually average diet food (see Kahneman and Miller 143).

Prototypes and other prior structures necessarily exist solely in the minds of individual authors. However, they are only to some extent distinct for individual authors. In other words, they are always idiolectal, in the sense that they exist only in the idiolects of individuals. However, they are only partially idiosyncratic. For our purposes, the key prototypes are the universal story patterns to which we will turn in the following section. These vary to some degree across individuals but are more similar than different.

The second component is a set of development principles that apply to the previously existing structures. Story prototypes are clearly not stories in themselves. They are, rather, very abstract outlines for possible stories. The same point holds for character prototypes (e.g., "romantic hero") or scene prototypes (e.g., "home"). Development principles apply to these abstract structures, guiding authors in the production of particular stories from the general structures. As should already be clear, such production is not a random process. It results from the complex operation of neural networks. That complex operation, like others, may be captured and rendered more comprehensible in terms of rules.

The third component is a set of evaluation principles that apply to the product that results from the application of development principles to general structures. Authors do not simply produce fully formed and final versions of literary works. They alter what they produce initially. This happens most obviously in revision after a first version has been committed to paper. But it also occurs even before anything is uttered. Development principles (or rather, their underlying networks) produce alternatives. One or another may have the greatest activation at any given moment. It may or may not fit the author's aims, however. As with any other sort of activity, when composing a story, people do not simply do the first thing that occurs to them. They modulate initial impulses, hesitate, and shift to alternatives – all before they engage in an initial action. We might at first think of revision as parallel to error correction, but our evaluation of actions is more than error correction. We are continually modulating impulses for action, regardless of whether we are composing a story or driving a car. Indeed, this is a crucial function of simulation. Again, simulation occurs not only long term ("What will happen if, tomorrow, I go to my department head and ask for a course release in the fall?"). It occurs in our moment-to-moment anticipations ("What if that driver doesn't see me in his rearview mirror?"). Our decisions in those cases too are not random but rather captured by rules.

The following analyses will often seem to suggest that these three components also constitute distinct compositional stages. However, this is only for ease of exposition and clarity of causal attribution. In fact, as the preceding comments indicate, they continually interact and alter each other. Suppose Doe is writing a romantic story, perhaps a story based to some extent on his own experiences. He begins with the romantic prototype, along with relevant exempla or instances (e.g., *Romeo and Juliet* or, to take a case from popular fiction, *Titanic*) – and, indeed, a range of other, relevant prototypes, subprototypes, and so on. He begins with these structures in two senses. First, they are there before his particular romantic experiences. Second, they are there as he begins to reflect on those experiences in order to write the story. In both cases, the romantic prototype and the other structures help select features from his experience, place them in causal relations with one another, relate them to possible outcomes, and sharpen emotional continuities and contrasts. At the same time, however, his experience begins to particularize the prototype. As a result of this specification, the precise configuration of his cognition – its particular complex of selecting, organizing, and orienting structures – changes. For example, some exempla become more prominent (thus the modeling function of *Romeo and Juliet* or *Titanic* may decline and be replaced by, say, Wong Kar-wai's much less prototypical *In the Mood for Love*). These exempla may even assume greater importance than the prototype. In addition, the relative significance of other prototypes and subprototypes will change.[1] Similarly, he may begin to focus on particular, recurring motifs that are separable from prototypes[2] (e.g., the motif of the journey away from home and the return home).

Moreover, as this is going on, he is continually evaluating what he writes, what he has written, and what he anticipates as the result of what he is writing and has written. His negative evaluation of a passage or scene may lead him to revise what he has done, or it may lead him to plan certain corrections later in the story. For example, he may feel that he is beginning to make the heroine too unsympathetic. He may then change some of what he has written, or he may include more sympathy-fostering moments later on. In short, the components are in continual interaction and mutual modification.[3] Nonetheless, it is valuable to separate them for clarity of exposition and explanation.

The primary prototypes involved in story production are commonly those of the cross-cultural genres – heroic, romantic, sacrificial, familial, and so on. The next section briefly outlines these, as they are the most crucial, recurring parts of the initial component of simulation (i.e., previously existing cognitive and affective structures). Subsequent sections consider development and evaluation principles, focusing in particular on the importance of character, a point introduced briefly in Chapter 1.

Universal Genres

Cross-cultural research in story structures indicates that a number of story prototypes occur in a wide range of unrelated traditions of literature and orature. The most prominent structures of this sort – the major genres – appear to be heroic, sacrificial, and romantic tragicomedies. Somewhat less prominent but also widespread structures – the minor genres – may be found in revenge, criminal investigation, familial separation, and seduction plots. Stories generally involve characters pursuing goals. These goals fall into categories or types, based on which emotion/motivational systems are most significantly engaged. Different configurations of motivational systems (along with some standard operations of the human mind) generate these genres.

Thus we may think of the genres first of all in terms of the emotion systems at play in producing them.[4]

Focusing on the social structure of society, the heroic plot prominently involves both group and individual pride, thus striving for individual authority within an in-group and in-group domination over out-groups. A standard version begins with a legitimate ruler or someone who should become the legitimate ruler of the society. This legitimate ruler is usurped unjustly by someone else in the home society. He or she is, as a result, removed from the home society in some form of exile (or imprisonment). During this period of exile, the home society is threatened by some outside force or invader. The invader may be a foreign leader who aided the usurper or may be a new character. In the full, comic version, the legitimate ruler returns from exile to protect the home society and reestablish his or her position. The personal pride of the ruler (and its conflict with that of the usurper) forms the usurpation sequence of the prototype. The group pride of the home society (and its conflict with that of the invader) forms the threat/defense sequence of the prototype.

The heroic plot may be followed by an epilogue of suffering. This epilogue explores the results of conflict and is shaped by the goal of working through either grief or guilt after destruction. It has two common versions related to these two emotions. In the simpler case, it merely represents the mourning of those who are left behind after the many deaths that occur in war. In the more complex case, it involves the hero in a second exile that now constitutes a spiritual chastening. This is typically a sort of atonement for the killing of some innocent victim (often a child) in the course of the war. At the end, he or she is able to return to the home society again, now wiser and less prone to conflict.

The sacrificial prototype concerns a more basic goal – procuring food and water or physical health, typically in conditions where this is very difficult, such as famine or epidemic disease. It is resolved not by the temporary provision of food, but by lasting abundance and health. This narrative commonly concerns the relationship between society and a divinity or superhuman realm. Some representative member of a human society or some adequately representative group of ordinary people has violated a divine prescription. This is commonly due in part to internal weakness, both personal and social; however, it is also because of the temptation created by some out-group member who has entered the society. The divine punishment for this violation is need deprivation – often the denial of food (e.g., through drought and famine) or the infliction of disease – imposed on the entire community. The violation requires a sacrifice, and there are two common versions of this sacrifice. The sacrificial victim may be the guilty party, either the in-group representative (e.g., a king who sinned) or the out-group "tempter" or both. Alternatively, the victim may be an innocent representative of the in-group. The sacrifice compensates for the initial violation and normalcy is restored, typically in an improved or even idealized form.

The romantic plot concerns the combination of sexual desire and attachment that constitutes romantic love. It begins with two people falling in love. They encounter some representative of social authority who prevents them from being united in an enduring way, most obviously through marriage. This social representative may be from various levels of society – commonly, the family, religious institutions, or the state. Often, the lovers are from antagonistic groups so that in-group/out-group divisions enter here as they do in the heroic and sacrificial prototypes. There is often a socially acceptable rival for one lover, a rival preferred by the social authority. Social disapproval commonly leads to the exile of one lover and the confinement of the other. Some significant accomplishment by or change in state of the demeaned lover (and/or some failure by the preferred rival) may produce an alteration that allows the lovers to be united. This is often accompanied by a larger social reconciliation.

The familial separation prototype is related to the romantic prototype. However, it involves only attachment concerns without the sexual component. It is intermediate between the major and minor groups. On the one hand, it is fairly common in different traditions. On the other hand, it tends to be less prominent; that is, it seems to occur less frequently as the main narrative in the most admired works in a tradition. It also appears somewhat less "autonomous" (i.e., it appears to occur somewhat less frequently on its own and more frequently as an adjunct to other structures) and somewhat more variable.[5] In any case, it commonly involves the separation of parents and children, sometimes by accident and sometimes by choice. Often, many years pass before either the children or the parents seek to end this separation. The search is usually a difficult one with moments of misrecognition. When the parents and children are finally reunited, the result is rarely simple. There is in many cases a high degree of ambivalence, and sometimes the reunion is very brief and unsatisfactory.

The seduction prototype takes up the other component of motivation in the romantic plot – sexual desire. This prototype involves a man who seduces a woman, professing love and promising marriage. He then abandons her, often when she is pregnant. (Sometimes the woman consents to the seduction in the hope of becoming pregnant.) The woman then pursues the man. The pursuit is difficult and may involve misrecognitions. The final reunion of the man and woman is, at best, highly ambivalent. In some cases, the man, woman, or both may die. In other cases, they are married, but the man's previous behavior inhibits the degree to which we can imagine that they will live "happily ever after."

The revenge plot is driven primarily by anger and disgust, both of which play a secondary role in heroic narratives. In revenge narratives, these feelings typically result from attachment loss. Specifically, the "hero" has suffered some harm. This may be sexual betrayal. In that case, the revenger knows about the partner's betrayal. Nonetheless, he or she is often ignorant of the circumstances in which the betrayal occurred. Moreover, he or she may be ambivalent about the revenge itself. Specifically, he or she may continue to have attachment bonds with the beloved, even while feeling compelled to harm or even kill him or her. More often, the harm is not sexual infidelity but the death of an attachment figure (e.g., a spouse). In this case, the revenger seeks the person who committed the harmful act. This is often a difficult process and commonly involves misrecognitions – often with the terrible consequence that innocents are murdered. In the end, the revenger may find and kill the initial murderer. This development is usually ambivalent, however. First, the revenger often ends up dead himself or herself. Second, whether or not the hero dies or lives, the beloved is not recovered; the grief remains. Finally, the process of the revenge has only multiplied the initial devastation, not reversed it.

The criminal investigation narrative commonly begins with a murder. However, there may be a complication in that the ultimate responsibility for the murder may lie with one character while the execution of the murder is undertaken by a second character. Some representative of social authority seeks the criminal. This is a difficult process and usually involves misrecognitions. If the investigator is upright, then these misrecognitions are unlikely to result in enduring harm (e.g., false executions). If the investigator is corrupt or otherwise flawed, however, the misrecognitions may have the same deleterious consequences as in the revenge plot. Ultimately, the upright investigator is likely to uncover the person who committed the murder. The punishment of the murderer follows. Typically, the criminal investigation narrative is less ambivalent than the other minor genres. However, the presence of corrupt investigators and the related occurrence of further suffering to innocents (e.g., in the execution of an innocent defendant) create a highly ambivalent version of this narrative. Moreover, even the upright investigator may punish only the agent of the crime, without affecting the person who devised and instigated it (or any larger structure responsible for it).

In addition to recurring genres, we may isolate recurring event sequences, character types, and scenes. To a great extent, these derive from the cross-cultural genres. For example, the sacrificial prototype generates character types such as the tempter, the sacrificial victim, and the priest or other intermediary between society and the heavens. Some of these elements are parts of more than one genre. Exile is a recurring narrative sequence of this sort. Recurring scenes (i.e., places) in all genres would include a character's dwelling, his or her home society (e.g., village), and an alien place. As these cases indicate, some character types, event sequences, and scenes – free motifs or, more briefly, motifs – are independent of specific narrative prototypes. Motifs beyond those found across prototypes (such as exile) may vary considerably from author to author. Therefore, rather than attempting a comprehensive overview – an impossible task in any case – we will consider cases as they arise in the course of particular analyses.

Development Principles

We may distinguish two kinds of development principle. First, there are principles that serve to alter a basic prototype or its representation. We may refer to these as alteration principles. Second, there are principles that serve to make abstract prototypes concrete. We may refer to these as specification principles.[6]

As just noted, alteration principles may bear on the prototype itself or the representation of the prototype – the way the prototype is presented to an audience. Thus discourse manipulation (e.g., the reordering of story events) is included here. Suppose Doe begins a film with the wedding of the loving couple. She cuts to the best man talking to one of the bridesmaids. He sighs and exclaims, "Thank God! I thought it would never happen!" The dewy-eyed bridesmaid inquires innocently, "But why not?" The best man then explains the wacky and tumultuous sequence of events that led to the wedding – the unlikely meeting of the couple, their initial alienation, their growing affection, the sinister interference of money-grubbing relatives and the doltish intervention of buffoonish rivals with strangely large overbites, the traffic jams, the car chases, the disheartening fiasco with the wedding cake, the loss and recovery of the wedding ring, and a strange series of mix-ups involving a police officer posing as a prostitute and identical twins. Framing the tale with this dialogue is a simple discursive change that conforms to an alteration principle. The general form of this discourse alteration principle might be something along the following lines: "Place an emotionally significant outcome before its causal explanation." It would commonly be combined with a metaprinciple to the following effect: "Motivate any discursive departures from story/discourse parallelism." Here, the motivation would be to provoke curiosity (in

Sternberg's term) and to assure the viewer beforehand that apparently harmful events are actually innocuous (thus they need not interfere with mirth).

Discourse manipulations bear not only on events but also on all the main components of a narrative. For example, temporal alteration in character appears when an important fact about a character – a fact that both explains and contextualizes his or her action – is concealed from the reader until the end of the story. A principle here might be something along the following lines: "Withhold explanatory information about a character – prominently including identity information." This is, in turn, qualified by another metaprinciple: "Supply adequate story information so that a reader is not disoriented."

Other alteration principles bear on the story. These include the multiplication or deletion of prototype elements and the insertion of nonprototype elements. The multiplication of events with slight variations is perhaps the most obvious. This practice is probably most familiar from oral tales.[7] We also find it in canonical literature, as in Lear's triple division of his kingdom and triple test of his daughters' love – the insertion and repetition of a motif of test and reward. *King Lear* is particularly apt to our concerns, for it shows that the variation is inseparable from differences in the characters involved (itself a matter of specification). The first and second tests and divisions are very similar because of the near indistinguishability of the characters Goneril and Regan. The third test and division are, however, distinctive. This is because of the character of Cordelia. In effect, we see the same abstract structure "run" or processed three times, with different characters determining the differences in the resulting episodes.

Ellipsis (the deletion of prototype elements) may be less common in standard forms of storytelling, but it is a sometimes obtrusive feature of modernist and postmodern storytelling, in which crucial narrative information may simply be absent. In many cases, that absence is balanced by a more intensive development of some limited segment of the story – often through character focus and elaboration, as when Robbe-Grillet dwells on the mental state of a jealous lover in *La Jalousie*.

We have already seen a case of the insertion of elements that are not part of the initial prototype – the test/reward event sequence motif in *King Lear*. In some cases, these elements are drawn from other prototypes. For example, the separation of lovers in a romantic plot may be connected with a war drawn from the heroic plot, and their reunion may be facilitated by the suffering or death of a scapegoat figure drawn from the sacrificial plot. As the case of *King Lear* suggests, however, the inserted elements are often free motifs. Examples would include event sequences such as the investigation of a secret or the undertaking of a journey and characters such as an investigator, suppliant, clown, or sage.

Indeed, not only may any plot include an investigator, any character may take on the (free motivic) role of an investigator. This brings us to another set of alteration principles – the fusion and subdivision of elements. These principles apply almost entirely to characters. As a number of writers have noted,[8] for a given set of character functions, one character may fulfill one or more than one function and one function may be fulfilled by one or more than one character. For example, in the sacrificial plot, as noted in the previous section, there is a sin that leads to communal devastation. That devastation can be reversed only by a sacrifice. The facts of sin and sacrifice entail two character functions – the sinner and the sacrificial victim. There is also, commonly, a deity responsible for the punishing devastation and the subsequent forgiveness. The sinner may be one character (e.g., a group leader) or many (e.g., an entire community). The sacrificial victim may be the same as the sinner or may be different. The Judeo-Christian story of the fall gives us two sinners, Adam and Eve, and a sacrificial victim, Jesus, who is different from the sinners – but who is the same as a (split) deity, an unusual and obviously emotionally effective variant.

Although alteration principles are certainly important, they only vary what is given in the prototypes themselves. They do not give us particular stories. Indeed, they become substantial only insofar as they operate on prototypes that are elaborated in concrete detail. This is where specification principles enter.

Specification principles begin with event types and character functions as well as broad divisions of scene (e.g., home place versus alien place). All three abstract structures must be specified. However, it is unlikely that the specification operates equally in all three cases. Authors may and often do particularize events without reference to characters. For example, an author may decide to write a heroic plot treating a nuclear war before he or she has determined anything about the people involved. Perhaps the most straightforward way of particularizing prototypical events, however, is by particularizing prototypical characters (and to a lesser extent circumstances).[9] What makes *Romeo and Juliet* different from *Abhijñānaśākuntalam*? In many ways, it is the characters. Romeo is highly passionate, prone to rashness. Moreover, he lives in a society peopled by feuding patriarchs and hot-headed youths. These are the characters who hinder his love. His helper is a scheming friar. Duṣyanta, in contrast, is a cultivated gentleman, somewhat inclined to melancholy, and skilled in arts of leisure, such as painting. His society is peopled by jealous wives and choleric sages. These are the characters who hinder his love. The helper function is taken up by a lazy and self-indulgent priest. In many ways, the differences in the narrative follow from these differences in character.

Of course, it is in principle possible that these authors began with the plot events and worked back to the character traits. In some cases, that may what happen. However, our ordinary processes of simulation involve projecting events based on our understanding of people with their intentions, goals, and dispositions. Even when we first think about some major event, such as war, our imagination of unfolding subsequent scenarios is based on how individuals – with their personalities, virtues and vices, intellects, and so on – would behave. Thus (to take a slightly outdated example) we might think, "How would Kim Jong Il react if George Bush ordered an invasion of North Korea?" In other words, we do not ordinarily start out imagining some situation, then working backward to agency. We do not usually think, "Let's imagine that North Korea invades South Korea. What sort of North Korean leader might undertake such an invasion?" The reasons for our agent-based imagination are straightforward. Most of the time, it is far more functional in the real world to think in this way. Here as elsewhere, there is no reason to believe that we follow one principle in our quotidian simulations and another principle in our literary simulations.[10]

As noted earlier in this section, character specification begins with character functions, commonly in relation to a genre. Character specification affects two things. First, it details and expands the character's motivations, feelings, decisions, and actions. Second, it alters and intensifies the reader's response to the character – including the reader's understanding of, feelings about, and evaluation of the character.

As discussed in Chapter 1, we understand other people through our theory of mind, our sense of those people as having distinct beliefs, experiences, and motives. Again, there are two commonly accepted modes of understanding other minds – inference and simulation. The two modes interact extensively – often it seems in the two-stage manner outlined in Chapter 1. Nonetheless, it is worth distinguishing between them theoretically. This is important as the two strategies are not always employed in the same proportions, and they do not always have the same emotional, evaluative, and other consequences.

Again, prototypes give us character functions – sinners, scapegoats, lovers, rivals, and so on. Alteration principles may divide or fuse these or add to the list. Specification principles operate on these functions to produce characters to whom we may respond as persons. The first step in this specification involves a fundamental division in types of character. This division is determined by our two fundamental sorts of response to persons – theoretical inference and simulation. Simulation is distinct from empathy (i.e., one can simulate someone else's thoughts without sharing their feelings). However, simulation is a necessary component of empathy that is sustained beyond immediate experiential responses (e.g., a pang of fear on hearing someone scream in fear). Thus lack of empathy is related to lack of simulation. For example, our empathy is inhibited with respect to members of out-groups.[11] This is presumably due in part to a diminished inclination to simulate their experiences and feelings. Put very simply, in responding to an in-group member – when that in-group membership is salient – we are likely to use a combination of simulation and inference in our theory of mind responses regarding that person, with simulation as the default (as discussed in Chapter 1). The simulation in such cases tends to foster empathy. In contrast, we may be more likely to rely on inference in the case of out-group members, or we may be more likely to shift to inference even if we spontaneously begin with simulation. Specifically, the out-grouping itself may create enough of a processing contradiction to inhibit simulation. One consequence of this is that we are less likely to empathize with out-group members. Moreover, we are likely to understand out-group members more mechanically. Simulation involves assimilating the other person to ourselves, and we commonly understand that our own motives, ideas, and feelings are changeable, that they are not rigidly fixed.[12] In contrast, we see out-groups as "less complex, less variable, less individuated" (Duckitt 81).

In this way, the first crucial division in character specification is between us and them, in-group and out-group. This division may be inflected by another division that has consequences for inference and simulation as well. That is the division into characters who are socially normative (i.e., characters who represent social categories and associated norms) and individualistic characters (i.e., characters with idiosyncratic preferences and affiliations, which often run contrary to social norms).[13] Generally, the latter seem more likely to provoke simulation and empathy than the former.

None of these categories absolutely precludes simulation, however. Indeed, generally speaking, the greater attention an author devotes to a given character, the more likely it is that the character will provoke simulation and associated empathy – even when that character is an out-group member.[14] In connection with this, perhaps individualistic characters are not more likely to provoke simulation simply because they are individualistic. Rather, any such tendency toward simulation may be the result of the greater attention and elaboration commonly extended to such characters.

Fundamental divisions in character are commonly affected by further, typological categories. Obviously, in the case of in-group/out-group divisions, the first typological categorizations are likely to be based on ideas about group identity, most commonly stereotypes. Broad ethnic, religious, national, and related categorizations clearly provide some specification of character functions. Suppose Smith wishes to write a heroic narrative and makes the hero a European-American and the enemy an Arab. This will entail certain likely plot developments. For example, based on stereotypes, it may lead to the inclusion of suicide bombing or the use of commercial airliners as weapons. It may lead to a broad characterization of the enemy as "fanatically" religious and thus uncompromising in his or her commitment to the destruction of the United States.

Other sorts of typological categorization do not divide along lines of ethnicity and culture per se. Instead, they address attitudes toward cultural origins and practices that may cross identity categories. For example, much literature from former British colonies involves a tacit typology of characters defined by their relation to colonial and indigenous cultures. Some characters are mimics, celebrating and (often badly) imitating European practices simply because they are European, rejecting indigenous practices simply because they are not European. Other characters are what we might call *orthodox*. They follow traditions of the home society in a way that is beneficial for the society and sensitive to changing social conditions. Still other characters are reactionary traditionalists or fundamentalists, asserting a narrow, rigid, oppressive – and, generally, inaccurate – form of tradition (often after having been mimics). There are also syncretists, who seek to combine different cultural practices.[15]

Divisions of this sort may be less simplistic and repetitive than divisions based on ethnicity or culture per se. Consider Rabindranath Tagore's novel *Gora*. One plot sequence – a romantic tragicomedy – makes one lover orthodox, with a strong tendency toward reactionary traditionalism (in response to European colonial denigration of indigenous beliefs), and the other a syncretist. This entails a range of narrative consequences that are intellectually challenging and emotionally effective. It seems unlikely that, other things being equal, a more standard narrative – for example, one in which the lovers came from different castes – would have been equally successful and distinctive.

Another common typological specification principle is familialization. This is the selection of an antagonist from the category of family members or, more generally, trusted attachment figures (thus including friends). This is an instance of a more general specification principle that adjures intensifying emotional effect through intensifying the sense of betrayal in conflict. This itself may be an instance of a still more general development principle that adjures minimizing expectation in order to enhance the gradient of change from one emotion to another. (One expects treachery from enemies, not from friends and relatives.)

Even the most fine-grained and culturally illuminating typological categorizations remain limited in their consequences for narrative specification. Stories remain threadbare if they are not particularized beyond typological selection. For such fuller particularization, we need, at the very least, individual traits, distinct from typologies. The obvious way of developing such individual traits is by transferring information about particular people who share some narratively relevant category with the character being simulated, including the category defined by the typologically dominant trait – for example, orthodoxy or, to take a trait from psychophysiological typology, melancholy. These particular people, the exempla mentioned at the beginning of this chapter, may be real or fictional, known directly or only by report. They prominently include ourselves. For instance, when James Joyce was writing *Ulysses*, he had to particularize Stephen Dedalus, a melancholic freethinker and poet. To do this, he drew extensively not only on his own biography but also on Hamlet, Milton's Satan, characters from Byron, and so on. More technically, these exempla were activated in his neural network and thus became sources for the fictional simulation.

Here the difference between simulation and inference enters again. An author may simply transfer features from an exemplum to the target character (e.g., having Stephen dress in black and brood, like Hamlet). Alternatively, an author may draw on exempla as sources for simulating particular ways of feeling, thinking, or acting (as when Joyce imagines how he himself would have felt in the partially autobiographical but partially altered circumstances of Stephen). The contrast here may be very stark. As a result, simulation may lead to developments that make causal sense to readers even when they cannot articulate that causal sense. For example, in simulation, we primarily experience the character's (or real person's) motivation as comprehensible through our imagination of his or her experiences and feelings. We may be able to articulate specific reasons for this motivation, or we may not. Indeed, in some cases, the discrepancy between our intuitive sense and our explanation of a given character's motives may be obtrusive. Perhaps this is the case with one of the most famous conundrums in the history of criticism – Hamlet's delay in exacting revenge for his father's murder. Critics have elevated Hamlet's delay to one of the great puzzles of literary interpretation. That may mean that readers find the contradiction between Hamlet's decision and his behavior to be incomprehensible. But it seems unlikely that we would find Hamlet so fascinating if we felt that Shakespeare's portrayal of the prince was merely inconsistent or opaque.[16] We should, in that case, see Hamlet's delay as a flaw rather than something to be explained. Our sense that it is explicable suggests that Hamlet's behavior does indeed feel plausible in simulation – even if we cannot articulate an explanation for it.

Such apparently anomalous plausibility (as we might call it) is not surprising. In simulation, we fundamentally rely on our own experience of motivation, decision, and action. For example, Joyce draws on his simulation of Hamlet to imagine Stephen Dedalus at some points rather than drawing (directly) on autobiography. In those cases, Joyce's use of his own experience has not ended; it has only been made indirect since his simulation of Hamlet relies on his own experience. This relation of simulation to personal experience should lead us to expect something along the lines of anomalous plausibility. In our own lives, we often make decisions that (like Hamlet) we are unable to follow through. Often we can give some sort of explanation for this discrepancy, but not always. In some cases, we are uncertain as to why we did or did not act in a certain way. If asked why, we cannot give an articulate and cogent response. If we do give a response, it may be little better than a guess. (On our frequent inability to explain our own emotions and actions, see Nisbett and Ross 226–227 and Frijda 464.)

Indeed, in many cases, even articulate, cogent explanations of our behavior do not really capture our motives and feelings. Explicit explanations abstract from complex motivational particularity. They select aspects of experience for purposes of causal alignment – Smith is writing a particular paper because she has been invited to a conference; Gora wears traditional clothing because he rejects colonialist mimeticism; Hamlet does not commit suicide because he fears hellfire. But these are at best simplifications. Take the first. Clearly, the set of psychological events that give rise to the action of writing an essay is highly complex. For particular purposes, Smith's invitation to the Zentrum für interdisziplinäre Forschung may be the most relevant precedent for the writing and thus the most relevant cause. However, it is clearly not the only cause of the writing (for example, she could have refused the invitation), and it is certainly not the sole cause or even an important cause of the particular argument of the essay. The general point holds regardless of whether one is speaking of one's own direct experience of oneself or one's simulation of someone else – including characters, such as Hamlet.

The discrepancy between an articulated causal account and direct or simulated experience bears on a range of mental phenomena, but it is perhaps most consequential in the case of emotion or motivation. One aspect of this merits particular attention. Our emotions or motivations almost invariably have some degree of ambivalence. In other words, there is almost always some conflict in our feelings. Our account of these feelings in causal explanations tends to eliminate that ambivalence, however. For example, I have written about a dozen versions of this chapter. My feelings about it are mixed. I even have ambivalence about aspects of the argument itself. I cannot say that I am 100 percent convinced of all its claims. I am largely convinced, but I would hardly say that I have no doubts. Nonetheless, in most contexts, I am very unlikely to note this ambivalence in explaining my composition and revision of this chapter.

All this too extends from the real world to character. It indicates that, through simulation, ambivalence is likely to be important to our experience and tacit understanding of character and narrative more generally – even though it is unlikely to enter into our explicit accounts of either. Indeed, one might argue that ambivalence is inseparable from the purposes of verbal art. This leads to the topic of evaluation principles.

Evaluation Principles

Evaluation principles are simply the principles that capture patterns in an author's judgments as to whether a work is likely to have the right impact. In verbal art, there are two common sorts of impact that concern authors and readers. One is the thematic point of the work. The other is its emotional force. In both cases, the author's evaluation of the work is primarily receptive rather than expressive.[17] In other words, it is primarily a matter of establishing the likely understanding or response of readers. An author necessarily combines the roles of writer (or speaker) and reader (or listener). The second role is particularly crucial in evaluation and revision. In keeping with general cognitive principles, none of this is peculiar to literary creation. We all engage in this sort of dual activity all the time. One might be about to make some political joke to a colleague, then stop oneself, worrying that the colleague might have different political views. Stopping oneself in this context is a version of revision based on receptive intent, one's projection of how one's addressee might understand and respond to what one is saying.[18] Indeed, even in such ordinary conversations, one often has two purposes – first, conveying some general idea (e.g., some political point); second, provoking some emotional response (e.g., mirth). One's evaluation is bound up with one's sense of how these will operate for the addressee. For example, one may judge that this addressee will feel offended rather than amused. Similarly, one may judge that the other person is not in a position to recognize some irony in the story and therefore might take away the wrong political message from the joke. Thus, even in ordinary conversation, we commonly develop and evaluate utterances by reference to thematic point and emotional force. Moreover, we judge that point and force through simulated reception.

Thematic point includes any general ideas or attitudes that the author wishes to convey to the reader through the work – more exactly, anything that the reader should transfer from the story to the world of his or her ordinary life. Most often, this transfer involves ethical or political/social concerns. For instance, a film about the Iraq War is likely to have a thematic purpose in affecting our attitude toward the war when we leave the theater. This is not to say that all works are didactic, involving precise thematic claims that we can articulate readily and concisely. Indeed, not all themes are self-conscious; not all authors have a clear and exact sense of what thematic ideas and attitudes they wish to convey. As with so much else, authors commonly evaluate the thematic impact of the work tacitly. They write something, then reread it, judging whether it feels right. In ethics and politics, as elsewhere, we may distinguish between self-conscious articulation or theory on the one hand, and simulation on the other. In some cases, we make moral judgments by invoking general principles (theories). However, we first of all rely on our "gut" (thus simulation), shifting to effortful inferential processing only when some problem arises. Both types of process enter into the authorial development and readerly experience of stories. Here too simulations tend to be more complex, variable, and ambivalent. They also tend to be more emotionally affecting – an important consequence since our moral and political concerns, in art and in life, are inseparable from our feelings.

Emotional force is most obviously a matter of enhancing the emotional effect of the work as a whole. That overarching goal, however, is qualified by local concerns – such as the need to sustain the reader's interest. Moreover, enhancing emotional effect does not necessarily mean producing the strongest emotion. It means, rather, producing the most satisfying emotion – or, in some cases, producing the most appropriate emotion given the thematic purposes of the work. (For example, a film opposing a current war may have the strongest thematic impact if the overall emotional effect of the work is disconcerting and thus in a sense unsatisfying.) Given the preceding analysis, we would expect emotion in either case to be, so to speak, impure, to involve some degree of multiplicity and conflict. In general, then, we might say that the main function of emotive evaluation principles is to manage and orient ambivalence. Certainly, there will be many cases where that ambivalence is minimal. For example, in many romantic tragicomedies, we just want the lovers to marry; in many heroic tragicomedies, we just want the evil invader to be repulsed. Nonetheless, here too the operation of the evaluation principles remains a form of shaping ambivalence, even if that shaping involves intensifying one emotion and inhibiting contradictory feelings (which are almost certainly there, even in effervescent comedies and dire melodramas).

Given the particularity of the simulations at issue, and given the centrality of emotional response to those particulars, it seems unlikely that evaluation principles are, most importantly, general precepts, rules along the lines of those set out by neoclassicists. There are probably some general precepts of this sort. Some of these are explicit in creative writing manuals, such as "show, don't tell." Others are implicit, but easily recognizable, such as "in developing concrete, perceptual details, draw particularly on properties that are emotionally consequential." It seems likely, however, that evaluation principles most often make reference to exempla rather than general categories. For instance, in evaluating a particular colonial character in a postcolonial novel, a writer might seek to determine if his or her passage has the same careful balance between sympathy and criticism as found in such cases as J. M. Coetzee's treatment of the Magistrate in *Waiting for the Barbarians*. This does not mean that the comparison is self-conscious.[19] Rather, the new author has had experiences of emotionally and thematically successful writing – writing that produces a desirable effect. That experience is retained in emotional memories. In evaluating his or her ongoing simulation of a new work, the author tacitly compares its effects with these emotional memories. That may or may not involve explicit attention to the initial source of that emotional memory. In the case of the preceding example, the new author would have an emotional memory of his or her experience of Coetzee's Magistrate along with other relevant and successful cases. In composing a new work, he or she will reread what he or she has written, seeking to ascertain whether it has the right impact. His or her sense of what constitutes the right impact is guided in part by the emotional memory of Coetzee's novel, among others, even if he or she never explicitly thinks about these works in the course of revision. In this context, he or she may feel that the new novel is too maudlin or lacking in emotional force (or perhaps it is perfect and needs no revision). In any event, as this suggests, an author's evaluation principles are probably most often bound up with partially shifting – although also partially stable – configurations of largely implicit exempla with their associated emotional effects. They are almost certainly not a result of guidelines giving necessary and sufficient conditions and may only rarely involve even schematic rules of thumb.

The point is at least consistent with research on the pragmatic consequences of emotionally salient exempla for practical decisions, such as choosing a car. It is well established that we are more persuaded to act in certain ways by emotionally strong instances (e.g., a bad experience with a Volvo), rather than general guidelines (e.g., statistics about Volvos; see Nisbett and Ross 15). It seems likely that this inclination is only intensified in relation to decisions regarding literary works. This is particularly so as the value of literary works is more centrally emotional than the value of, say, automobiles.

In evaluation, as elsewhere, character is central. We do judge actions as moral or immoral, joyous or lamentable, and so forth. Actions, however, obviously do not occur independently of agents, and the moral praise or blame – as well as the emotion-producing effects of actions – are inseparable from persons. Our ethical relationship to the world is primarily a relationship to people; our emotional relationship to the world is largely a relationship to people also. Our ethical and emotional relationship to stories is, then, profoundly a relationship to people as well. But is there the same sort of directional orientation in evaluation as there is in developmental principles, where character seems to be the primary source for narrative specification? That is less clear. We may qualify our response to an act on the basis of our understanding of the person, but we may also qualify our response to a person due to our understanding of the act. As a result, character may not guide evaluation in the same way it appears to guide narrative specification. Nevertheless, our willingness to exculpate a character for apparent crimes and our tendency to experience one or another emotion in response to a character's actions (e.g., killing) and experiences (e.g., being imprisoned) are often inseparable from whether we categorize the character as us or them, and whether we infer or simulate his or her experiences. Indeed, our very understanding of what the relevant events are (e.g., aggression or self-defense) may be affected by our response to the characters involved. In this respect, then, character may indeed play a guiding role in evaluation, both that of the author and that of readers.

Conclusion

Particular stories commonly begin with prototypes and other general structures. The most important prototypes are derived from emotion systems and define cross-cultural genres. Some of these genres show a high degree of autonomy (i.e., likelihood of defining the main or only plot in a narrative) and appear prominently in highly esteemed narratives of verbal art across cultures and periods. Others show less autonomy and, although they occur across cultures, tend to be found in a more limited range of historical periods; they may also be more likely to appear in ephemeral works. The former are the major genres – romantic, heroic, and sacrificial tragicomedy. These bear on romantic love, individual and group pride, and hunger or physical well-being. The heroic plot often includes an epilogue (the epilogue of suffering), which in effect constitutes a further genre, related to guilt or remorse.

Its inconsistent presence in heroic plots makes it in some ways intermediate between the major and minor groups. The second, less autonomous group comprises the minor genres – seduction, revenge, criminal investigation, and familial separation. The cross-cultural and transhistorical recurrence of the last, however, suggests that it too might be viewed as intermediate between the two groups. These genres bear on sexual desire, anger at attachment violation, guilt attribution, and attachment respectively.

These prototypes are developed through alteration principles (including event/explanation reversal, identity concealment, varied repetition, ellipsis, synthesis of prototypes, and insertion of motifs) and specification principles (including typological categorization, trait transfer, and theory of mind simulation). Authors continually assess and revise developments through ongoing processes of evaluation relative to emotional and thematic goals. Evaluative judgments are often mediated by tacit comparison with the effects of exemplary earlier works – works that revealed to the author some emotional or thematic possibilities of literature. Emotional goals involve facilitating the most thematically appropriate and/or the most satisfying emotional response on the part of readers (perhaps readers from a particular, target audience). More precisely, for almost any narrative that provokes more than fleeting simulation, a reader's or spectator's emotional response is likely to be, in some respects, ambivalent. In those cases, the emotional purposes of the work are, at least in part, to organize and direct that ambivalence into an experience that is either intrinsically satisfying or that is best coordinated with the work's thematic purposes.

Much development and even evaluation operate crucially through characters. Both quotidian and literary simulation ordinarily proceed by placing particular characters in particular situations in order to envision outcomes. Our emotional response and ethical judgment are inseparable from our disposition toward characters as well. The operation of character in all these areas – story particularization, emotional response, and ethical judgment – often crucially involves the opposition between in-group and out-group categorization and the related difference between simulation of mental states and inference to mental states.

3

A Narrative Idiolect

Shakespeare's Heroic Stories

Up to this point, the theoretical analysis has been fairly general. For example, while acknowledging variability in principle, it has in practical terms considered prototypes as relatively uniform cognitive structures shared by different authors. But one of the fundamental implications of a cognitive approach to literature is that we cannot treat prototypes or other structures as autonomous or as operating on some sort of generic mind.[1] It is, again, individual authors' minds that make stories. Those individual authors must have enough in common to interact and communicate. However, they do not, strictly speaking, share prototypes or principles – not to mention precise neural networks (as emphasized by Edelman; see also Chapter 2 of Goldblum). Rather, there will be small but often significant differences. Those differences necessarily play a role in what leads Shakespeare to create works that are different from Austen's or Faulkner's works.

At the same time, the preceding account of simulation suggests that an author's particular cognitive structures (e.g., the precise details of his or her prototypes) and personal emotional orientations (e.g., as guided by emotional memories) will have some degree of internal consistency. A person's cognitive structures may not be entirely stable, but in all likelihood they do not change randomly, swiftly, or extensively. They at least partially maintain distinctive contents and processes. These continuous idiolectal features will result in narrative patterns that are, at some level, characteristic. In other words, we would expect there to be both differences across works by different authors and similarities across works by a single author. A central part of the cognitive analysis of how authors' minds make stories is necessarily a consideration of what these continuous cognitive features might be and how they operate in generating individual works. That is the topic both of this chapter and Chapter 4.

Shakespearean Patterns

Anyone who is familiar with Shakespeare's canon is likely to be aware that there are many continuities across his plays. Given this, it is unsurprising that story patterns in Shakespeare have been noticed by other critics. However, there has been relatively little systematic exploration of the topic. Helmut Bonheim takes up the idea of the narreme, a minimal narrative unit. Although narremes, like Northrop Frye's archetypes, commonly recur across different authors' works, particular versions and clusters of narremes may be distinctive of a given author. However, Bonheim notes that "Shakespeare criticism has given [narremes] scant notice" (1). His point is not confined to use of the word *narreme*. It covers systematic treatment of Shakespearean story patterns more generally. Indeed, in keeping with Bonheim's judgment, McAlindon begins his essay "What Is a Shakespearean Tragedy?" by citing "an eminent Shakespearean scholar [who] famously remarked that there is no such thing as Shakespearean Tragedy: there are only Shakespearean tragedies" (1). In other words, there are only the particular works, no overarching continuities.[2]

When critics have isolated patterns in Shakespeare's work, these patterns have tended to be very general. Moreover, they are often based on the standard generic divisions of the Shakespeare canon – history, comedy, tragedy, and romance – as the quote from McAlindon suggests.[3] But this is a theoretically problematic classification. "History" refers to story topic; "comedy" and "tragedy" refer to story outcome and overall emotional tone. Only "romance" seems even to aim at something like a story trajectory. The problem here is in part that critics have not had a sense of the universal narrative genres. Such a sense would have led them to organize their initial data differently. For example, in the approach adopted here, heroic plays include *Henry V* (a history), *Hamlet* (a tragedy), and *The Tempest* (a romance). Blind to the universal patterns instantiated in the plays, critics have necessarily been blind to the ways in which Shakespeare distinctively varied these patterns.[4]

A well-known case may be found in Theodore Spencer's account of the history plays: "An existing order is violated, the consequent conflict and turmoil are portrayed, and order is restored by the destruction of the force or forces that initially violated it" (72). There are two problems with this account. First, it is too general. It applies to such a wide range of works that it tells us little about Shakespeare. Second, it is too specific. The statement of the beginning and middle could apply to most universal genres. However, the conclusion applies only to some cases of a few universal genres. It points most obviously to the heroic plot (which is appropriate). It treats only part of the heroic reso-lution, however, and it applies to some versions of the sacrificial, revenge, and other genres as well. In short, it does not seem to be successful in isolating a general pattern or a distinctively Shakespearean pattern.

We see the same sorts of problem in more recent efforts, such as McAlindon's often insightful observations about Shakespearean tragedy. For example, McAlindon stresses the "transformation of the community and its represen-tative hero" and "the collapse of an order in which … ethical opposites have hitherto been kept in balance" (7). The points are quite general and virtually a logical consequence of the heroic structure. Later, he ties Shakespearean tragedy "loosely" to "anger and ambition … and, on the other hand, love and grief" (10). These emotions roughly distinguish heroic and romantic plots, both of which may be tragic. But they do so without the narrative detail of the cross-cultural prototype, not to mention Shakespeare's idiolectal specifi-cation of that prototype.[5]

Similar points apply even when critics happen to focus on plays that are pro-totypical heroic tragicomedies. For example, Fergusson isolates the following pattern in *Hamlet, Macbeth,* and *King Lear*: "The de facto ruler … creates a situation in his reign in which 'God's truth' is lost to sight.… A series of blind struggles follows," leading to "visions of anarchy," and so on (Fergusson 167). To some extent, this recapitulates part of the heroic structure. However, it does so in a somewhat vague way. Moreover, Fergusson finds a different pattern in heroic works such as *Julius Caesar* (see 170–172). This is not to say there is no value in Fergusson's pattern abstraction. Quite the contrary, it con-tributes to sensitive analyses. However, it seems to miss the main generative principles of the stories.

One of the few critical analyses that begins to capture significant patterns across Shakespeare's works is Bonheim's essay on narremes. Bonheim has a keen eye for isolating such patterns. In consequence, he catalogs a range of significant continuities in Shakespeare's canon, and his project is aided by rejection of strict adherence to traditional genre categories. However, his work is inhibited by two problems. The first is the usual one – failure to recog-nize the universal genres. Bonheim's acute sensitivity is shown by the fact that he recognizes "usurpation play" as an important category in Shakespeare's works (6). He has thus isolated the usurpation component of the heroic plot. However, he gives this as an example of a purely ad hoc category that we "gen-erate … as we go along" (6). In fact, it is crucial that usurpation is a recurring pattern across cultures and time periods. Without noting this, we cannot rec-ognize what is distinctive about Shakespeare (or what is shared). To put the point a little harshly, this is a bit like trying to figure out what is distinctive about Jones and observing that he has a nose and a pair of arms – or perhaps, in fairness to Bonheim, it might be more like observing that Jones has an endocrine system, but the general point is the same.

The second problem with Bonheim's approach is also shared by other critics – it is unsystematic. It is unsystematic in its catalog of narremes. It is also unsystematic in the psychological structure that it involves. This has results for both description and explanation. As to description, Bonheim fails to distinguish, for example, isolated motifs from large story structures. This is the result of not having the cross-cultural patterns available for his analysis. He is also unable to distinguish different levels of structure – abstract schemas, standard or average cases (prototypes), and particular instances. The second point derives from his structuralism, which does not involve the rigorously developed mental architecture of contemporary cognitive science. This, in turn, leads to the explanatory problems. Bonheim and others writing on patterns in Shakespeare's works have not drawn on the sort of psychological principles that would move their observations beyond a catalog of recurrences to explanatory principles.

Similar points apply to Honigmann's valuable overview of self-repetitions in Shakespeare. Honigmann actually has something like a sense of narrative idiolect. Thus he explains the particularity of Shakespeare's *King John* in the following way: "Shakespeare's previous explorations of character, scenic development and of his drama's great variety of technical devices, would have steered him ... towards a play consisting of structural elements such as those of *King John*" (183).[6] Indeed, he could almost have had in mind parallel distributed processing when he remarks that "self-repetitions form a network that links every play to the rest of the canon" (182). But the self-repetitions he isolates (e.g., "prattling, pathetic boys" [175], the "siege of a city," "ambiguous prophecy" [176], and so on) seem to constitute a somewhat random and not always very distinctive set. As usual, the problems often relate to the absence of a full sense of the universal genres – although Honigmann does repeatedly recognize elements of those genres (e.g., in referring to the "usurper" character [176]).

Needless to say, the following discussion is very far from anything like a full explanation of Shakespeare's plays. Through the principles articulated in the preceding chapters and further developed here, however, it proposes at least the elements of an explanation of some important continuities. Specifically, it begins to articulate an account of some basic principles that contribute to the distinctiveness of Shakespeare's heroic plays. In short, it does not simply list some features that turn up more than once in Shakespeare's works but also sets out to explore how his mind made stories, specifically, heroic stories. To do this, the bulk of the discussion will focus on five particular works – four that are highly characteristic; one that is not. However, in order to orient ourselves before going on to these specific plays, it is valuable to outline a few of his most common preferences, some of the things that make his particularizing simulation of the heroic plot different from that of other authors.

Shakespeare's Narrative Idiolect

Clearly, Shakespeare drew on universal story prototypes, prominently heroic and romantic. Unsurprisingly, he also took up standard development principles and motifs. He used some only occasionally. He used others more consistently. For example, one standard development principle, familialization, is also one of Shakespeare's most common strategies. In keeping with a cross-culturally common principle, this familialization is sometimes literal (as in *King Lear*), but at other times it is a matter of imagery or a character's associations, as in Lady Macbeth's linking of Duncan with her father ("Had he not resembled/My father as he slept, I had done 't" [II.ii.12–13]). More significantly, Shakespeare intensified or extended some development principles in partially distinctive ways. Consider descriptive alignment, a common development principle that establishes parallels across different components in a narrative (e.g., setting a character's violent grief during a violent storm). Shakespeare might parallel three or four components rather than the more common two. Thus Lear's madness (a disruption of reason) mirrors the disruption of the state (due to his dispossession), which in turn mirrors the disruption in his family (due to the rule of the children over the parent), which in turn mirrors the disruption in nature (due to the terrible storm).

Shakespeare sometimes takes up a common motif but alters it in characteristic and consequential ways. For instance, the killing of an innocent youth is a fairly widespread cross-cultural motif in heroic plots. This killing is often performed by the hero or someone else on the "good" side. As such, it is a common trigger for the epilogue of suffering. Shakespeare incorporates such a murder with some frequency. However, he most often attributes this killing to the enemy or "bad" side (insofar as this is precisely determinable). In keeping with this propensity, Shakespeare's plays rarely involve an epilogue of suffering. Thus Macbeth murders Macduff's son; King John orders the murder of Arthur (and causes his death, although in a somewhat more complex way than one might at first imagine); France kills all the youths who guard the luggage in *Henry V* ("'Tis certain there's not a boy left alive" [IV.vii.5]); and Richard III kills his nephews.

Shakespeare also makes use of less widespread, sometimes even idiosyncratic, principles and motifs. One is his intriguing characterization of figures seeking a change in power (whether through usurpation or restoration) as suicidal. Examples include Cassius, Brutus, Hamlet, Lady Macbeth, and Arthur ("As good to die and go as die and stay" [*King John* IV.iii.8]), as well as the poisoned monk (*King John* V.vi.24–31). Antony and Cleopatra vary this pattern only slightly.

A motif – or rather, the combination of a motif and a development principle – also apparently peculiar to Shakespeare is the death of a hero's (often the usurper's) beloved, frequently through suicide, and usually at a moment of particular conflict and suffering. This is presumably a technique of emotional intensification. As a character suffers political trials, he or she is suddenly faced with a deep personal loss as well. Thus Brutus learns of his beloved wife's suicide just before he battles Octavius; Macbeth receives news that his wife has killed herself just as he prepares for his final battle; Hamlet returns from exile and an attempt on his life to find Ophelia dead, perhaps by suicide. Antony and Cleopatra present a complex version. Antony commits suicide when he hears a false report of Cleopatra's suicide just after his defeat; then Cleopatra, also following defeat, learns of Antony's suicide and commits suicide herself. There are some more distant, but nonetheless recognizable, variants also, as when King John discovers that his mother has died just as he learns of a rebellion and an invasion (see IV.ii.110–121) or when York learns that his "sister Gloucester" has died at the very moment when "a tide of woes/ Comes rushing on this woeful land" (II.ii.90, 98–99). In some ways the most striking variant concerns Albany and Goneril. Goneril commits suicide more or less at the moment of Albany's triumph. In this case, the event is not so much sorrowful as horrible, a continuation of the terrible devastation that marks this play, even in "success."

There is even a structural feature of the heroic prototype that is altered in Shakespeare – recurrently, thus not as an exceptional variant produced by some accidental confluence of factors. Specifically, for Shakespeare, the exiled ruler rarely redeems himself by defending the home society against an invasion by another nation. Rather, the exiled ruler is joined with the other nation and invasion. Examples include King Lear, Arthur in King John, Malcolm in *Macbeth*, Coriolanus, and, with a slight alteration, Hamlet (in his concluding support for Fortinbras).

Needless to say, there are more features that collectively distinguish Shakespeare from other authors. In a short chapter, one can hardly name – not to mention explore and develop – all these. It may happen, however, that there are further, superordinate patterns organizing sets of particular development principles, motifs, and prototype variants that characterize a writer. We find a striking case of this in Shakespeare. Specifically, Shakespeare's use of familial-ization, his intensification of the suffering of the usurper figure (through the death of his or her beloved and his or her own suicidal tendencies), and his association of the deposed ruler with the invading enemy, all tend to make the heroic plot much more ethically ambiguous and emotionally ambivalent.

To understand the significance of this, we need to pause for a moment and consider the usual political function of heroic plots. Cross-culturally, heroic tragicomedies have operated with astonishing frequency to cultivate a sense of devotion to and pride in a national in-group, a sense of opposition to an out-group (including anger toward that group), and a sense of respect for hierarchies of authority within the in-group. The first and second are most clearly related to the invasion sequence, where a national out-group threatens the national in-group. The third (regarding hierarchy) derives primarily from the usurpation sequence, in which internal social order is disrupted.

There are three development principles that are particularly crucial to the political function of heroic tragicomedy. The first is a form of alignment. The ideologically functional operation of alignment in heroic plots is not simply a matter of contingent parallels across facts (e.g., violent grief and violent storms). Rather, it involves the integration of norms – moral, spiritual, and social. Specifically, the social norms of the national in-group are presented as identical with transcendental moral norms, which are in turn presented as identical with divine preferences. Thus, in the usurpation sequence, the usurper violates social law (e.g., fealty), the higher ethical norms (e.g., loy-alty) that underwrite the social law, and the divine will that underlies both (e.g., "divine right" for English kings or the "mandate of heaven" for Chinese monarchs). Likewise, in the invasion sequence, the home society is ethi-cally and spiritually superior to the foreign, invading society. Here too the in-group's norms are aligned with ethical principles and divine prescriptions. Even when it appears to be the aggressor, the home society is in fact act-ing defensively – not merely protecting life and property but also, and more importantly, the norms that guarantee life and property.

The second and third development principles are related to this. They both concern the construction of the plot. The former involves establishing an absolute origin to the heroic narrative; the latter mirrors this in establishing an absolute conclusion. The prototypical heroic structure in principle allows the addition of earlier or later events, backstories, and epilogues. But ethical and divine alignment entail a limitation on both the forward and backward extensions of the story. Specifically, the evil of usurpation and invasion rests on the absolute and singular origin of conflict. The usurpation must be the first act of internal disruption, the initiation of the series of events constitut-ing the story. It cannot be a response to prior usurpations or prior injustices, for, if it is, the narrative cannot function to foster respect for social order. In keeping with this, the invasion must be the start of external conflict. If it responds to prior violations by the home society, then the functional align-ment of norms is disturbed. Similarly, given divine sanction, there must be an absolute end point to the story, a happy conclusion in which good triumphs due to providence or some comparable divine principle. At the same time, that triumph itself is evidence of divine authorization. Because the godly side must win, whoever wins must be the godly side. If there are other stories to tell after the restoration of the rightful ruler or the repulsion of the enemy attack, then they are not continuations of this story. They are, rather, new stories with their own absolute and singular origins and their own providen-tial conclusions.

In sum, the political function of the heroic plot is enabled by the alignment of norms with the ruler and the home society; the construal of usurpation and foreign attack as pure, historyless origins; and the determination of a providential, all-resolving conclusion.

Presidential speeches and government propaganda are fairly brazen in emplotting national history in these terms.[7] It is relatively rare for canonical literary works to be entirely unequivocal on normative alignment, absolute origins, or providence. Canonical works regularly develop at least some sort of complexity regarding both abstract rights and human sympathy. Indeed, we see this (at least partial) recognition of ethical complexity and this ambiv-alence in the recurring epilogue of suffering. Even with this complexity and ambivalence, however, the broader justice of the home society and its hier-archy is rarely questioned even in the epilogue of suffering itself. Indeed, the epilogue of suffering may reinforce the sense of hierarchical, in-group right-ness by stressing the humane feeling and ultimate wisdom of the national leader.

This is altered in Shakespeare's heroic plays through the idiolectal features outlined above. Indeed, in those plays even the division between usurper and rightful ruler or that between defenders of the home society and invaders is not entirely straightforward. Admittedly, one can in most cases plump for one side or the other. But the rights of the rightful ruler are rarely unequivocal; the justice of the home society in war is rarely unquestionable. Even the death of innocents, as it operates in Shakespeare, is consistent with this. Specifically, the doubtful legitimacy of in-group/out-group divisions and in-group hier-archies is not a matter of isolable incidents, such as the killing of a guilt-less youth, rare deviations that necessitate temporary penance in an epilogue of suffering. This doubtfulness is, rather, the result of a more encompassing absence of morally functional properties distinguishing "our" side from the enemy or the putatively legitimate leaders from everyone else.

In short, perhaps the most remarkable feature of Shakespeare's heroic plots is that, with hardly an exception, they are not designed in such a way as to take up the usual political functions readily. Indeed, they routinely run contrary to the standard requirements of hierarchical and nationalistic function.[8] Thus Shakespeare's plays rarely present either usurpation or war as having an absolute and singular origin. They regularly indicate that there is a history of claims and counterclaims, a history of conflicts and injustices (or at least hurts and perceived injustices) that precede any usurpation or invasion. It is usually unclear whether there is any isolable origin to this sequence, or even whether it makes sense to ask about such an origin. In keeping with this, despite his intensification of descriptive alignment (e.g., setting up nature, mind, family, and society in parallel), Shakespeare most often disaligns the normative registers. Indeed, most authors intensify this alignment, extending it from norms to a broader set of values, including emotional preference (e.g., sympathy) and prudential superiority (e.g., regarding the relative skills in leadership possessed by the rival rulers), along with legal right, moral right, and divine choice. Shakespeare rarely constructs his plots in such a way that these five registers operate in parallel.[9]

Many authors at many times and in many cultures display a degree of ambivalence regarding emotional preference and even moral right. However, this rarely affects the central issues of the story. It is, rather, a matter of consequences. Most often, the in-group should win the battle, but the suffering of the out-group excites our sympathy and makes us feel that they should not be punished too severely, and that the in-group itself is guilty of some moral violations as well. Again, this is what gives rise to the epilogue of suffering. But Shakespeare commonly goes well beyond this. First, our personal preferences or sympathy may be divided and changeable. Particularly when paying careful attention, audience members are likely to find that the qualities of characters change, often systematically, such that a character will draw our sympathy in one scene only to lose it in another. The reasons for both usurpation and restoration are, most often, partially convincing and partially unconvincing. The legal status of a particular ruler is rarely self-evident. The legal right to a disputed piece of land (in a threat/defense sequence) is rarely well established in the play itself. Ethical issues are usually mixed up as well, at least in the sense that no side appears to be engaging in strictly moral actions. For example, it is repeatedly unclear whether a given war is a matter of self-defense on one side and aggression on the other – in part because, in case after case, the precise origin of the conflict is not specifiable. Moral principles clash and lead to contradictory conclusions, as do legal principles (e.g., supporting an illegitimate ruler may be unjust, but bloody insurrection – especially using foreign troops – may be even more unjust). Legal right is not always consistent with prudence (e.g., rebelling against an illegitimate ruler may be justified but bad for the home society). In Shakespeare's heroic tragedies (as in life), the implications of these registers do not accumulate in force toward a single conclusion but rather pull in different directions.[10]

In keeping with this, the sides are not clearly divided into normatively consistent groups. Even when we have clear preferences for particular characters and actions, even when some characters seem to be choosing a moral option or to have a reasonable claim to legal right, those characters are not always on the same side. Conversely, the "evil" and unsympathetic characters are not necessarily bunched together and isolated from the rest. They too are sprinkled about, located in different camps. Indeed, Shakespeare's use of familialization and other techniques – including psychologically complex representations of characters from both sides, representations that show us members of each group in their own regular, human thoughts and actions – leads to a blurring of even preexisting in-group/out-group distinctions drawn from history. We might expect a clear division between English and Scottish, Danish and Norwegian, Trojan and Greek, and a straightforward sense of author and audience identification with one over the other. But this is not the case. Even the distinction between English and French, although not wholly undermined, is by no means absolute.

Finally, there is rarely any clear indication of divine preference. Shakespeare does regularly deal with the issue of providence, and his characters routinely make statements about divine intervention in human affairs. The actual events in the works, however, are almost entirely inconsistent with these statements. This is true for two reasons: the first bearing on legal and moral issues, the second on personal sympathy. Regarding the former, the goodness of one side and thus the goodness of one outcome are, again, rarely unequivocal. Therefore, even when a story ends with the "right" side winning, ambiguity about this "rightness" makes it difficult to see this triumph as the working out of a divine plan. As to sympathy, even when the story arrives at our "preferred final situation" (as Tan would put it), it does not do so by "surgical" means (to use the popular military phrase). Conflict is not discriminating. Even when we have clear preferences for characters (and, again, this is not always the case), Shakespeare usually punishes the "good" along with the "evil." Goneril and Regan die, but so does Cordelia; Edmund is about to die, but there are suggestions of Kent's death as well; and Lear dies in despair. Moreover, even the suffering of the evil characters can be moving, can create a sense of their humanity, and thus produce an aversion to their pain. It is hard to accept such endings as the best of all possible worlds, shaped by an omnipotent and benevolent deity.

The bulk of this chapter goes through a selection of Shakespeare's heroic plays, focusing on this political complexity and ambivalence, thus the ways Shakespeare's idiolect differed from more typical developments. In order to clarify the nationalistic "dysfunction" of most Shakespearean heroic plots, however, it is useful to begin with a play – perhaps unique among Shakespeare's works – that is apparently unequivocal in serving the usual nationalistic purposes of heroic tragicomedy.[11]

Henry V

Although it includes a brief and unsuccessful usurpation, *Henry V* is primarily a threat/defense narrative. There is an apparent peculiarity in that the invasion is performed by the in-group against an out-group, but this is presented as a final defeat of a prior attack not treated directly in the play. Thus it is a truncated version of the threat/defense sequence, treating only the defense portion.

The play begins with a praise poem on the king. This sort of eulogizing is a common part of heroic works – although rare in Shakespeare – and it might give rise to an expectation of straightforward nationalism. However, the opening scenes suggest some of the ambivalence that is characteristic of Shakespeare's other plays. Specifically, the idea to invade France is proposed by the Catholic hierarchy – hardly guarantors of righteousness in Elizabethan England. To make matters worse, their reasons are entirely a matter of self-interest. Moreover, the legal exposition putatively demonstrating the right of King Henry is convoluted and not altogether believable. The entire sequence suggests deep uncertainty about the absolute and singular origin of the conflict and about the English king's rights.

In other Shakespeare plays, such ambivalence would be continued and extended. But this is where *Henry V* is different. The subsequent development of the story involves a highly nonambivalent, nationalistic use of the invasion/defense plot. The alignment of values is particularly noteworthy. For example, in a manner all too familiar to Americans (and Iraqis) after the presidency of George W. Bush, the national leader makes it clear that all atrocities of the war are the fault of the enemy leader (here, the French king) for not surrendering his usurped title (see II.iv.102–110). Later, the barbarous slaughter of prisoners of war is represented simply as a response to French perfidy in the killing of innocent boys (see IV.vii.1–67). In other words, the absolute and singular origin of that particular act – the killing of prisoners – is the (by this account, unprovoked) French slaughter of innocents. The English have not committed a crime. The death of the French prisoners falls on the heads of the French themselves. In short, the moral and legal rights are with the English – or, rather, with Henry, whose violent acts are implicitly identified as the acts of England. Indeed, even prudence favors Henry, for his leadership resulted in fewer than thirty casualties for the English and a great harvest of ten thousand dead Frenchmen (IV.viii.82–83, 105–108). Emotionally, this is unlikely to foster ambivalence because the suffering of the French is invisible.

Unsurprisingly, all this feeds into the providentialism of the play and the clear identification of the English with the party of God. Indeed, we find this divine alignment from the opening act, despite the ambiguities noted earlier. The argument for war involves the citation of scripture (I.ii.98) and the explanation that killing is necessary to fulfill "the will of God" (I.ii.289). Shortly after this argument, the usurpation sequence reinforces Henry's divinely appointed station. The rebels are characterized as "inhuman" (II.ii.93) and "evil" (101) and are associated with "devils" (114), the "fiend" (111), "hell" (113), "damnation" (115), and so forth. Even the rebels say that it is the work of God that the rebellion was discovered and foiled (151, 157) and confess it a "damned enterprise" (164). Moreover, the rebels regret their rebellion. In connection with this, they are so joyous about their failure, and even about their deaths, that we are not faced with their suffering – quite the contrary. We therefore have no reason to feel compassion for them.

The use of providentialism recurs in Henry's speech at Harfleur. This speech concludes with the assertion of divine support for the home society and for the hierarchy of that society: "God for Harry, England and Saint George!" (III.i.34), the image of St. George serving implicitly to dehumanize the French as a dragon. The St. Crispin's Day speech reinforces these themes, enhancing the role of providence (and thus the divine associations of the English) by stressing the physical inferiority of the English troops. On achieving victory, Henry calls out, "Praised be God, and not our strength for it!" (IV.vii.89). Subsequently, Henry proclaims that no one may speak of the number killed by the English without explaining that "God fought for us" (IV.viii.122).

Perhaps the most perverse use of providential thought comes in Henry's conversation with Bates and Williams. Bates and Williams raise the issue of whether it might not be wrong to kill so many people. In hearing this, one might wonder briefly if there is a sudden reentry of ambivalence into the play. But the objection to the war is introduced only to allow Henry to answer it. His argument is that God uses war to punish the guilty, so that, far from violating God's principles by killing, the leader who prosecutes a war is actually providing the means for God's justice (IV.i.170–176). In addition, those who are innocent and die in battle go to heaven. For them, death in war is "advantage" (185). In short, a just war is just for everyone, guilty and innocent.

Like any other work, *Henry V* can be interpreted as ironic.[12] Moreover, a given production may stress the illogic of its arguments. Nonetheless, with small changes reflecting the alterations in time and place, the arguments are precisely those used by governments and military organizations throughout the world and throughout history. It is not clear what led to this. The play may be self-conscious propagandizing on Shakespeare's part or an attempt to gain favor; it may suggest external interference (e.g., some form of political constraint); it may represent a brief alteration in Shakespeare's unconscious processes – that is, a change in the way his prototypes, motifs, development principles, and evaluation principles (in short, his simulations) operated to generate a heroic plot. We can, however, eliminate two possible explanations. It does not indicate some youthful jingoism, nor does it result from conservatism developing with age (middle thirties, in this case). The political complexity and emotional ambivalence discussed above characterize Shakespeare's plays both before and after *Henry V*. They even pervade the work Shakespeare composed at the same time. Indeed, although almost exactly contemporary with *Henry V*, *Julius Caesar* is a clear case of Shakespearean ambivalence in heroic tragedy.[13]

Julius Caesar

Shakespeare's play about the most famous Roman ruler takes up the standard heroic structure, including both the usurpation and invasion sequences, although with some twists. There is an initial rebellion with a usurpation of Caesar. Caesar is killed, so there is no issue of exiling him. The function of the heir is divided between Octavius and Marc Antony. Octavius is already away from Rome, and there is some initial uncertainty regarding Marc Antony. However, rather than Marc Antony being exiled, the usurpers are themselves exiled and Octavius returns. The usurpers then attack Rome and are defeated by Marc Antony (and, to a lesser extent, Octavius). Thus we have the usurpation sequence followed by the threat/defense sequence, with the difference that the usurpation is overturned before the invasion. In connection with the invasion, however, the heirs remain critical for the defense of the home society. (This is a case where Shakespeare comes close to the more usual pro-totype of the usurped ruler returning to defeat external attackers.)

Yet none of this is straightforward. Indeed, Shakespeare develops ambivalence so systematically that one suspects it was a self-conscious strategy, worked into the play methodically. The opening pages mention Pompey as a leader usurped by Caesar (I.i.39–40, 53–54). This not only undermines any clear sense that the rebels are usurping right rule, but also undermines the notion that there is a single, absolute origin to the conflict represented in the play. The references to Pompey suggest an extended and ongoing sequence of usurpations. Such references turn up at crucial points in the play. A prominent instance occurs when the murder of Caesar takes place at the foot of Pompey's statue (III.i.114–116). The current act of usurpation is thereby conjoined directly with the earlier act. The location of the murder at Pompey's statue is subsequently recalled in Marc Antony's speech (III.ii.190), providing a brief reminder of ambiguity in a passage that otherwise indicates the perfidy of the rebellion. Another important reference is found near the end of the play, when Cassius compares himself to Pompey (V.i.74). The comparison suggests – contrary to all appearances at this point – that the forces of Octavius and Marc Antony are the usurping/invading army (like those of Caesar when he crossed the Rubicon).

After the opening, we experience many of the events along with Brutus and in many ways think through the story from his point of view. In Murray Smith's terms, we are "aligned" with his perspective and experiences. Such alignment is typically "conjoined with sympathy."[14] In this case, then, our alignment tends to foster sympathy for Brutus and his side in the conflict. Nevertheless, we actually see the brutality of the murder of Caesar and the obscene ritual of the murderers bathing their hands in Caesar's blood. Moreover, we hear Caesar's exclamation of astonishment at Brutus's personal betrayal, "Et tu, Brute?" (III.i.77). That is not all. Prior to the murder, Brutus seems to consider very carefully the arguments for killing Caesar and to act on the basis of moral principle. However, the reasoning is prospective and conjectural. It all concerns what Caesar might do, not what he is currently doing. In this way, Brutus condemns Caesar on what are, in effect, imaginary grounds. Worse still, the reasoning entails a comparable condemnation of Brutus himself. Brutus's entire argument regarding what might happen to Caesar if he is crowned – the change in his nature leading to "abuse of greatness" (II.i.18) – applies no less to the rebels themselves, including Brutus. This is indicated most clearly by the cries of the Plebeians after Brutus's speech: "Let him be Caesar" and "Caesar's better parts/Shall be crowned in Brutus" (III.ii.52–54).[15]

Following the murder, Mark Antony's speech is more powerful than Brutus's speech. That, and the points just discussed, might sway us against the rebels. But, in the following scene, we are faced with Marc Antony's own brutality and the ruling triumvirate's own bloodbath – later numbered at 70 or 100 senators killed, including Cicero (IV.iii.172–177).[16] Along the same lines, Marc Antony's speech appeals to the shared interests of the right rulers and the common people, thus prudential considerations, largely by reference to Caesar's will. But, once the common people are out of earshot, he immediately tries to limit what will be paid out from that will: "Fetch the will hither, and we shall determine/ How to cut off some charge in legacies" (IV.i.8–9). In this way, he at least partially defeats his own prudential argument as well as his implicit claims to virtue, insofar as these derive from his solicitousness for the well-being of the common people. Moreover, some subsequent developments not only diminish our sympathy for the rulers but also enhance our sympathy for the rebels. Perhaps most importantly, we witness Brutus's personal miseries, including that over the suicide of his wife (the output of a recurring development principle, as already noted). This tends to foster sympathy for him – sympathy that most audience members are not likely to have for Marc Antony or Octavius.

In much of what follows, Shakespeare not only balances our sympathies and evaluations, he works systematically to undermine any differences between the two sides. For example, the scenes with Portia mirror those with Calpurnia; a conflict between Cassius and Brutus (IV.iii) is followed by a conflict between Octavius and Marc Antony (V.i). More significantly, Brutus defeats Octavius in war while Marc Antony defeats Cassius (V.iii.51–53). This suggests not only that the two sides are mirror images of one another, but also that competence is not the monopoly of one side, nor is divine preference (certainly not of the sort that allowed Henry V to defeat a vastly larger French force with almost no casualties to his own side). The near indistinguishability of the two sides continues to Marc Antony's final speech in which he praises Brutus as "the noblest Roman of them all" (V.v.68) and to Octavius's statement that Brutus's corpse will stay in Octavius's tent until it receives the honors of burial (76–79). This is precisely what one would expect for a dead hero on the side of Octavius and Antony, not a dead enemy.

Needless to say, Marc Antony's final praise of Brutus does not mean that Brutus was right. This is not a concluding resolution in favor of the rebels. Indeed, Marc Antony's speech equally stresses the injustice of the other conspirators, and it indicates his own generosity of spirit, just as Octavius's surrender of his tent to the dead Brutus implies his own decency. Above all, audience members cannot help but be aware that everyone is only worse off for all the fighting and killing. In retrospect, Brutus's justification of engaging in murder for "love [of] country" (III.ii.33) seems thoroughly implausible.

Thus the play runs directly against the triumphalistic patriotism that marked *Henry V*. There is no absolute and single origin to conflict and no stable lining up of values. At each point in the cycle of violence, either side could have ended the killing. When they do not, the result is not only massive death but despair and suicide as well.[17] In this respect also we see the two sides mirroring one another.

Finally, in keeping with the close parallel between the two sides, the play offers a remarkable criticism of group identification. Indeed, in one scene, it effectively undermines the entire idea of in-group/out-group opposition. Inspired by Marc Antony's speech, a mob first confuses Cinna the poet with Cinna the conspirator. Then, faced with the error, they decide to kill Cinna the poet anyway. As one of them puts it, "It is no matter, his name's Cinna; pluck but his name out of his heart" (III.iii.33–34). This may seem an isolated and accidental matter. But it is not. Shakespeare shows the absurdity of killing one "Cinna" due to anger over the acts of another "Cinna." The point holds equally for killing one "Frenchman" (or ten thousand "Frenchmen" – or Iraqis or Afghanis) due to the acts of another. There is no more reason to blame other Frenchmen than to blame other Cinnas.

For our purposes, the key point here is that these patterns result from Shakespeare's narrative idiolect. We have already noted some peculiarities of his heroic prototype and development principles – for example, the undermining of a singular origin to the conflict and the disruption of normative alignment. We may add two further points here. First, Shakespeare engages in relatively full simulation of characters independent of their (apparent) in-group or out-group status. Second, perhaps at the level of evaluations, he seems to follow a principle of something like emotional balance. As one set of characters is presented more favorably, that provokes a sort of emotional compensation – either criticism of the (previously) favored group or elevation of the (previously) disfavored group. (This is a subprinciple of the disruption of normative alignment.) Shakespeare does not always follow these two principles as thoroughly as he does in *Julius Caesar*. However, they define a recurring tendency. Once again, all this is in keeping with the works' overarching thematic criticism of the usual nationalistic functions of heroic stories.

Richard II

It would be convenient if it turned out that *Julius Caesar* was a sort of turning point, with earlier heroic plays fitting well with the usual nationalistic function of the genre and later plays moving toward ambivalence. That is not the case, however, as we may see from such works as *Richard II*, which preceded *Henry V* by several years.

Richard II focuses on the usurpation sequence, although it does so almost in slow motion, dividing the usurpation into stages – thereby revealing another one of Shakespeare's development principles. (We find something similar in *King Lear*.) The theme of usurpation is asserted at the outset when Mowbray and Bolingbroke accuse one another. In connection with this, the idea of providence – at least in the form found in *Henry V* – is almost immediately undermined as Richard shows no faith that a contest between the two will actually prove who is right and who is wrong. From this opening, Richard seems eminently reasonable in attempting to forestall the likely consequences should either of these nobles kill the other, thus perhaps initiating a cycle of violence. In the second scene, however, we hear that Richard is himself a usurper. Indeed, he is reported to be responsible for the very murder debated by Mowbray and Bolingbroke. This certainly taints Richard's character. It does not, however, undermine his actions regarding the duel. Even if he is guilty of the relevant murder,[18] it seems that he has nothing to lose by allowing the duel to proceed. Should Bolingbroke be killed, that eliminates one of Richard's enemies. However, if Mowbray is killed, then (we may infer from events later in the play) that silences someone who might have testified to Richard's guilt. Thus preventing the duel remains the reasonable act it seemed at first.

After these preliminaries, Bolingbroke is exiled. In keeping with the standard structure, immediately after the exile of Bolingbroke, the story turns to a threat, in this case from Ireland. In the usual manner of Shakespeare's (slightly modified) prototypical structure, Bolingbroke does not return to fend off this threat. Rather, he makes use of the opportunity to stage his own invasion, supported by the Duke of Brittany. In this way, Shakespeare doubles the foreign-attack sequence. (Multiplication of this sort is another development principle used by Shakespeare.) In part drawing our sympathy toward Bolingbroke, Shakespeare presents a series of complaints against Richard (e.g., II.i.246–255). But right after this, we witness the affection Richard's wife has for him (II.ii). This helps rehumanize Richard and tends to foster compassion for his side in the conflict. Sympathy is not the only wavering value here, however. Law too is unclear. York states that legal right is on the side of Richard (II.iv.167–168), whereas Bolingbroke claims illegal dealings on Richard's part (II.iii.128–135). Bolingbroke then goes on to order executions with very flimsy justifications (III.i), a point with both legal and emotional ramifications. The ambivalence cultivated throughout the play (with its intensification through familialization) is stated directly by York when he says, regarding Richard and Bolingbroke, "Both are my kinsmen./Th'one is my sovereign, whom both my oath/And duty bids defend; t'other again/Is my kinsman, whom the King hath wronged,/Whom conscience and my kindred bids to right" (II.ii.111–115).[19]

In direct contradiction of providentialism and the alignment of right with might, once Richard's defeat is certain, virtually all our sympathy is with him. The one exception to this is the trial regarding Gloucester's murder. But first, the trial is inconclusive (as both sides have reason to lie), and second, the purges engaged in by Bolingbroke seem worse than anything done by Richard. Indeed, in a perversion of the idea of providence, we find Bolingbroke himself playing God in making his decisions as to whether others should live or die. In one such instance he is explicitly called "god on earth" (V.iii.135) – a sort of ultimate usurpation, but one not punished by divine intervention. In short, the only providence this play appears to accept, at least in the short term, is the providence of powerful rulers.

The play ends with Bolingbroke's rejection of the henchman he used to kill Richard and Bolingbroke's vow to "make a voyage to the Holy Land,/To wash this blood off from my guilty hand" (V.vi.49–50). The rejection may function to indicate some moral decency on Bolingbroke's part, some lingering conscience. But it may equally operate to indicate that Bolingbroke lacks even that basic "honor among thieves" that we find in, for example, Macbeth. The pilgrimage is a projected epilogue of suffering. It is a Christian specification of the temporary exile, the time of repentance and spiritual renewal, that precedes full accession to kingship in the complete prototypical structure. But here too there is ambiguity. The epilogue of suffering is usually the act of the rightful ruler who has been usurped and restored, but it is not obvious that Bolingbroke fits this description. More importantly, the vow of the pilgrimage has the ambiguity of all epilogues of suffering. On the one hand, it is an expression of remorse and an act of penance. On the other hand, it is a cheap way of freeing oneself from guilt, purging one's conscience and currying divine favor, without making any genuine sacrifice. In this respect, Claudius is far preferable to Bolingbroke in admitting that he cannot beg forgiveness for his murder of King Hamlet, "Since I am still possess'd/Of those effects for which I did the murther:/My crown, mine own ambition, and my queen" (III.iii.53–55). Of course, Shakespeare – and his audience – may not have recognized the ambiguity in Bolingbroke's final speech. But that only partially modifies – perhaps even enhances – the ambivalence of the play. The speech in that case gives the audience some reason to sympathize with Bolingbroke's feelings of remorse and to admire his spiritual dedication. Nonetheless, this hardly counterbalances the sympathy most audience members are likely to have developed for Richard after his defeat. Either way, we continue to see

Shakespeare's development principles at work, most obviously those of normative disalignment and emotional balance.

Hamlet

Most of the action in *Hamlet* concerns usurpation. At least at one level, the
play elaborates and complicates the restoration part of this sequence. Thus
it gives us another instance of what might be called Shakespeare's principle of prolongation (the "slow motion" mentioned in relation to *Richard
II*). Before the play begins, Claudius has usurped the kingdom from King
Hamlet and thus prevented Prince Hamlet from gaining the throne. (The latter is the common preventive usurpation variant.) In keeping with the usual
structure, Hamlet is exiled. He returns shortly before an enemy army enters
the kingdom. Following Shakespeare's somewhat idiosyncratic prototype,
he sides with the entering army. In a variation on this structure, the invading army comes with a peaceful purpose. Moreover, the invading king only
stakes his claim when the royal family of the home society has done itself in.
Thus Hamlet does not join an invading army in battle. Rather, he in effect
bequeaths the kingdom to the invader.

But, here again, things are curiouser than this summary indicates. Most
importantly, there are suggestions that Hamlet is himself in some way the
usurper. Thus some things happen to Hamlet that typically happen to the
usurper. For example, he suffers the loss of his beloved, perhaps through
suicide, at the moment when his sufferings are accumulating toward a final
defeat.

The play begins with a motif used elsewhere by Shakespeare, the return
of the usurped victim's ghost. But here – in keeping with ambiguity about
which character plays which prototypical role – the spirit does not haunt the
(apparent) usurper, as in the case of Caesar's ghost, the ghost of Banquo, or
the ghosts in *Richard III*. Indeed, initially we are unsure of the reason for
the ghost's appearance. He is wearing the armor he wore when he defeated
Norway decades earlier, and we immediately hear that Denmark is currently
preparing for an invasion from Norway. In other words, the play begins with
a very strong suggestion that it will present the threat/defense scenario from
the heroic plot. Here, as elsewhere in Shakespeare, the situation is almost
immediately confused when we learn that King Hamlet won the disputed
territory on a wager. Although Horatio asserts that the entire process was
"ratified by law" (I.i.87), no argument is presented, and it is difficult to see
how Denmark can justly claim the land. In any case, it is clear that the territory did once belong to Norway and thus that there is no simple, single

origin to this conflict (i.e., a simple decision by Norway to invade land that was immemorially Danish). Moreover, the fact that the names are identical in the two generations – Hamlet and Fortinbras – may suggest just the sort of nontelic, nonprovidential cycle of violence that we saw in the earlier plays.

Of course, as it turns out, the ghost's presence results from the other part of the heroic plot – not invasion, but usurpation. The ghost tells the story of how Claudius murdered him to gain the throne. The idea is plausible, but we are uncertain about the nature of the ghost. Hamlet himself says that the ghost may be "a spirit of health, or goblin damn'd," bringing "airs from heaven, or blasts from hell" (I.iv.40, 41). Subsequently, the ghost confesses himself to be suffering "sulph'rous and tormenting flames" (I.v.3–4), although only "for a certain term" (10). In other words, he claims to have departed life, neither for heaven nor for hell, but for purgatory. This claim does not entirely resolve the issue. Indeed, it may confuse things further. Shakespeare's Catholic audience members may have taken the ghost's assertion as perfectly reasonable. But the Protestants could have seen this as evidence that the ghost was untrustworthy, that he was lying in his reference to purgatory, a nonexistent place, a Catholic fiction.[20] Hamlet himself continues to doubt the provenance of the ghost, wondering if he is "a dev'l" who "abuses me to damn me" (II.ii.579, 583). Even when we learn that the ghost has spoken truthfully about the murder, his own nature remains uncertain. As Watts points out, "Even a veracious ghost could still be diabolic, since the Devil can tell the truth to suit his purposes" (Watts "Where" 18).

Nevertheless, I imagine that most audience members are willing to accept that the ghost is telling the truth, not only about Claudius (a point confirmed later in the play) but about his own identity and condition as well. (Even Protestant audience members may accept that purgatory is real in a fiction, even if it is a fiction in reality.) This gives Hamlet at least a partial justification for setting out to kill Claudius. Moreover, the entire play focuses on Hamlet. We share his point of view, and, what is crucial here, we know his suicidal despair. We see him love, act in friendship, joke, and feel hurt by Ophelia's apparent rejection. He is a full person for us, and a person whose father evidently has been murdered. Thus we have strong reasons for supporting him, for seeing his case as right and Claudius's as wrong.

Yet killing Claudius remains the killing of a king, thus an act of treason in many ways directly comparable to Claudius's killing of King Hamlet.[21] Indeed, the parallel goes beyond the act itself to the motivation. Hamlet desires to right a wrong. His goal is restoration. But the restoration is, of course, his own (as heir to King Hamlet), and part of his motivation is the simple desire to be king. Thus he tells Rosencrantz and Guildenstern that he suffers grief because he "lack[s] advancement" (III.ii.320). Elsewhere, he explains that Claudius "popp'd in between th'election and my hopes" (V.ii.65). Hamlet is, at least to some degree, motivated by the very feeling of ambition that drove Claudius to murder King Hamlet initially (for Claudius's motivation, see III.iii.55). The identification is perhaps most striking in *The Mousetrap*, where the usurper is not the king's brother (Claudius's relation to King Hamlet) but his nephew (Prince Hamlet's relation to Claudius).

Beyond all this, regicide is not merely a legal and moral issue but also a prudential one, for the murder of the king affects the entire society. Although said in flattery, Rosencrantz's comments on the life of a king are not invalid. He refers to the king as "that spirit upon whose weal depends and rests/The lives of many" (III.iii.14–15), explaining that a king "Dies not alone, but … doth draw/What's near it with it" (16–17). More generally, a single murder is never an absolute end and resolution – especially when it is the murder of a ruler (whether rightful or usurping). One killing is invariably a source of further death and destruction, a point borne out by Claudius's and Hamlet's various murders in the course of the play. Such sequences are routinely part of Shakespeare's simulation of violent acts.

The rightness of Hamlet's cause is enhanced when we learn at last that Claudius did in fact commit the murder, as claimed by the ghost (III.iii.36–38). The force of this revelation, however, is diminished by a series of events surrounding it. First, Hamlet himself never hears Claudius's confession. His evidence of the murder is all circumstantial.[22] *Our* knowledge that Claudius is the murderer hardly justifies Hamlet's revenge. Second, along with Claudius's confession, we learn about his feelings of guilt. This at least creates some sympathy for, in Hawkes's words, "the pitiable human situation … of a man torn by the conflicting demands of criminal passion and remorse" (183). Perhaps more significantly, it is difficult to align Hamlet with the good and the divine when he has to restrain his impulse to kill his mother (see III.ii.367–378), who presumably knew nothing of the murder.[23] Moreover, in this speech, Hamlet explicitly associates his undertaking with "hell itself" (III.ii.368). Along the same lines, there is some excess in Hamlet's insistence that Claudius not merely die but also go to hell (see III.iii.95). After all, Hamlet's father is suffering only purgatory. Finally, the whole scene between Hamlet and Gertrude disturbs any easy admiration for Hamlet. First, despite his earlier resolution, he seems poised to murder his mother, who cries out, "Thou wilt not murther me?/Help ho!" (III.iv.21–22). Immediately following this, he does kill Polonius and shows no real remorse, but is, rather, quite "callous," as Foakes puts it (Foakes 93). Rather than recognizing that he has committed murder, he engages in a repellent fantasy of his mother's sexual relations with

Claudius ("In the rank sweat of an enseamed bed ... honeying and making love" [III.iv.92–93]).

At this point, one might wonder if the play is establishing Claudius as a flawed, but rightful ruler and Hamlet as the usurper.[24] But here Shakespeare's principle of emotional balance enters again. Specifically, Claudius initiates the plot to kill Hamlet. His subsequent scheming with Laertes only compounds the fault. These actions weigh heavily against Claudius – both morally and emotively. Yet, even in this part of the play, things are not simple. Between Claudius's two plots, Hamlet has forged orders for the king of England to kill Rosencrantz and Guildenstern, although there is no reason to believe that they knew anything about the plot on Hamlet's life. Hamlet even admits to killing them simply because they became involved in royal affairs. "They are not near my conscience," he tells Horatio. He goes on to explain that their death is their own fault because "'tis dangerous when the baser nature comes/Between the pass and fell incensed points/Of mighty opposites" (V.ii.58–62).[25] We do not, however, see these deaths. We only hear about them, which diminishes their emotional force. Moreover, it is easy for an audience member, caught up in the events, to unthinkingly assume that Rosencrantz and Guildenstern were necessarily parties to the plot against Hamlet's life – although, at the same time, it is important that Hamlet himself does not use this as his excuse.

In short, the play derives from the usurpation sequence. But, like the other plays we have considered (except *Henry V*), it is insistently ambivalent. It systematically disaligns different values and feelings. It indicates that heroic violence is a potentially unending cycle with no absolute origin in unjustified and unprovoked individual evil (e.g., the mere greed of Fortinbras or Claudius) and no providential resolution. One point where this ambivalence is strikingly articulated occurs when Hamlet compares himself to Laertes. Hamlet's relation to Claudius, in this view, is the same as Laertes's relation to Hamlet: "By the image of my cause I see/The portraiture of his" (V.ii.77–78). Of course, Laertes is on the side of Claudius, against Hamlet. The parallel further indicates that neither side can be seen as generally right or wrong. What might seem to justify one side justifies its opposite as well.

The few references to providence sustain or even advance the work's ambivalence. Here as in other plays, "some ultimately beneficent, supernatural plan ... is expressly invoked" only "to be shattered time and again by fresh horrors" (in Kiernan Ryan's words [96]), horrors that do not bear on one side only. That is not all. At one point, the play invokes providence with such palpable irony that it becomes almost impossible to take the idea seriously. When threatened by Laertes, Claudius affirms the divine determination of political events, claiming that Laertes cannot simply choose to rebel, for the king is protected by God. Addressing Gertrude, who is trying to restrain Laertes, he says, "Let him go ... do not fear our person:/There's such divinity doth hedge a king/That treason can but peep to what it would" (IV.v.122–124). Of course, the entire story we are witnessing would be impossible if this were true. Claudius knows perfectly well that no divinity hedges a king, regardless of whether he is legitimate or a usurper, and that treason encounters no supernatural barriers. After all, he has successfully murdered a king himself. Given this, an audience member can only conclude that Claudius's claims – and, more generally, the standard alignment of God and ruler – are merely self-conscious deceit and propaganda.

The play ends with a no less ambivalent treatment of the invasion sequence. Hamlet gives his "voice" to Fortinbras as the new ruler (V.ii.338). This is a strange choice, given that Fortinbras should have been the paradigm of the enemy, but it is consistent with Shakespeare's idiolectal prototype. In part, it shows a mixing up of in-group and out-group. In part, it represents a simple recognition that peace is better than war and that, without a peaceful ceding to Fortinbras, a war might follow. The idea is in keeping with Hamlet's earlier account of Fortinbras – an account that seriously questions the nationalistic function of heroic plots.[26] Hamlet meets a captain in Fortinbras's army, who explains that the troops are heading off to war over "a little patch of ground/ That hath in it no profit but the name" (IV.iv.16–17). Hamlet summarizes the theme, "Two thousand souls and twenty thousand ducats/Will not debate the question of this straw" (25–26). He goes on to explain Fortinbras's action as the result of "spirit with divine ambition puff'd" (49). Renaissance audience members should have recognized "divine ambition" as the sin of spiritual pride, a more intense and more damnable form of the mundane ambition and pride that motivated Claudius and motivates Hamlet. But here the danger is not a single murder. It is "the imminent death of twenty thousand men" fighting "for a fantasy and trick of fame" (60–61) – precisely the fate that is both perpetuated and occluded by heroic tragicomedy even to the present day.

The Tempest

It should be clear that plays such as *King John*, *Richard III*, *Titus Andronicus*, *King Lear*, *Macbeth*, and *Coriolanus* are robust, if highly complex instances of heroic plots, including the usual components. Other works, such as *Troilus and Cressida*, *Antony and Cleopatra*, and *Cymbeline*, include partial heroic plots or elements of heroic plots as well.[27] There is no need to treat all these works here. The preceding analyses – treating the alliance of the exiled leader with the invader, normative disalignment, the independence of character simulation from in-group/out-group status, and other of Shakespeare's idiolectal principles – may be extended to these works more or less straightforwardly. Of course, there is necessarily some variability in the precise complex of principles operating in each case. After all, there are necessarily some differences among an author's works along with the continuities; otherwise they would not count as different works. Nonetheless, the continuities remain.

In conclusion, however, it is valuable to consider a play that is not so obviously an instance of heroic tragicomedy – *The Tempest*. At first blush, it may seem that *The Tempest* is a romantic plot, and it is, to a degree. But it is also a heroic plot, despite its lack of "heroism." *The Tempest* is valuable to consider in part because, like *Henry V*, it is a comedy, but it is a comedy that is consistent with the treatment of heroic structures in the other plays. That treatment, as we have seen, undermines the standard political function of heroic tragicomedy, yet Shakespeare does this, in part, by making the vision of those plays deeply tragic. In short, those works show us what is wrong with the propagandistic uses of the heroic structure. But they offer no positive alternative. Of course, *Henry V* is positive, but that is only because it accepts the nationalist ideology exposed in the other plays, deviating from Shakespeare's ordinary prototype and development and evaluation principles. In contrast with both cases, *The Tempest* suggests how the heroic plot may be specified in such a way as to resist its standard ideological function – thus following Shakespeare's usual idiolectal principles – while still permitting a comic conclusion.

Although it may not be evident at first, *The Tempest* is, at its heart, a play about usurpation. Like *Hamlet*, it focuses on the restoration part of the usurpation sequence, also with some prolongation. Unlike *Hamlet*, however, it eschews violence as a means to attain restoration. That, it seems, is what allows it to be a comedy – in striking contrast with *Henry V* where the comic conclusion is premised on mass murder. Put differently, the play returns to the brief moment from early in Shakespeare's career – the moment of *Henry V* – when he evidently believed that a comic resolution to a heroic plot was possible (assuming the development of that earlier play was not determined by political expediency or constraint). However, it retains the insights and attitudes of the other heroic plays, the crucial simulative principle that violence leads to violence, the development principle that there is no direct and evident providential decision by which God chooses one side over the other in conflict, the balance-inspiring evaluation principle that good and evil are not doled out as wholes. In short, it preserves the humane sense of ambivalence we have been treating, but it nonetheless allows a positive ending.

The fundamental usurpation in the play is obvious. It is a familial betrayal by which a brother usurps a brother (like *Hamlet*). It is preceded by Prospero's delegation of authority to Antonio – a Shakespearean motif that we also see in *King Lear* and, in a different form, in *Titus Andronicus*. Alonso then joins with Antonio in an invasion sequence. "A treacherous army" (I.ii.128) enters Milan, and Prospero is exiled. Here, in a surprisingly standard variation on the prototype, the usurper joins with the invading army rather than the exiled ruler doing so. This to some extent reduces the ambivalence of the plot, for Antonio is wrong on both counts: He has no right to rule, and he has betrayed his society to an invader. Yet Antonio does have some claim in terms of merit and ability. As in *King Lear*, it is not entirely unreasonable for someone who has all the responsibilities of rule to expect the title and ultimate authority of office as well. Moreover, he is not bloodthirsty. The rebels and invaders do not kill Prospero and his daughter. That not only affects our emotional attitude toward the usurpers (contrast a play in which Prospero and Miranda narrowly escape an attempted execution). In many ways, this one reticence, the fact that "they durst not … set/A mark so bloody on the business" (I.ii.140–143), allows the peaceful and comic resolution at the end of the play.

Of course, none of this makes Antonio or his ally, Alonso, sympathetic. We know Prospero intimately, whereas we know Antonio and Alonso only distantly. Moreover, law and moral principles clearly favor Prospero. Yet the mere fact that Prospero is so adept at magic taints his actions and his character. His power is too close to witchcraft, too near to demonic practices. Moreover, the side of Antonio and Alonso is not without its positive merits. The compassionate Neapolitan, Gonzalo, who helped Prospero and Miranda at the moment of usurpation, remains with Alonso's party. Alonso's son, Ferdinand, appears generally admirable. He is certainly not guilty of his father's crime. Any general attack on the side of Antonio and Alonso would be wrong in this context, for it would result in the suffering of innocents – the inevitable result of war, as the other plays show. In short, there is not a simple division of good on one side and evil on the other.

Beyond this, we develop sympathy with Alonso when the first of two usurpation subplots begins. Specifically, the play concerns not only the restoration of Prospero, but equally treats the failed usurpation of Alonso by Sebastian and Antonio. Indeed, this plot is worse, for it rests on the death of Alonso. This murderous project does operate to make Antonio a more damnable figure, but it establishes a parallel between Alonso and Prospero. Although this conspiracy does not mitigate Alonso's earlier crime, it makes the danger to his life more salient than his past treachery. In addition, the parallel with Prospero (along with Ferdinand's developing romance with Miranda) helps undermine what would otherwise be a simple in-group/out-group division between Naples and Milan. This establishment of parallels between antagonists is also a recurring principle in Shakespeare.

The third usurpation plot – manifesting Shakespeare's development principle of narrative repetition with variation – complicates the situation still further. It concerns Stephano, Trinculo, and Caliban, who seek to usurp Prospero. This is perhaps the point in the play where ambivalence arises most significantly. In some ways, the usurpation plot of this bibulous crew is farcical. However, there are serious elements to it. For example, Caliban treats wine as if it is sacred and Stephano as if he were a deity. On the one hand, this is absurd. On the other hand, it is difficult not to recall that, in Christianity, there is a close association between wine and sacredness. Indeed, Christian Europeans, encountering Caliban on an island, would have tried to convert him to a doctrine that preached precisely that God appeared in human form and poured out sacred wine to his followers.

More importantly, it is far from clear that this is the usurpation part of a usurpation sequence. In many ways, it is a failed restoration, with the usual Shakespearean variation of the deposed ruler (here, Caliban) allying himself with invaders (here, Stephano and Trinculo). Early in the play, Caliban offers a strong argument that "this island's mine, by Sycorax my mother,/Which thou tak'st from me" (I.ii.334–335). We are never given good reason to believe this is untrue. As Wheeler points out, "Caliban's experience of betrayal closely parallels Prospero's story of an inherited claim usurped by someone he trusted" (Wheeler 141). Thus we have a triple parallel across antagonists – Alonso is parallel to Prospero, who is in turn parallel with Caliban. But there is a difference. Alonso remains the usurper of Prospero, and Prospero remains the usurper of Caliban. Caliban does not appear to have usurped anyone.

The subsequent revelation of attempted sex crimes certainly makes Caliban less sympathetic, but it does not entirely degrade him. First, the accusation is milder than what we would call *rape* today: "Thou didst seek to violate/ The honor of my child" (I.ii.349–350). Any attempt to have sexual relations without marriage – including the sorts of profession of love that apparently passed from Hamlet to Ophelia – could in principle be characterized in these terms. As long as Caliban bypassed the authority of Prospero in the matter, he was seeking to violate Miranda's honor. Moreover, this does not seem to bear on the issue of usurpation – although Prospero presents it as his primary argument against Caliban's claims. Finally, even relevant arguments would have no real force here. After all, Prospero is not a judge in some international criminal court, empowered to decide on the deposing of foreign rulers. Admittedly, he articulates another argument elsewhere – that Sycorax was not born on the island but exiled there. However, it is not clear how this is relevant either, as Caliban's claim to the island remains prior to that of Prospero. Stephano's assertion of ownership of the island – an assertion that simply ignores Prospero – appears to be a mirror image of Prospero's own assertion, with its simple ignoring of Sycorax and Caliban. Indeed, Stephano's claim even involves the same liberatory rhetoric. Prospero implicitly justifies his domination of the island and of Ariel by the assertion that he freed Ariel from the pains imposed on him by Sycorax. In the same way, Stephano will liberate Caliban from the "tyrant" Prospero, as Caliban calls him (III.i.155).

Of course, Prospero repeatedly links Caliban with demonic origins and practices, as when he says that Caliban was "got by the devil himself" (I.ii.322). This may seem to undermine any ambivalence suggested elsewhere, but it does not, ultimately, produce the simple godly/satanic division one might expect in this context. Indeed, Caliban more convincingly, if implicitly, links Prospero with demonic practices when he claims that "by sorcery he got this isle;/From me he got it" (III.ii.50–51). Unsurprisingly, this too requires qual-ification. Most importantly, Prospero's use of sorcery is never fatal. It causes pain to Caliban, but it frees Ariel from pain. In causing the tempest at the out-set, Prospero is careful to keep everyone alive. Again, it is not that Prospero is the villain. It is just that there is no simple alignment of sides and values – or even a perfectly clear division of in-group and out-group.

The conclusion of the play is, again, comic. Prospero is restored, and he is restored entirely by policy – manipulative policy, but policy nonetheless, not murder.[28] The play hints at the sorts of violence that produce the epilogue of suffering. Ariel explains to Prospero that "the King,/His brother, and yours abide all three distracted.... That if you now beheld them your affections/ Would become tender" (V.i.12–13, 18–19). Prospero does not press further but responds, "And mine shall" (20). Rather than exacting revenge, he will stop before the cruelty that leads to remorse – and to a cycle of violence. He explains that "they being penitent,/The sole drift of my purpose doth extend/ Not a frown further" (V.i.28–30). Clearly, repentance is necessary. If Prospero became duke again but Alonso and Antonio had no remorse for their prior usurpation, they would be likely to seek out any opportunity to repeat it. But, Prospero explains, he does not ask anything beyond this necessary condition, not even to the extent of a single frown. In keeping with the general attitude manifest in his heroic plays, Shakespeare here indicates that forgiveness and reconciliation are the only way to end the cycle of usurpations and invasions. That is the clear suggestion of the final lines, when Prospero addresses the audience, asking them, "As you from crimes would pardoned be,/Let your indulgence set me free" (Epilogue 20). To prevent further harm, Prospero refrains from revealing the treachery of Sebastian and Antonio (V.i.126–129).

He punishes the plot of Stephano and Trinculo only with housekeeping (V.i.292–294).

There is still something missing here, however. We have considered the Italian characters. But what about the characters Prospero found already on the island? Ariel is freed. Caliban is subjected to the same punishment as Stephano and Trinculo, but what is to happen to him after that? Prospero's departure suggests that perhaps he has regained dominion over the island, that this usurpation too has ended in restoration (cf. Omesco 164). In light of postcolonial interpretations of the play,[29] this may seem slight. One might have wished Prospero to be remorseful over Caliban (perhaps even over Ariel) as Alonso is remorseful over Prospero. Perhaps this is hoping for too much. Or perhaps not. The epilogue to the play presents us with a vision of Prospero trapped, "confined" (Epilogue 4) on the island, as Ariel was "confine[d]" in the tree (I.ii.275) or Caliban was "confined" in the rock (I.ii.364). Prospero is, in this way, closely parallel with the islanders, thus linked with them and not only with the Italians.[30] The point blurs the in-group/out-group division, in keeping with a central development principle of Shakespeare – roughly, "When in-group/out-group divisions begin to form, make it to some degree ambiguous which is actually the in-group and which is the out-group." In addition, Prospero himself asks forgiveness. In a context that so clearly suggests Ariel and Caliban, the sins that he repents in this brief epilogue of suffering are almost certainly his treatment of these prior inhabitants of the island.

This multiplication of remorse, compassion, and forgiveness – extended from the characters to the real world members of the audience at the end – culminates Shakespeare's vision, or revision, of the heroic plot. It involves all the ambivalence of the other heroic plays, but it uses that ambivalence positively to produce a comedy, however muted. The usurpation plot is finished. Restorations finally succeed. Invasions are ultimately reversed. But these standard resolutions are not achieved by the good exterminating the evil. They are achieved by flawed people acting together with empathy, penitence, and mercy.[31]

Conclusion

The preceding analyses illustrate key features of the simulation of narratives. Specifically, they indicate that distinctive features of the author's narrative idiolect are crucial in the production of particular works. In other words, an author's narrative production is a function of his or her narrative idiolect (which governs simulation), just as his or her sentence production is a function of his or her linguistic idiolect. Moreover, here as elsewhere, an awareness of authorial narrative idiolect may inflect our thematic interpretation of and emotional response to particular works.

With respect to Shakespeare, these analyses indicate several points. First, a large number of Shakespeare's plays fall into the general, cross-cultural pattern of heroic tragicomedy. Like any author, Shakespeare specified the heroic prototype in ways that are themselves patterned. The development principles and motifs he employed in particularizing that prototype are largely universal. These include descriptive (as opposed to normative) alignment, event and character repetition with variation, and prolonged elaboration of prototype segments (e.g., the usurpation proper). However, the exact force of these principles and motifs as well as the hierarchized complexes they formed in their precise variants were unique to him.

One overarching pattern in Shakespeare's narrative idiolect was a systematic undermining of the main ideological functions of heroic tragicomedy. This resulted from several development and evaluation principles, including theory of mind simulation for out-group members, normative disalignment (including the cultivation of ambivalence), parallelism across antagonists, and ambiguity over in- versus out-group status. This undermining also derived from peculiarities of Shakespeare's idiolectal heroic prototype itself, such as his tendency to link the rightful ruler with invasion.

At the same time, *Henry V* shows that Shakespeare's work is not entirely uniform. Rather, Shakespeare could violate his own idiolectal principles. It is unsurprising that this violation involved a turn to the more standard prototypical structure.

4

Principles and Parameters of Storytelling

The Trajectory of Racine's Romantic Tragedies

The sorts of recurring patterns we have been considering in Shakespeare's heroic tragicomedies are far from unique. Patterns of some sort should be discernable in the canon of any author. Again, this is a matter of continuities in the author's narrative idiolect. In another terminology, it is a function of cognitive entrenchment.

Nonetheless, in Shakespeare and other authors, entrenchment is not absolute, inflexible, or fully determinative. Shakespeare wrote different plays. He did not simply keep reproducing *The Comedy of Errors*. Even his most characteristic heroic works are clearly distinct from one another. Thus there is necessarily some degree of cognitive plasticity as well (a point that is particularly obvious with *Henry V*).

Mere change is not all that is at issue here. Authors never simply reproduce the same work. Nonetheless, we sometimes refer to authors or other artists as "repeating themselves." This does not mean simply manifesting closely related surface properties. Ultimately, the difference between repetitive and nonrepetitive literature has to do with the reader's or viewer's emotional and intellectual engagement. That engagement has a number of possible sources, but it is necessarily bound up with the reader's expectations regarding an author, thus the variability of the author's work. In some cases, we say that an author's work has altered systematically. In other words, it does not simply vary a recurring structure but rather follows out a trajectory of change. This chapter considers some of what is involved in such systematic alteration.

Before turning to that topic, however, we should recall the components of narrative idiolect. These include the following:

Cross-cultural story prototypes, both major and minor (as well as more historically and culturally specific genre patterns).
Character and scene prototypes (connected with the story prototypes).

Event, character, and scene motifs.

Processes for changing these "prior structures," particularly prototypes – thus alteration principles.

Individual instances of event, character, and scene categories, both literary and biographical – in other words, exempla. These are often recruited by specification principles.

Processes that particularize prior structures – thus specification principles. These commonly draw on exempla.

Processes for evaluating one's narratives and engaging in corrective revision for emotional or thematic deficits – thus evaluation principles. These prominently include tacit comparison with exempla.

These components of an authorial idiolect are not immutable. But they are fairly enduring. The durability accounts for the constancies across an author's canon – isolating and explaining such constancies is one task in understanding such a canon.

Again, when we isolate the narrative idiolect of an author, we are studying entrenchment, inferring relatively constant structures, processes, and contents. But this constancy should not be understood too narrowly. In many cases, it is possible to isolate alternative structures, processes, and contents within an authorial idiolect. For example, one might argue that Tagore's stories of attachment separation develop differently if the separation is due to social constraint (e.g., the economics of dowry) or if the separation is due to ideology (e.g., the social stigma of violating normative gender roles). In other words, one might argue that there are two versions of his idiolectal attachment prototype, one for each type of causal condition.

As this suggests, we may model the authorial idiolectal prototypes and variants as complexes of principles with parameters. Thus Tagore's simulation of attachment separation may develop by setting a causal parameter to social constraint (e.g., where family members are separated due to financial need) or to ideology (e.g., where family members are separated due to the gender ideology that rigidly segregates male and female activities). Note that we engage in simulation with small parametric shifts all the time in ordinary life. It is well established that "counterfactual thinking usually involves minimal departures from reality" (Van Boven, Kane, and McGraw 133). Indeed, "constructing a counterfactual thought implicitly involves laying out a causal chain of events in a sequence of actions and mutating one step in the process to construct an alternate reality" (Wong, Galinsky, Kray 162). The same point holds for hypotheticals. Thus the junior editor of a collection might imagine how the notoriously prickly Jones would react if she asked him to revise his essay. The result is unappealing. She then reimagines the scenario with her senior coeditor asking. The result of the second simulation may be different. This sort of imagination with small parameter shifts is crucial to the functionality of simulation. Indeed, this ability to hold most of the components constant and slightly alter a small number of specific elements is what allows us to vary and improve plans for action. Because this ability underlies the imagination of trajectories of action in real life, we would expect it to underlie that imagination in fictional narrative as well.[1]

To refer to principles and parameters is to draw an idiom from theoretical linguistics. In linguistic principles and parameters theory, language is understood as defined by a set of innate principles that have limited variables.[2] These govern, for example, whether adjectives go before or after nouns. By this theory, language universality may be accounted for by the principles and the limitation of the parameters. At the same time, language variation may be accounted for by different complexes of parameter settings. These complexes are further constrained by the order in which the parameters are set and the consequences one parameter setting has for others.[3]

Needless to say, the present analysis is not an instance of linguistic principles and parameters theory. Indeed, nothing in the following discussion in any way presupposes the validity of any particular linguistic theory. Rather, here as elsewhere, the linguistic theory is valuable for establishing and illustrating a kind of cognitive architecture. As Mark Baker, one of the major writers on linguistic principles and parameters, explains, the idea of principles and parameters "is most commonly associated with the Chomskyan approach to formal generative linguistics.... The idea is, however, a very general one, and it can also be used in the context of other views" ("Parameters" 582). The general idea, then, presents us with a way of understanding the operation of rules in more complex, systematic ways. It thereby enhances the descriptive precision and explanatory power of our rule-based analyses.

Of course, we need to specify this architecture in ways that are most relevant to narrative study. In some cases, the parameters of a narrative idiolect are very much like those in linguistic theory, comprising a limited number of specified alternatives. As such, the principles and parameters should account for the fixed part of authorial idiolect, and the complexes of parameter settings should account for variation. There is, however, an important difference between language and storytelling. The parameters of an author's narrative idiolect are not set once and for all in childhood. They are, rather, set with each new story. Moreover, there are possibilities for the addition of new principles and/or parameters.[4]

Confining ourselves for the moment to the case where principles and parametric alternatives are already established, we still face the question of how the parameters are set in particular cases. Since they are not set socially and for all stories, they must be set at the time individual stories are created. This setting presumably results from the integration of the cognitive elements listed above. Most obviously, individual characters and scenes not only may but must be integrated with narrative prototypes if the prototypes are to be expanded and particularized – if they are to become real stories and not just outlines for possible stories. That is, once again, why the insertion of particular characters into narrative prototypes seems to be especially important for the generation of specific stories. That point has renewed significance here as the integration of idiolectal character into idiolectal prototype involves processes that are particularly well modeled by parameter setting. Specifically, we may think of character simulation in part as a matter of setting character parameters (for sex, generation, etc.). Once a character is inserted into a story structure, these parameter settings guide further parameter settings for the story itself. (Recall that parameter specification for stories commonly underlies and enables story simulation.)

Extending these points, and linking them with the treatment of mental architecture in Chapter 1, we may isolate a structure of the following sort. Most fundamentally, we have neural networks of strongly and weakly connected properties and relations. The relatively enduring aspects of these networks may be captured in sets of principles – development and evaluation principles, as well as the principles that constitute prototypes. The variability of the outputs of the enduring structures will be captured by parameters for those principles.[5] For example, we will see that one standard development principle in Racine's narrative idiolect is to double his male protagonists. This doubling is further affected by variables such as whether the two are of the same generation or different generations, friends or relations, and so on. Cutting across the division between development and evaluation principles, we may distinguish basic principles and metaprinciples. Metaprinciples govern the application of basic principles, often constraining their application. For example, one metaprinciple of Racine's first and second plays may be something along the following lines: "maintain emotional consistency for a given character with respect to a given object." For example, if Hémon loves Antigone, keep him loving Antigone.

Principles may cluster together to form standard action sequences for a particular author. They may also aggregate with respect to characters or scenes. Thus some principles will tend to co-occur with respect to the doubled protagonists or their attachment figures, such as the sister of brother protagonists or the mother of those protagonists. In some cases, these aggregations may appear consistent enough to constitute types. Indeed, in discussing Racine's first play it will be convenient to introduce clusters of character principles as if they were character types. An account of the present sort differs crucially from an account based on character types, however. Specifically, the fundamental reality of the authorial idiolect is actually given in the highly diffuse and always somewhat unstable neural networks. Even the principles are approximate generalizations from those – and the putative character types are merely approximate generalizations from the principles. In other words, any reference to something along the lines of a character type is shorthand for an aggregative tendency of principles – which is itself shorthand for the enduring and variable features of the neural network that defines authorial narrative idiolect. These points apply to authorial versions of the universal prototypes as well as more idiosyncratic patterns. Nonetheless, the former tend to be far more consistent and stable than the latter. Thus I will continue to refer to these prototypes as fundamental – though by no means unalterable – structures.

The obvious way of treating authorial idiolect is by reference to the canon as a whole, considered synchronically (as in Chapter 3). However, an author composes works in a sequence. The precise composition and operation of narrative idiolect – including general principles and specified parameters – changes in the course of his or her life. In other words, there is, once again, entrenchment and plasticity. Indeed, the specification of one work subtly alters the precise configuration of principles that will interact to produce the next work. Examining this process of change constitutes a diachronic study. Moreover, if we are able to isolate trends across diachronic changes, then we will also have a trajectory study.

Diachronic study is made difficult by the fact that authors often write different works simultaneously and revise them repeatedly over long periods. However, some authors do give us a neat, chronologically organized canon to work with. Racine is a good case. His earliest dramatic works have not survived; however, his subsequent writings present as tidy a chronicle of composition as we are likely to find. This chapter will consider these plays in sequence, seeking to infer the common principles of Racine's plays as well as the changes that occurred across the career of his writings – including what most readers recognize as a vast improvement in literary quality from *La Thébaïd* to *Phèdre*.[6]

Racine is also an unusually apt author for this sort of study in that he nicely illustrates the parametric formation of a narrative trajectory. Specifically, it is arguable that, from one play to the next, Racine begins by making small changes in the situations, events, and, above all, characters or the relations among characters. These small changes can generally be seen as selections from a limited number of options, thus as settings of parameters. These parameter settings have widespread consequences for the resulting play. For example, suppose we have two (heterosexual) lovers. One axis of parametric variation would concern political power. There are three values: the man has more political power; the woman has more political power; the two are roughly equal in political power.[7] It may seem that the first two value settings would have the same outcome and thus be equivalent. That is not the case, however, since other parameters affect men and women differently. As a result, setting the political power parameter one way (say, in favor of the woman) will not simply produce a mirror image of setting it the other way (in favor of the man). Parametric axes that operate in Racine's specification of character relations include the following: sex (male or female), age (with the parameters varying first by generation, then by older/younger within a generation), attachment profile (attached, indifferent, alienated), sexual status (possible sexual partner or not, then, if a possible sexual partner, socially legitimate or not), familial relation (parent/child, sibling), and political authority (superior, inferior).[8]

A Note on the Analysis of Racine's Work

Unsurprisingly, the consistency of Racine's canon has not gone unnoticed. For instance, in his lucid and scholarly introduction to Racine, Tobin points out the recurrence of "warring brothers" in *La Thébaïd* and *Mithridate* (9). More significantly, he refers to recurring features in the later plays, beginning with *Bérénice*, specifically, "a love interest, a relatively uncomplicated plot, striking rhetorical passages, and a highly poetic use of time" (8). These are valuable observations, but they hardly even suggest the extensive patterns found in Racine's tragedies or their trajectory across his career. They are also unsystematic.

Pavel examines *Bajazet* in relation to a more encompassing pattern. Specifically, he isolates a narrative structure that involves a disturbed universe and, at the end, a reestablished universe; the disturbed universe comprises an initial situation and either a transgression or a lack, whereas the reestablished universe includes mediation and a dénouement (121). The idea is plausible, but it is clearly very general (and also not integrated with a well-defined cognitive architecture).

Heyndels is more particular to Racine. She distinguishes, first, cases where the hero dies because it is not possible to resolve the surrounding contradictions. There are two subtypes of this – cases in which things work out for other characters and cases in which they do not. Then there is a final type in which the hero does not die but rather lives with the contradictions (156–157). This is a suggestive organization of Racine's canon. But it remains at a very high level of abstraction, telling us relatively little about the detail of Racine's narrative idiolect and virtually nothing about the trajectory of his writings.

Other critics have treated recurring motifs. A good example is Morel's isolation of a character type that turns up repeatedly in Racine's plays – the character who is denied the status of tragic hero or heroine, despite manifesting "qualities" that "would normally bear a tragic destiny" (90–91). Analyses of this sort are certainly valuable but much more limited in scope than the present study.[9]

Perhaps the three major precursors for the present study are Lucien Goldmann, Roland Barthes, and Charles Mauron. These are perhaps the three most important and influential critics of Racine as well. Their works are illuminating, often brilliant explorations of Racine. I do not mean to compare the present, relatively brief analysis with their far more elaborate and comprehensive studies. Nonetheless, in terms of the present project, their treatment of narrative continuities and changes in Racine's work are either somewhat general or unsystematic (Goldmann and Barthes) or limited by their theoretical approach (Mauron).

Goldmann examines the Jansenist background to Racine's plays, setting out to isolate Racine's worldview. This worldview has broad thematic consequences, but it is more limited in its implications for the details of story development. For example, Goldmann stresses the "moment when man becomes fully tragic by refusing the world and life" (317). This is extremely general – indeed, so general that it is not entirely clear when it does or does not occur in a story. Elsewhere, Goldmann asserts that "we find the same world in all Racine's plays, each of which differs from its fellows ... solely by emphasizing a different aspect of it." But here he is referring primarily to characters being "under the power of the same amoral and unreflecting love" (321).

Barthes too isolated patterns in the work. Thus he comments that we could "make one essential tragedy" out of all Racine's tragedies. But, once again, this tends to be very general. For example, he notes that we find "the father, ... the women, ... the brothers, ... lastly, the son" (9). The point is undoubtedly valid and, in Barthes's analyses, revealing, but it is only the start of an idiolectal analysis. Barthes does make more detailed observations about recurring structure as well. Although insightful, these are often also problematic. For example, he comments on the set of "viriloid women" (13), including Axiane and Roxanne. The following analyses will suggest that there is a pattern here, but it is a matter of setting parameters such that the character with power is female, a parameter setting with consequences throughout the story. This is not to say that Barthes in any way ignores the issue of power. Indeed, one of the most valuable aspects of his analysis is his recognition that power relations and romantic relations are intertwined in the plays.

Perhaps the discussion closest to the present analysis is that of Charles Mauron. Mauron begins his study with the question of whether, despite apparent differences, there might not be "more profound structural analogies" unknown even to "the author himself" (25). In isolating these recurring structures, Mauron even makes some of the same specific connections (e.g., between Néron and Pyrrhus, and between Mithridate and Agamemnon). However, Mauron's psychoanalytic presuppositions orient his project very differently – most obviously in his tendency to allegorize elements of psychoanalytic mental organization (e.g., the ego and the superego). This leads to very consequential differences in both the description and explanation of patterns in Racine's work.

La Thébaïd ou Les Frères Ennemis
(The Thebiad or The Enemy Brothers)

Racine's *Thébaïd* is a strange work.[10] It combines elements of all three major genres (and even hints of minor genres) in such a way that it is never clear which genre dominates.[11] That tends to make the play seem diffuse – narratively, emotionally, and ideologically. Nonetheless, the play shows some subtle and, as we will see, characteristic narrative complications that prefigure or prepare for the more unified works that follow.

The backstory to the narrative is that Polynice and Étéocle should be co-heirs to the throne of Thebes, ruling in alternate years. Étéocle, however, has refused to step down as king. Thus we have a usurpation. But it is already a peculiar one, for the usurper is himself a legitimate ruler. Moreover, the usurped brother has taken up the actions of the usurper, in the version where he is allied with the invader (a shift we have seen in Shakespeare). Specifically, Polynice, aided by his father-in-law, has brought an army to fight against Thebes. Thus he has joined with an enemy to stage an invasion. In keeping with this, the populace seems to favor Étéocle as king.

The heroic plot continues with Jocaste and Antigone urging the warring brothers to reconcile and Créon manipulating the brothers in such a way as to exacerbate their antagonism. The result is that the brothers kill one another. This leaves the kingdom in the hands of Créon. However, the events leading to this also leave Créon without an heir – a common condition of a ruler at the beginning of a heroic plot rather than the end.

In addition to this heroic plot, there is a very undeveloped sacrificial plot. Étéocle explains that there is fear of hunger. An oracle suggests that a sacrifice is in order – specifically, the sacrifice of the "last" of the ruling family. Hearing this, Créon's son, Ménécée, kills himself. This is explicitly explained as a "sacrifice" to "efface" past "crimes" with "blood" (I: 62; my translation). The war, however, continues; the death was "in vain" (I: 63). This plot recurs when Créon, at the end of the play, announces that he is truly the "last" of this family and kills himself, fulfilling the "oracles" of "heaven" (I: 89).

As to romance, Antigone and Hémon are in love. They are separated by the war, which ultimately kills Hémon. In an unexpected development, Créon (Hémon's father) explains that Hémon's death removes an obstacle to his own pursuit of Antigone. However, before he can advance his plans in this direction, Antigone commits suicide.

Although we are dealing with only one play, we can begin to infer some distinctive aspects of Racine's narrative idiolect at those points where he introduces unusual features into a standard prototypes. With respect to character, these features could include the following. First, we have a political division between two roughly equal characters who should be joined. For ease of identification, we might refer to these as *rival protagonists*. The antagonism between the rivals is partially assuaged by an attachment figure from the same generation (Antigone) and one from the parental generation (Jocaste), both female. We may refer to these as *reconciler* figures. It seems best to treat the attachment parameter or function separately from the reconciliation function so that we might say that, in this case, the reconcilers are also attachment figures.[12] Moreover, they have the generation parameter set differently and neither is a possible sexual partner. In contrast with both, there is a (male) figure from the parental generation (Créon) who intensifies this antagonism to his own benefit. We may refer to this as an *antagonizer*. At the same time, it is important to note that he is not neutral between the protagonists. He serves as an adviser for Étéocle.

The antagonizer character here, Créon, has another peculiarity that appears in the romantic plot. He is an interfering parent and also a rival. The existence of these two character functions is obviously not peculiar to Racine. Their combination, however, is unusual. Commonly, an author's idiolect may be thought of as having a principle that defines romantic blocking characters such that there are some, mutually exclusive, parameters (i.e., choosing one entails rejecting the other). What is noteworthy here is that parent and rival are not mutually exclusive parameters in Racine's idiolect. When both are selected, we have the parent/rival figure. (This probably results from Racine's internalization of the Oedipus story as an important literary model.)

There are some idiolectally significant events as well. These include the mutual killing of the rival protagonists, the death of the son/rival (Hémon), and the suicide of the beloved (Antigone). The last is less distinctive than the others, as it is a recurring feature of romantic tragedies, most obviously in Japanese love-suicide plays, although also in such European works as *Romeo and Juliet*.

There are also at least partially distinctive thematic and emotional concerns that have consequences for the story. These prominently include the development of shame and pride – more precisely, pride in social esteem, thus honor – as perhaps the primary motivating factors for the heroes, in addition to romantic love. In the heroic prototype, the emotions governing social aspirations within the in-group are prototypically the desire for authority or power (a form of greed) and the desire for esteem or honor (a form of pride). Racine greatly stresses the latter, and pairs it with an extreme sensitivity to shame. In contrast, desire for authority becomes more prominent than pride in rather villainous characters, such as Créon. Indeed, contending leaders in Racine's works are often distinguished fundamentally by this parameter – that is, by whether they are motivated primarily by ambition (thus greed) or pride. The former are (despised) villains, whereas the latter are closer to rival heroes.

Alexandre le Grand (Alexander the Great)

Racine's second surviving play is, arguably, far more successful than the first.[13] It shows considerable aesthetic advancement, yet at the same time, it is clearly continuous with *La Thébaïd* in its narrative structure.[14]

The play concerns two kings of India, Porus and Taxile, who are faced with an invasion by Alexandre. This is the standard threat/defense sequence from the heroic prototype. However, it is modified by the doubling of the in-group ruler into the rival protagonists. Of course, for the two to be actual rivals, they need to be in conflict with one another. In keeping with this, Taxile comes to ally himself with Alexandre. Thus we have the scenario of *La Thébaïd*: There are two legitimate rulers. One of them, however, joins with an invader and thus operates as a usurper. There are a couple of small differences from the earlier play. First, Porus, unlike Étéocle, is not usurping Taxile's position. Second, the invasion precedes the betrayal of one protagonist by the other. The two small (parametric) changes are related. Because Porus does not usurp Taxile's kingdom, something else must serve as the provoking incident that leads him into conflict with his rival protagonist. There is also the parametric change that the rival protagonists are initially comrades rather than brothers (although Racine does refer to them as metaphorical brothers at one point [153]).

Just as Racine had reconcilers and antagonizers in the earlier play, he has them here as well. Moreover, he has two women, one of whom, Cléofile, is (like Antigone) a sister to one of the protagonists. (Obviously, she cannot be sister to both as they are not brothers.) In *La Thébaïd*, Antigone played a somewhat more mixed role than indicated in the previous section. On the one hand, she sought to reconcile the brothers. At the same time, however, she drove her lover, Hémon, to fight along with the invading army of Polynice (I: 52). In this way, she was also an antagonizer. Cléofile is in part a version of Antigone; however, there is a parametric change. She seeks to reconcile her brother Taxile not with Porus but with Alexandre. Thus she enhances the antagonism of the male heroes by allying her brother with the invader. In contrast, Antigone (somewhat incoherently) sought to reconcile the heroes/brothers, while allying her lover with the invader. Both result in the death of an attachment figure (Taxile in one case and Hémon in the other).

Cléofile can push Taxile toward Alexandre because the latter has already suggested an alliance. In this way, Alexandre is related to Créon. He is a character who benefits materially by setting the rival protagonists against one another. Moreover, he is allied with one against the other. It may seem initially that Alexandre is unlike Créon in not being duplicitous. To some extent, this is true. However, this is less a matter of setting a character parameter than of simulatively following through a simpler change in the character's situation. Créon does not have political authority independent of Étéocle. Alexandre, in contrast, is an independent monarch who is far more powerful than Taxile. Duplicity is much more likely in the former situation than in the latter.

Créon's romantic interest in Antigone carries through to *Alexandre* as well, for Alexandre is in love with Cléofile. Here we see two small parametric shifts. First, Alexandre appears to have genuine romantic attachment to Cléofile, whereas the depth of Créon's feelings for Antigone is less clear. Second, the love, in this case, is reciprocated, and this affects the end of the play. Taxile dies. Like Antigone at the end of *La Thébaïd*, Cléofile is deeply affected by this loss. As a result, her response to Alexandre's expressions of feeling are muted. Before committing suicide, Antigone asked Créon to leave her in solitude to mourn (I: 85–86). Similarly, at the end of the second play, Cléofile explains that she cannot speak but can only weep over her loss (I: 155). However, the parametric shift from a deceased lover (Antigone/Hémon) to a deceased brother (Cléofile/Taxile) and the associated shift from nonreciprocated (Créon/Antigone) to reciprocated (Alexandre/Cléofile) love have consequences for the final result of the play. Cléofile does not kill herself. She simply goes into mourning for her brother, leaving open the possibility of eventual union with Alexandre.

Jocaste appears to be changed utterly in the new work, but this is largely the result of a single parameter shift. The principles that gave rise to Jocaste in the first play have now generated the character of Axiane. Like Jocaste, she is a queen. She is also the major reconciler between the protagonists. Finally, she is an attachment figure for both protagonists. In keeping with her position as an attachment figure, she uses her own well-being as an argument for the unity of Taxile and Porus (I: 118), just as Jocaste stresses the harm done to her by the conflict between Étéocle and Polynice (I: 44–45). In this case, however, the parameter is not set to mother but rather to beloved.

This small character alteration has significant consequences for the story. The most obvious is that it presents us with a love triangle. In keeping with the usual structure of the romantic prototype, Alexandre is the social authority who sides with the unloved rival (Taxile) over the true beloved (Porus). Intensifying the emotional effects of this conflict, Racine has Taxile abduct and imprison Axiane. This takes up one common action of the blocking figure in the romantic plot.

While Axiane is imprisoned, a false report arrives stating that Porus has been killed. This provides an opportunity for Alexandre and Taxile to plead Taxile's case. There was a version of this false report motif in *La Thébaïd*. In that case, the false report was that Polynice had *not* died in the combat with Étéocle. Here, then, we have an idiolectal narrative motif, with a parametric shift (roughly, "false report of death/survival").[15]

While in prison, and under the impression that Porus has died, Axiane suggests that she will commit suicide, like Jocaste. Fortunately, she succumbs neither to the enticements of Taxile nor to the promptings of despair, for it turns out that Porus is alive. In fact, Taxile dies. Here again there is a combat between the rivals, as between Étéocle and Polynice; however, the parameter was set not to "mutual killing," but to the hero killing the rival.

At this point, there is a change in Alexandre, somewhat parallel to the change in Créon at the end of *La Thébaïd*. Following Antigone's death, Créon recognizes that his acquisition of the kingdom was all in vain. Unlike Créon, Alexandre has not lost any attachment figures. Moreover, there is no oracle stating that his death is necessary. Thus there is no issue of despair or sacrificial suicide as with Créon. Nonetheless, he no longer desires to rule the place he has taken such pains to possess. In this sense, his acquisition of the kingdom has been in vain. Since he no longer has to repay Taxile for his services, he can now allow the marriage of Axiane and Porus and surrender back the land he has conquered. This, so to speak, redemption of Alexandre – in contrast with Créon's death – is allowed by the fact that Alexandre shares with Porus a fundamental motivation of pride or desire for honor. This distinguishes both from the less "elevated," greed-driven characters, such as Créon. Indeed, it is another parameter shift. As such, this case nicely illustrates the value of a principles and parameters model, as opposed to a simpler mapping of character types without internal variables, as there is not a simple one-to-one, typological mapping of Créon onto Alexandre.

Andromaque

Racine's third play in many ways marks an aesthetic breakthrough, compared to which the earlier works are little better than juvenilia. Tobin expresses the view of many critics when he writes that the premiere of *Andromaque* was "one of the signal moments in the history of world theater" (42). This breakthrough is related to Racine's more complex use of his idiolectal principles and his cultivation of character ambivalence, in which different emotional parameters are selected simultaneously or in alternation, even if they are mutually exclusive.[16] The ambivalence at issue in this play typically involves the two key complexes of emotion in Racine's plays generally – romantic love and pride (or shame), which is to say, the emotions associated with the prominent romantic and heroic narrative prototypes.[17]

As the story begins, Andromaque, the widow of Hector, has been awarded to Pyrrhus in the division of spoils from the Trojan War. Andromaque is accompanied by her son, Astyanax. Astyanax was supposed to have been killed by the Greeks. Through a substitution, Andromaque managed to save him; however, his survival is continually threatened. Pyrrhus is in love with Andromaque, but his feelings are not reciprocated. He uses threats against Astyanax to convince Andromaque to marry him. The threats come from the Greeks generally, who demand that Pyrrhus hand over the child. Thus the play is pervaded by the threat that this innocent child will be murdered in the cause of a war that is now over.

In keeping with this crucial narrative conflict, a central ideological concern of the play is reconciliation after war. On the one hand, Pyrrhus and Andromaque argue forcefully that it is wrong to kill the boy (although Pyrrhus is not always consistent in acting on the arguments). On the other hand, Racine dramatizes the difficulty of forgiveness by presenting us with Andromaque's vivid memories of the trauma she experienced as her family was brutally killed by the Greeks, including Pyrrhus. Once again, we have parametric shifts with respect to the earlier plays – first, a shift from the period of war to postwar conditions; second, a shift from a relatively benevolent conquest driven only by pride (Alexandre) to a devastating conquest driven by greed (as evidenced in the division of Trojan spoils).

From the perspective of the present study, the crucial point about Astyanax is that Racine has reached back to *La Thébaïd* and taken up the figure of Ménécée. In this case, however, he has integrated the youth's story into the heroic rather than the sacrificial plot. In keeping with this shift in genre, Astyanax is continually threatened with murder rather than being driven to suicide.

Needless to say, this sacrificial element is not the only idiolectal feature that continues from the earlier works. The most obvious is that the play concerns rival protagonists. Moreover, one of these kills the other. One is seen as a traitor to the main society, one is loved by a woman who is to some degree shared by both, and so on. But, in each case, the complexity of the relations and even of the individual character properties is remarkable. Indeed, it is already significant that we cannot simply introduce the rival protagonists together at the beginning, as when saying "there were two brothers" or "there were two kings of India."

Before turning to the rival male protagonist, we need to introduce another female protagonist – Hermione, who loves Pyrrhus and was to marry him. Initially, her love seems to have been reciprocated, but she has been replaced in Pyrrhus's affections by Andromaque.

Now we may introduce the second male protagonist – Oreste. He is in love with Hermione, but Hermione has rejected him for Pyrrhus. He has been sent by the Greeks to take Astyanax. In the process, he hopes to change things with Hermione.

Much of the play concerns the shifting feelings of the characters – their "tortured humanity," as Tobin puts it (47). Hermione is alternately devoted to Pyrrhus and filled with murderous rage against him, due largely to feelings of betrayal and humiliation (see I: 217).[18] (In Racine's plays, hate and rage commonly result from humiliation and a sense of betrayal in an attachment relation. In other words, this is a standard motivational complex in his narrative idiolect.) Fluctuating ambivalence is also found in Pyrrhus with respect to Andromaque. Oreste too exhibits some of these swings. In each case, the changes are due to strong romantic feelings combined with rejection by the beloved. Only Andromaque remains fixed in her love and loyalty. But she too suffers ambivalence as she cannot determine whether she should marry a man she loathes (Pyrrhus), thereby saving her child, or sacrifice her child to abstract principles of loyalty to a dead husband and noncooperation with the enemy.

In the end, Andromaque agrees to marry Pyrrhus, thus saving her child. However, she has determined that she will kill herself immediately after the wedding, leaving Pyrrhus with his promise to act as a father to the boy.

Hearing of the marriage, Hermione convinces Oreste to kill Pyrrhus. Pyrrhus is killed. But, when Oreste returns after the murder, Hermione denounces him, then goes and commits suicide herself. In the meantime, Andromaque establishes herself as queen. His life now in danger, Oreste cannot bring himself to leave but seems to see the restless spirits of Pyrrhus and Hermione before him. The play ends as his companions agree that he must be brought away to the ships in order to escape.

It is easy to see how this play developed out of Racine's evolving idiolectal narrative principles. Oreste is the dispreferred lover (for Hermione) as Taxile is the dispreferred lover (for Axiane) in *Alexandre le Grand* and Étéocle is the dispreferred brother (for Antigone) in *La Thébaïd* (see I: 82). Oreste seeks Pyrrhus for combat as Étéocle and Polynice or Taxile and Porus face one another – although in this case it is the outsider, Oreste, who emerges as the victor. This is, again, a simple parameter shift. In the case of *La Thébaïd*, both protagonists were killed; in the case of *Alexandre*, the invader/usurper was killed; here, the rightful ruler is killed. This covers three of the four logical possibilities (the fourth being that neither is killed).

The reference to Pyrrhus as the rightful ruler leads to a second set of connections. In some ways, Oreste is the usurper. But he is also the representative of official (Greek) authority. In this respect, Pyrrhus is not the rightful ruler but the betrayer of Greece, a rebel against that larger authority, just as Étéocle was a sort of usurper in Thebes, a betrayer of a larger authority there. In this case, however, the mixing of character functions is not the result of a simple rule (that the two kings should alternate in occupying the throne). Rather, it is the result of a complex political situation and, more importantly, a contradiction between moral obligations. Specifically, Racine presents Pyrrhus's quasi-rebellion against his fellow Greeks as morally and emotionally justified, even if Pyrrhus's motives are held inconsistently and are not entirely the right ones. In connection with this, the play – not unlike many works that present an epilogue of suffering – shows an embryonic understanding of what we would refer to as war crimes. Specifically, it exhibits a sense of empathy that works against the crimes that provoke the epilogue of suffering, prominently the murder of innocents.

Other complexities appear in Hermione. In *Alexandre le Grand*, Cléofile worries that Alexandre will tire of her. Alexandre strongly denies this, and the play suggests that he is right to do so. However, if one simply shifts this parameter, so that her fear comes true, then we have Hermione's situation. Following from this – and from the Racinian motivational complex of humiliation and a sense of attachment betrayal – Hermione, filled with rage and hate, urges Oreste to kill Pyrrhus. Thus she serves the antagonizing function of Cléofile (as well as Antigone). However, in the case of *Andromaque*, this is all emotionally intensified by the fact that she loves Pyrrhus. Thus Hermione becomes responsible for the death of the one person she truly cares for. Her suicide is a version of the suicide of Antigone after the deaths of Polynice and Hémon; it is also a version of the grief of Cléofile after the death of Taxile. Nonetheless, Antigone and Cléofile seem rather starkly unambivalent, whereas Hermione is intensely ambivalent. This difference, it seems, is less a matter of setting a parameter (ambivalent versus unambivalent) than it is a matter of clustering parameters and limiting them relative to context. In other words, what seems to have happened here is that Racine has honed his use of principles and parameters to the point where he can alternate different and contradictory parameter settings for a single character. One could think of this as a metaprinciple – roughly, "allow/disallow emotional contradiction" – with the parameter setting here ("allow") guiding the operation of first order, character principles.

At the end of the play, the despairing madness of Oreste is a version of the despair of Créon, which concludes *La Thébaïd*. There are, of course, changes. First, Créon evokes and imagines the afterlife of Antigone and Hémon, but he does not see them. In contrast, for Oreste, the images of Hermione and Pyrrhus are vivid, hallucinatory perceptions (I: 224). This is a simple variation on guilt and the results of despair, perhaps related to the parameter of generational difference between the two (with the older Créon being less prone to nervous excitement). A second change is that there is no sacrificial context to motivate Oreste's suicide. More significantly, we see a difference in ambivalence here as well. Oreste has been emotionally conflicted about his actions from the start. This is much less true of Créon, despite his familial relations with the victims of his plotting. Indeed, Créon's lack of ambivalence is almost inhuman. Also, we see here the parametric differences between romantic love (Oreste) and what seems something more like simple lust (Créon). There is in addition a clear difference in sensitivity to issues of honor between the two.

Beyond these points, in *Alexandre*, Taxile cannot win the love of his captive, Axiane, even when it appears that Porus is dead. Changing Axiane's situation so that she has a child whose life is threatened, we arrive at the simulation of Andromaque. Moreover, Axiane is an autonomous queen with military authority and firm resolve before her capture by Taxile. The parametric shift in Andromaque's character is simply to having that authority and resolve against the enemy after Pyrrhus's death.

Ideologically, it is noteworthy that the strength and authority of this female protagonist grows with each play. In *La Thébaïd*, Jocaste cannot assume a role as queen but can only plead with her sons, then kill herself in despair. Axiane is a powerful queen, but she still seems dependent on the degree to which she can inspire belligerence in kings – specifically, Porus and Taxile. Andromaque, in contrast, seems to rally her kingdom with a force that even Pyrrhus could not manage. This too could be understood in parametric terms – roughly, (1) no female authority; (2) dependent female authority; (3) derivative female authority (i.e., authority that derives from a man, but is maintained autonomously).[19]

In short, *Andromaque* takes up largely the same principles that we have seen in the preceding plays, partially altering their parameters. However, it shows greater flexibility in the degree to which characters change their motivations in the course of changing circumstances. In keeping with this, we may add that it evidences a more complex sense of the role of norms in motivation as well.

Phrasing these points in a more algorithmic way, we may say that *Andromaque* manifests differences in two processes. The first is the increased integration of contradictory properties and relations. This may derive from the parameterization of a metaprinciple – that is, the addition of parameters to a previously existing metaprinciple. This is particularly the case with respect to contradictory emotions, thus ambivalence. One could understand the process in the following way. Racine initially had a metaprinciple requiring emotional consistency for a character and object (e.g., a lover and beloved). The addition of parameters enabled two alterations. First, it became possible to change one's primary attachment object, but probably only once. Second, it became possible for this attachment to involve a single continuous feeling (e.g., romantic love) or an alteration between related but opposed feelings (such as romantic love and rage at attachment betrayal). This ambivalence allows a more dynamic interaction between character and event, precisely because changing contexts trigger the changes in the emotion.

The second process that defines the difference of *Andromaque* is an enhanced parameterization of motivation and a correlated integration of thematic and motivational concerns. Racine presents at least the rudiments of a two-stage account of motivation. One stage involves emotion systems; the other involves a regulation of emotion systems by reference to norms – norms that themselves have emotional force. Thus we find Pyrrhus motivated by his feelings for Andromaque but also considering the justice of murdering Astyanax, an act with intrinsic emotional valence as well as thematic consequence. This contrasts rather starkly with the imposition of an arbitrary and nonmotivational precept in *La Thébaïd* (the rule that the brothers should switch the kingship every year) and the violent insouciance of Alexandre, who happily prosecutes a war for glory, with no apparent regulative consideration of norms.

In both changes from earlier works, we see the sort of enhanced cognitive flexibility and nuance that we would expect from an increased mastery of any skill – here, Racine's skill as a playwright. At the same time, the analysis of these changes in terms of principles and parameters allows us to better understand the processes involved. In this case, such increased skill is a matter of adding possible parametric variation in formerly invariable (or less variable) principles.[20]

Britannicus

Andromaque partially begins with the possibilities feared by Cléofile in *Alexandre le Grand*. In a sense, Racine asks – what would happen if Alexandre fell in love with someone else after he is brought together with Cléofile? *Britannicus* continues with this line of development, through Néron, Octavie, and Junie.[21] It also takes up the ending of *Andromaque*, in effect asking – what will happen to a strong queen once her son reaches the age to rule? Racine addresses this small parameter shift through Agrippine and her son, Néron. In a more general way, the play continues Racine's increasingly flexible and dynamic use of principles, which is characteristic of his work after *Andromaque*.

By this point in our discussion, readers unfamiliar with the play should not be surprised to discover that it has rival male protagonists. There are also two female protagonists and two important advisers. The rivals are Britannicus and Néron. Having treated comrades in *Alexandre the Great* and *Andromaque*, Racine now returns to brothers – or rather stepbrothers, in this case. Through the manipulations of Agrippine, Néron has come to the throne, in effect usurping his stepbrother Britannicus. However, Britannicus does not appear to have any particular ambitions for the throne. Part of Néron's success is also because of his marriage. He married Britannicus's sister, Octavie. This deprived Silanus of his beloved and led to his death. Now, like Pyrrhus, Néron has fallen in love with someone else – Silanus's sister, Junie.[22] At the beginning of the play, he has arrested and confined her. Here we have only a small variation on Pyrrhus's relation to Andromaque, primarily in initial conditions. Junie is not a war captive, thus she is imprisoned, not handed over to Néron as part of the spoils of victory. Moreover, Néron was not at war with her family, so her bereavement cannot be the result of war. But the key point is that, like Pyrrhus with Andromaque, Néron is at least partially responsible for the death of someone Junie loved. Thus she has particular antagonism toward him that makes him an unlikely candidate for her affection. Moreover – and this will not surprise readers either – she and Britannicus are in love.[23]

Thus Néron is a version of Étéocle and Taxile in the usurpation narrative and a version of Pyrrhus in the love triangle narrative. Similarly, Britannicus takes up the position of Polynice, Porus, and Oreste, but without their violence. He is simply a lover. Indeed, despite the fact that the play is named after him, he is a relatively underdeveloped character, reduced almost entirely to his affection for Junie. This fits with a somewhat unexpected development of the rival protagonists. In the earlier plays, there may have been some preference for one protagonist over the other, but it was not generally a matter of a "good" character and a "bad" character. There is little difference between Étéocle and Polynice. Taxile is definitely inferior to Porus, but he does not seem wholly bad – although certainly he comes closest. Both Pyrrhus and Oreste have good and bad points; as with Étéocle and Polynice, it would be difficult to choose between them. But, in the case of Étéocle and Polynice, that is because these characters are rather one dimensional. In the case of Pyrrhus and Oreste, it is the very complexity of the characters that makes them difficult to hierarchize. This is not true of Néron and Britannicus, and this is in part the result of Britannicus's relative flatness.

As to the female characters, Agrippine continues the trajectory that runs from Jocaste through Axiane and Andromaque. In connection with this, Agrippine takes over a surprising characteristic from Jocaste and Axiane. These two characters were, in our initial terminology, reconcilers. They sought to bring the rivals together, and they did this in the context of war. Despite her role in bringing Néron to power, and despite the usual role of a parent in romantic plots, she actually works to end the brothers' romantic conflict over Junie. Thus she works on behalf of the lovers. This is, in effect, a shift of the reconciler character from the heroic to the romantic structure.

Junie is, like Britannicus, a sort of purified version of earlier lovers. She is related to Antigone in being romantically associated with the initially usurped side (in Antigone's case, Polynice's follower, Hémon, rather than Polynice himself, since the latter was disallowed by the brother/sister relation). She is also a variant on Axiane, as she is a captive to the inferior protagonist and in love with the superior protagonist.

There are two other significant characters in the play, Burrhus and Narcisse. Both are related to Créon in his role as adviser to Étéocle. The difference between Burrhus and Narcisse is largely the result of the switching of a single parameter bearing on motivation. Burrhus is interested in the well-being of the state, while Narcisse is self-interested. This leads to a further difference.

Burrhus can be honest, while Narcisse must be duplicitous. Moreover, Burrhus is conciliatory and Narcisse is divisive.

There are some complications in the narrative, such as a misunderstanding and partial alienation of the lovers. This is a common motif, not particular to Racine's narrative idiolect. Specifically, Junie has to reject Britannicus so as to prevent Néron from killing him. (This is a variation on the dilemma of Andromaque.) This briefly leads Britannicus to distrust Junie. But they are soon reconciled after a chance meeting allows Junie to explain everything, unobserved by Néron.

Much of the play involves Agrippine seeking to reestablish her authority over Néron, particularly in the area of his behavior toward Junie and Britannicus. Ultimately, she convinces him to be reconciled with his brother. Narcisse, however, influences Néron to reverse this decision. We have once again a one-on-one encounter of the brothers. There is an unexpected shift as the meeting is not a battle. It is, rather, the sharing of a cup in apparent reconciliation. Nonetheless, the outcome is the same. One rival kills the other. In this case, Néron poisons Britannicus. Here, we might expect the suicide of Junie, parallel to that undertaken by Antigone and Hermione and contemplated by Axiane. At first, it does indeed seem that Junie has committed suicide. However, Racine shifts to another sort of inaccessibility. Junie finds refuge in the cult of the vestal virgins. This preserves her chastity and associates her with the spiritual realm – two crucial results of suicide – but it does so while keeping her alive. Moreover, this incorporates the motif of popular support experienced by Andromaque, for Junie is protected from Narcisse (acting on behalf of Néron) by "the people" (I: 365). The unspeakable Narcisse is killed in the course of the ending. This sort of punishment for an evil character is so common that we do not need to seek a reason for it in any peculiarity of Racine's narrative idiolect.

Bérénice

Bérénice is overtly continuous with *Britannicus* in the sense that Titus, one hero of the play, more than once cites Néron as a negative model for his own behavior (I: 395, 398). In this way, Racine develops Titus as a sort of response to Néron. However, in terms of development principles, the play is closer to *Andromaque* and even *Alexandre le Grand*.[24]

Once again, we have a play that begins with rivals. One is a conquering Roman emperor, Titus. The other is a local ruler from the Middle East, Antiochus, who has collaborated with that emperor. It hardly needs saying that the configuration here is that of Alexandre and Taxile, but there has been a parameter shift. Now, the collaboration is right – or, if not right, it is at least the side favored by the perspective of the implied author. Relative to *Alexandre*, however, the play is simplified. The rival protagonists are Titus and Antiochus, with the Porus character eliminated. This is complemented by another reduction in which Cléofile and Axiane are combined. Indeed, the entire heroic portion of the plot has been removed. We now have only a love triangle. As this suggests, Antiochus and Titus both love the one major female character, Bérénice, the queen of Palestine. In parallel with Antiochus and Taxile, she derives from the same complex of principles as Axiane, with the change that – like Cléofile – she supports collaboration with the invading emperor. In addition, her situation is varied in that the emperor and the collaborator are the rivals for her love, rather than two invaded rulers (as in *Alexandre*). Given these changes, she could in principle favor either Antiochus or Titus. Drawing another element from Cléofile, Racine has her favor Titus.

In previous plays, Racine has generally developed two sources of tension in his stories. With the heroic plot gone, he requires another source if this pattern is to continue. He takes this new source of tension from the usual romantic story in which society and its representatives inhibit the union of the lovers. Moreover, the inhibition is due to the usual factors – identity categories. Bérénice is not Roman. Indeed, there is a direct conflict with Roman law, stressed by Titus's advisor, Paulin (see I: 395), who takes up a relatively benign version of the standard social representative/blocking character. Since Titus is emperor, this leads thematically to a version of the cross-cultural conflict between duty and love.

The story develops in a fairly straightforward way. Like Oreste, Antiochus has wandered aimlessly because of his frustrated love (I: 391). Eventually, he ends up in Rome and has a meeting with Bérénice who rejects his love, as Hermione rejects Oreste's love. Shortly after this, Bérénice finds Titus cold. There are hints of a jealousy plot, but they come to nothing. This is a recurring technique in Racine's work. He sometimes introduces the possibility of a standard plot line, only to derail it (as with the possible alienation of Britannicus and Junie). Much of the play addresses Titus's ambivalence regarding the duty/love conflict. He determines that he must choose duty over love. In *Andromaque*, Pyrrhus chooses Oreste to present Hermione at their wedding. In a similarly ironic moment, Titus chooses Antiochus to tell Bérénice that she must leave Rome forever. Moreover, he asks Antiochus to accompany her in this departure. This is, in a sense, the precise opposite of the scene in *Andromaque*. However, it is ambivalent. On the one hand, Titus is (unknowingly) giving Antiochus the woman he (Antiochus) loves. On the other hand, if Bérénice continues to spurn Antiochus's love, then this task will only make things worse for Antiochus, by in effect tantalizing him with the prospect of a love he can never have. When Antiochus tells Bérénice the bad news, she does not believe him. After meeting with Titus, however, she realizes it is true and determines (of course) to commit suicide (I: 421). Fortunately, however, she suddenly recovers from her distress and ends the play by proclaiming that she will leave, allowing Titus to take up his imperial duties, but telling Antiochus that he must go and never approach her again. Like Andromaque, she will remain forever faithful to her love. Like Junie, in place of suicide, she chooses chastity and devotion to a higher or greater principle – here, social duty rather than religious piety, as in Junie's case.

Bajazet

The usual rival men – the brothers, Amurat and Bajazet – appear in *Bajazet*.[25] However, they are by no means the protagonists of the play. Indeed, one of them is only an offstage agent, never actually appearing before the audience. The play begins with Roxane as acting sultan. Amurat, the sultan, is away at war. Before the action of the play, Amurat had sent word that his brother, Bajazet, should be killed. Here, Racine returns to the heroic plot, treating it in a complex, if somewhat indirect manner. Specifically, Amurat seems to fear usurpation. As a result, he is going to kill Bajazet preemptively. This sets in motion a series of events that – had they worked out – would have resulted in usurpation. Similarly, reports from the battlefield suggest that Amurat's aggressive warfare has produced danger from a national enemy of the sort we commonly find in the threat/defense sequence of the heroic plot. Eventually, Amurat is victorious in both narrative sequences. However, none of this is really at the foreground of *Bajazet*. Rather, this play once again focuses on the love triangle component of the romantic prototype.

The sultan's vizier, Acomat, takes up the role of Créon in manipulating the situation in favor of one brother (Bajazet). Specifically, he brings Roxane together with Bajazet in such a way that she falls in love with him. As a result, she does not have him executed. Rather, she plans to make him the sultan. Acomat will, of course, be the adviser to this new sultan. Moreover, he will be given Atalide, a member of the royal family, as his wife. Unfortunately, Bajazet is not in love with Roxane but with Atalide. Moreover, Roxane will make Bajazet the new sultan only if he agrees to marry her.

Amurat, in pursuing his brother's death, is a variant of Néron, and Bajazet is a variant of Britannicus (more technically, they are parallel instances of the same evolving complexes of principles). As to Roxane, she derives from

Axiane, Andromache, and Bérénice, but without their fidelity to an initial bond. Indeed, her preference for Bajazet is a simple parameter shift, as if Bérénice had chosen Antiochus. At the same time, Roxane partially manifests principles previously associated with Néron, Pyrrhus, and Taxile. She keeps her beloved in prison until he agrees to marry her, separating the true lover and beloved of the story. The incorporation of these principles produces a predatory, powerful female. Again, this is roughly parallel to the predatory, powerful male (e.g., Néron or Pyrrhus). However, the relative insecurity of her position, produced by the simple shift from male to female, almost necessarily makes her more sympathetic, as more vulnerable.

Atalide too derives from earlier female characters, most obviously Antigone, with Acomat in the position of Créon in this respect as well. But Racine synthesizes Atalide's derivation from Antigone with principles drawn from male characters such as Porus and Britannicus. Specifically, she finds herself in romantic conflict with a politically more-powerful rival.

Much of the play involves Atalide's vacillation regarding just what Bajazet should do, Bajazet's own somewhat contradictory (but emotionally realistic) behavior, and Roxane's fluctuations as she suspects that Bajazet does not really love her, then feels that he does, then again experiences doubts. The climax comes when several incidents occur. Amurat sends a messenger to ensure that Bajazet has been killed. This obviously forces Roxane to make a decision. She must determine whether to establish Bajazet as sultan before Amurat returns and takes action. This is a version of the Greek pressure to kill Astyanax and Pyrrhus's need to determine whether he will marry Andromaque – and, of course, Andromaque's decision as well. As with Andromaque and Pyrrhus, this involves ambivalence on Bajazet's part and on Roxane's. Andromaque ultimately decides on marriage out of concern for an attachment figure, Astyanax. In a variation, out of concern for an attachment figure (Atalide), Bajazet appears to decide on marriage. Here, a standard motif, popular in many literary traditions, enters – the misplaced letter. Due to concern over Atalide's jealousy, Bajazet makes the mistake of writing a profession of his love. This ends up in the hands of Roxane. She vows to kill both Bajazet and Atalide, just as one might anticipate.

At this point, an unexpected event occurs. Acomat leads an uprising in the palace. This is, of course, self-interested. It nonetheless partially removes Acomat from the cluster of principles that define harmful advisers (such as Créon). Rather, it places him in an event that recalls Porus's final advance against Alexandre and Taxile or the final battle of Polynice and Étéocle. The end result is also a variant of these – the threatening usurper, Roxane, is killed. But so is the rightful ruler and lover, Bajazet. Acomat tells Atalide that it is necessary to escape to the waiting ships. Like the stunned Oreste, Atalide does not follow. Instead, she commits suicide like Antigone and Hermione.

One might argue that *Bajazet* marks another turning point in Racine's writing. Like *Andromaque*, it is clearly continuous with what went before. Also like *Andromaque*, it is an emotionally complex play that stresses ambivalence. Specifically, romantic love involves strong egocentric elements and strong empathic elements. Usually, these are not in conflict (e.g., they both make injury to the beloved highly aversive). In some circumstances, however, they may produce opposed actional outcomes and opposed qualities of experience. We see this particularly in Atalide's conflict over the relationship between Bajazet and Roxane. On the one hand, she wants his sexual fidelity. On the other hand, she recognizes that he will be killed if he does not agree to marry Roxane. Indeed, she believes she has convinced him to accept the marriage but then blames him for doing so. Although seemingly irrational, this behavior is impeccable in its emotional logic. Indeed, it is a version of the ambivalence that drives Hermione but with slight parametric changes (e.g., in the source of the danger to the beloved's life).

The play is also morally complex – and psychologically complex about moral decisions. The characters seem to be divisible into the "good guys" (Bajazet and Atalide) and the "bad guys" (Roxane and Amurat). But Roxane is more sympathetic than this suggests. Moreover, the good guys are not really innocent, even if their deceptions result from their desperate circumstances. Finally, Acomat is at first clearly a bad guy, but he appears much more benevolent at the end of the play. Here we see something like a principle of emotional balance, although one not nearly so systematic as what we found in Shakespeare. Perhaps it is best considered a metaprinciple to the following effect: "Allow characters' moral behavior to be governed significantly by external circumstances (and not simply by personal traits)."

Moreover, Racine complicates the moral problems as well as the decision process. Specifically, he makes it clear that there is not always a simple moral choice. All the characters face moral dilemmas that are difficult to resolve and that are inextricable from their own emotions and interests. For example, Roxane owes loyalty to the sultan and is bound to obey his orders, but his order is to kill someone who is innocent – a dilemma already faced by Pyrrhus in *Andromaque*.

But these are not the reasons that the play is, arguably, a breakthrough. Rather, small changes accumulate in Racine's application of development principles until the point where there is a sort of gestalt shift or *reconfiguration*, as we might call it. As already noted, in earlier plays, Racine's development principles evolved with respect to his female characters. Part of this evolution relates to alterations in women's political authority. *Bajazet* suggests a discourse parameter bearing on this political authority – whether the authority is or is not within the scope of the direct emplotment (roughly, what we see on stage). Racine placed Andromaque in a position of authority after the play bearing her name. He placed Agrippine in that position before the action of *Britannicus*. He placed Axiane and Bérénice in that position outside the action of *Alexandre le Grand* and *Bérénice*. In *Bajazet*, however, Roxane is in charge of the empire while the events are unfolding. Thus her position of authority is integral to the story's elaboration and specification. Once again, it might seem that this will simply produce a mirror image of the stories in which men have the positions of authority. However, this is not a matriarchy. The society is still fundamentally patriarchal, even though an exceptional woman has managed to gain some degree of (temporary) dominance. As a result, the position of this (female) leader is more fragile, and the balance of power is more complex. In keeping with this, the female characters in *Bajazet* draw on both the development principles for female characters in earlier plays *and those for male characters*. The result, again, is a sort of reconfiguration in which the possible interconnections (or configurations) of principles change significantly. Put simply, the metaprinciple that segregated principles by gender has been compromised. This greatly expands the possibilities for combinations and interactions of character traits, relations, actions, and so on.

Mithridate

To some extent, *Mithridate* takes up the new configurational possibilities opened by *Bajazet* and puts them through a reverse transformation – that is, a parallel change across parameter settings. By shifting a woman into a position of (temporary) power, Racine produced novel relations, conditions, and events. He now in part translates this dominant woman (Roxane) back into a man (Mithridate). In short, he allows the integration of principles across sexes for male as well as female characters.[26]

Specifically, the play concerns a king, Mithridate; his sons, Xipharès and Pharnace; and Monime, who is betrothed to Mithridate. Just as Amurat is away in battle at the start of *Bajazet*, Mithridate is away in battle at the start of this play. Moreover, just as mistaken reports about Amurat reach his kingdom, mistaken reports about Mithridate reach his sons and fiancée. In this case, the mistaken report is the same as it was for Porus during the battle against Alexandre – that he has died. On hearing this (false) report, both Pharnace and Xipharès become suitors for Monime's hand. Pharnace is a

Taxile-like traitor, conspiring with the Romans against whom his father has been at war. In contrast, Xipharès is a Porus-like loyal and brave defender of the home society. Clearly, there is emotional intensification relative to the earlier play in that this is not only a matter of loyalty to country and a division between friends. It is a matter of filial loyalty and a division between brothers. As we would expect from Axiane (and Junie), Monime has no interest in Pharnace, but loves Xipharès. To reduce emotional and moral complications, Racine makes it clear that Xipharès and Monime fell in love before Mithridate had any feelings for her.

At this point, one might expect a normal love triangle plot with the standard two protagonists, perhaps leading the poor girl to suicide after the good brother dies. This would be in keeping with the general distribution of gender roles in Racine's idiolect. Consider, for example, suicide. We may distinguish two types of suicide. The first is the noble suicide of the sacrificial plot. We find this in Ménécée and Créon. The second is the despairing suicide of the romantic plot (often in combination with the heroic plot), what we find in Antigone, Hermione, and Atalide as well as the plans of Andromaque, Axiane, and Bérénice and the initial hints in the case of Junie. The suicide of Jocaste fits the general pattern as well, although the type of attachment loss is different in this case (familial rather than romantic).[27] This might lead us to expect despairing suicide for Monime – or at least plans for or hints of it.

But Mithridate returns. Monime tells Xipharès that they are never to see one another and that she will honor her duty to her fiancé. This loyalty is a trait most obviously related to Andromaque, with several parameter changes – first, she is not yet married; second, she loves Xipharès, not Mithridate; third, Xipharès is loyal to Mithridate, not involved in his murder. There is a perhaps less obvious but more important element drawn from *Bajazet*. Monime's decision serves to protect Xipharès from his father's anger. (Racine has prepared us to expect murderous jealousy from Mithridate.) In this respect, she draws on principles from both Atalide and Bajazet. Of course, here too Andromaque is an important instance of the same type, although she is protecting a son. In short, Racine's simulations of all these characters share key development principles, with isolated parametric variations.

Mithridate knows about Pharnace's relations with the Romans and thus his tendency toward usurpation. In response to this – and Pharnace's courting of Monime – he determines to exile him. Suspecting that his brother has betrayed him, Pharnace tells Mithridate that Xipharès too had wooed Monime. In fact, Xipharès had not betrayed Pharnace. This is, then, an instance of misguided revenge, a standard element in the revenge prototype, which briefly surfaces here. Like Roxane with Bajazet, Mithridate worries about how to determine Monime's true feelings. He does not find a letter, but he does trick her into admitting her love. Like Roxane, Mithridate suffers emotional conflicts between despair, guilt, and anger. Ultimately, anger is predominant. In consequence, Xipharès must escape or be killed, and Monime must marry Mithridate or be killed. This is, of course, directly parallel with the climax of *Bajazet*. Readers familiar with such works as *Othello* might find these developments not only unexceptional but also quite in keeping with gender stereotypes. However, to this point in his career, Racine has developed the murderous rage of jealousy, with its wrenching ambivalence, most thoroughly in connection with women – Hermione and Roxane. (This may derive in part from the exemplum of Medea.) In *Mithridate*, this gender division is no longer maintained.

At this point in *Bajazet*, the abortive usurpation led by Acomat interrupts the tragedy. Similarly, a Roman-assisted usurpation attempt interrupts *Mithridate*. It is led by Pharnace, thus intensifying the emotional force of the earlier play's uprising by familializing it. Mithridate believes that Xipharès has joined the rebellion as well. After fighting for a while, he despairs of victory and determines to kill himself. This is clearly a suicide of despair, not sacrifice. Its relation to the romantic plot is shown by the fact that, just before undertaking the act, he sends someone to kill Monime. This gender shift in despairing suicide is qualified by the fact that the heroic component is more prominent here than in the cases of the women (although it did figure in the case of Antigone). Nonetheless, this is a clear instance of shifting gender or, more accurately, allowing a gender variable where formerly there was a (more or less) fixed value.[28]

As it turns out, Xipharès has not betrayed Mithridate. He leads a group of loyal soldiers who rout the Romans and Pharnace – the comic conclusion to the standard usurpation and defense scenarios from the heroic prototype. As the battle ends, Xipharès discovers what his father has done. Mithridate then realizes his mistake in sending someone to kill Monime. He rescinds the order, which fortunately has not yet been executed. On his deathbed, Mithridate blesses the union of Monime and Xipharès.

In this play, then, Racine takes up some aspects of *Bajazet* (as well as other plays) but changes the sex of the characters once again. This produces further innovations. Rather than the expected fraternal love triangle, we have a drama of male, attachment-based jealousy of the sort Racine developed previously through female characters. In connection with this, he shifts the largely female act of despairing suicide to a man as well. In addition to extending the gender parameterization and reconfiguration of principles initiated in *Bajazet, Mithridate* also continues to exhibit Racine's enhanced fluency in the use of his increasingly parameterized, idiolectal principles.

Iphigénie

Of the plays we are considering, *Iphigénie* is the most unusual.[29] This is because the combination of genres is different. Most often, Racine combines the romantic plot with elements of the heroic plot. In this play, however, the second genre is sacrificial. Integrating the romantic structure with a sacrificial (rather than a heroic) narrative necessarily produces different results, not only for the work as a whole but even for the precise development of the romance. Interestingly, this in some ways makes the work more traditionally romantic.

The story begins with the Greek fleet stranded at Aulide, unable to leave for Troy. The priest, Calchas, determines that Iphigénie must be sacrificed to enable the Greek departure. Agamemnon has sent for her, using the ploy that she is to be married to Achille. We can already guess from this that the sacrificial plot will conflict with the romantic plot. Indeed, Agamemnon is in some ways taking up an extreme version of the interfering father figure. He is not only going to prevent his daughter from marrying the man she loves, he is actually going to have her killed. In other words, the initial situation introduces both a sacrificial and a romantic plot. As with the heroic and romantic plots in other works, Racine is faced with the task of integrating the two. Agamemnon's ruse is the beginning of that integration.

As the play opens, Agamemnon is suffering from the ambivalence we have come to expect from murderous protagonists in Racine's plays – particularly those who would murder attachment figures (Hermione, Roxane, and Mithridate). He has actually had a change of heart and now sends someone with a message to stop Iphigénie from coming. The message claims that Achille no longer wants to be married because he has fallen in love with Ériphile, one of his captives. This is a fascinating use of a key part of *Andromaque*. Here, Racine derives the relations among Iphigénie, Ériphile, and Achille from Hermione, Andromaque, and Pyrrhus. However, these are not the real relations among the characters in the new play. They are, rather, the relations in a (counterfactual) fiction contained within the story.

Iphigénie and her mother, Clytemnestre, have gotten lost. Having taken the wrong path, they do not meet the messenger but rather arrive at Aulide. As it happens, they have brought along Ériphile, in order to help her discover her parentage. Even from the single instance of a letter in *Bajazet*, one might expect Agamemnon's letter to turn up and cause problems. It does. Clytemnestre receives the letter and plans to leave. This leads to a brief jealousy-based misunderstanding between the lovers, of the sort we have seen before (with Britannicus/Junie and Bajazet/Atalide). In keeping with Racine's usual principles, it turns out that Ériphile actually is in love with Achille.

Once the minor crisis of jealousy is resolved, the lovers seem to be headed for a wedding when they suddenly learn that Agamemnon is going to have Iphigénie killed. There is much debate over this issue, and the main opposition is between the lovers. Achille, in keeping with his warrior character, wants to fight. Iphigénie, in contrast, is an instance of Racine's willing sacrificial victim, a figure manifest earlier in Ménécée but now with the shift in gender we might expect after *Bajazet*. Indeed, here we see the complement of the preceding play. Mithridate commits a despairing suicide, shifting this form from female to male. For Iphigénie, in contrast, the parameter shift concerns sacrificial suicide, changing it from male to female. We have already seen that Agamemnon is highly ambivalent about killing Iphigénie and is prone to change his mind. In keeping with this, and in parallel with Mithridate's change of heart about Monime's death, he does change his mind, urging Iphigénie to escape.

Here, once more, we see the usual processes generating plot particularization. Again, this particularization results from Racine giving the characters certain traits – either standard (Achille as a somewhat hot-headed fighter) or derived from Racine's more idiolectal principles (e.g., the sacrificial victim embracing his or her sacrifice). He then places those characters in an integrated romantic/sacrificial plot.

In keeping with Racine's idiolectal principles, Ériphile is the rejected lover here, and, like Pharnace, she tries to destroy the happiness of the true lovers by betraying their secret. As such, she reports Iphigénie's imminent escape to Calchas. Following the pattern of the preceding two plays (*Bajazet* and *Mithridate*), this triggers an uprising in the camp. Like Xipharès battling Pharnace and his allies, Achille defeats the hostile forces. This prevents Iphigénie's death directly, only a slight alteration from the preceding play in which Xipharès's victory indirectly prevents the death of Monime.

At this point we have something of a surprise. Calchas announces that everything was a big mix-up. It turns out that Ériphile was actually born with the name Iphigénie and the gods really wanted *her* sacrificed. This may seem to be an entirely new element; however, it is a complex variant of the "mistaken announcement" motif found in the preceding plays, combined with the mandated sacrifice that appeared in *La Thébaïd*. Indeed, we in effect saw a version of this when Créon's self-sacrifice (as the "last" of the ruling family) had to be added to the mistaken self-sacrifice of Ménécée. The result of this is not the straightforward sacrifice of Ériphile by Calchas. Rather, the willing victim pattern in Racine's narrative idiolect and the tendency for spurned lovers to commit suicide combine to produce the ending where Ériphile sacrifices herself. In other words, Ériphile now fuses the two sorts of suicide – despairing and sacrificial (as Créon did earlier).

Again, *Iphigénie* is a peculiar play in Racine's canon. Personally, I find it very engaging. In fact, it is one of my favorite plays. At the same time, however, it seems clear that this is rather a rough-hewn play in comparison with many of Racine's works, at least those beginning with *Andromaque*. This is not surprising. The play is a sort of detour from the main line of Racine's narrative trajectory. He had time to refine his narrative skills with the heroic and romantic plots. This was not the case up to this point with the sacrificial plot. In shifting genres, Racine was almost beginning again. At the same time, the shift freed Racine from some of the perhaps overused principles – regarding usurpation and invasion – that he had used so effectively in his earlier works. This gives the play a freshness that may partially account for my reaction at least.

Part of this freshness involves the rather implausible ending. Up to the last moment, we do not know how this situation can be resolved. Racine is constrained by the "history" of the Trojan War. He cannot give us a play with no sacrifice. Moreover, it is likely that most readers very much want Iphigénie not to be killed. Ériphile has been alternately cruel and despondent in the course of the play; it is also not clear what kind of future she can have with the Greeks. Indeed, that is part of the reason for her despair. All this is likely to make viewers less invested in her continued life.[30] It does not mean, however, that we want to see her murdered. Her sacrificial suicide solves these various problems.[31]

Indeed, these points about likely audience effect suggest that narrative structure, with its causal connections, may not be the primary place to look for Racine's narrative evolution in this play. Perhaps the main advancement manifest in *Iphigénie* is, rather, in Racine's understanding of the emotional responses of an audience – in part, at the level of evaluation principles. Tobin has a similar idea when he refers to Racine having "his fingers on the public's pulse" (113). However, this is not simply attunement to gross public opinion, as we would find in the marketing of prime time television programs. It suggests, rather, a growing recognition of the subtlety and ambivalence of emotional response that one may expect from an audience, a recognition manifest in more nuanced and accurate simulations of the work's reception. Just as *Andromaque* shows greater sensitivity to the emotional complexity of characters, perhaps *Iphigénie* presents us with Racine's increased sensitivity to the emotional complexity of audience response. The point fits the reception of the play. Stegmann explains that the play was a "triumph without precedent," with Racine praised as "a magician of emotion" (128).

Phèdre

Racine's final play before his dozen-year hiatus is, again, widely considered his masterpiece.[32] It does in many ways show a culmination in the evolution of his development and evaluation principles. At the same time, however, it shows relatively little in the way of innovation. Rather, it follows the trajectory that we have been tracing from *La Thébaïd* on. It is particularly consistent with the post-reconfiguration plays that begin with *Bajazet*. In some ways, it is a culmination precisely because it could almost serve as the prototype of this group of plays (even though a prototype is technically an abstraction from all the plays of this class – including *Phèdre*).[33]

Specifically, the play involves rival male characters – a father and son whose conflict over a woman extends back to Créon and Hémon in *La Thébaïd*, although it is more fully developed in the conflict between Mithridate and Xipharès in *Mithridate*. There are, of course, parametric changes here. First, this love triangle does not involve the two men – Thésée and Hippolyte – loving the same woman, Phèdre. Rather, Thésée loves Phèdre, who loves Hippolyte, who loves Aricie – who, fortunately, loves Hippolyte. In this respect, it is more closely related to *Bajazet* with its fraternal rivals. Second, unlike in *Mithridate*, the marriage of the father to the woman precedes the development of the rivalry. In keeping with the *Bajazet* connection, the rival male characters are not really at the center of the play. Rather, the central character is Phèdre, the powerful female figure, a sort of viceroy for the absent ruler. As in *Bajazet*, she is paired with her own rival, of whom she is initially unaware.

The play begins with the recurring Racinian condition of an absent ruler. In the manner with which we are familiar, this suggests a usurpation plot without really developing it. Indeed, in this case, Aricie's brothers had tried to take the throne from Thésée. As is often the case in real usurpations (and sometimes in fictional ones), the right to the throne is not entirely clear (see Hippolyte on Aricie's ancestral entitlements [II: 217]). In principle, the point could increase the ambivalence of the work; however, it seems simply to favor Aricie and Hippolyte, in effect making Thésée the usurper. In any event,

Thésée killed the brothers, preserving only Aricie. Taking up the motif of
legal constraint on the lovers union (found in *Bérénice*), Racine has Thésée
institute a law forbidding the marriage of Aricie. The purpose of the law is the
same as the purpose of killing Astyanax in *Andromaque* (to end an enemy's
lineage). However, Aricie is not the same type of character as Andromaque.
Rather, her precursors are the lovers forbidden by the will of a ruler, such as
Junie (of *Britannicus*) and Atalide (of *Bajazet*). Of course, in this case, there is
the small parametric change that the lovers are forbidden for reasons of state
(as in *Bérénice*), not due to the desire of the ruler. There is a further complication as well. By introducing a law forbidding Aricie's marriage, Racine creates
two forbidden women in the same play – Aricie and Phèdre. This allows possibilities for greater complexity in the emotional, ethical, legal, and other inter-
relations of the characters and thus of the story development. Furthermore,
Racine emotionally intensifies the legal prohibition – which affects Hippolyte
most directly – by associating it with Hippolyte's father.

Like Xipharès, Hippolyte is a model of filial piety. He considers leaving to
search for his father. However, as in *Mithridate*, the rumor spreads that the
absent king is dead. Just as Pharnace and Xipharès both confess their love to
their otherwise forbidden beloved, Hippolyte confesses his love to Aricie and
Phèdre confesses her love to Hippolyte.[34] In both cases, there is emotional
intensification due to the contrast with prior expectations. Hippolyte has, to
this point, been apparently indifferent to women. Phèdre has been positively
hostile to Hippolyte.

Even readers unfamiliar with the play will not be surprised to hear that,
as in the case of *Mithridate*, the rumors of Thésée's death were greatly
exaggerated.[35] (One may also recall the false report of Polynice's survival in *La
Thébaïd* and the false report of Porus's death in *Alexandre le Grand*.) Thésée
returns, but, of course, everything has changed because of this one misunderstanding – a standard Racinian technique. In *Mithridate*, Mithridate knows
about Pharnace's treachery. Thinking Xipharès has betrayed him, Pharnace
tells Mithridate about Xipharès's love of Monime. Drawing on the same
development principles, Racine has Phèdre fear that Hippolyte will betray
her to Thésée. She is convinced of this particularly by her nurse, Oenone.
Oenone then tells Thésée that Hippolyte has pursued Phèdre. Thésée's jealousy is aroused. By accident, he manages to get Hippolyte to confess his love
for Aricie, two small parametric shifts from Mithridate's tricking Monime
into exposing Xipharès's love. (The two shifts are from the forbidden woman
to the son and from intentional elicitation in discussion to accidental elicitation in discussion.) Furious with Hippolyte's behavior, Thésée curses him.
This is to some degree a matter of anger over insubordination, but it also

includes rage at attachment betrayal, continuing the gender shift that began with *Bajazet*.

Although still a love plot, *Phèdre* at this point also becomes, in part, a revenge narrative as well, with Thésée directly referring to vengeance (II: 238). This is part of an increased flexibility in Racine's use of genre – a flexibility already seen in the partially sacrificial structure of *Iphigénie* (although the revenge structure is perhaps not as great a departure from the heroic plot as is the sacrificial structure). In connection with this, we see the usual problems with revenge. Most importantly, the agent of the crime is misidentified. Moreover, the "repayment" of the crime is in excess of the crime itself. The result is, ultimately, a string of unnecessary deaths with resulting misery for those remaining behind. Thésée does show some ambivalence, as we would expect from Racine's principles of character emotion. Nonetheless, he persists in his anger long enough to cause harm.

Phèdre too has ambivalence. Like Atalide or Hermione, she alternates between egocentric concerns and empathic concerns for her beloved. In keeping with this, she is convinced by Oenone but then condemns her (much like Hermione condemns Oreste). Oenone is in some ways a version of the sinister advisers we have seen in earlier plays, starting with Créon. Here, however, there is a striking parametric difference, which adds emotional force to the play. She does not seem to be guided by a deceitful calculation of her own interests. Rather, she seems genuinely to want to protect Phèdre. When Phèdre somewhat cruelly denounces her, Oenone can only feel that Phèdre is right. Her few lines admitting this to herself are arguably among the most affecting in the play. Having come to the conclusion that she has failed to aid Phèdre and, falling into despair over the loss of this attachment relation, she commits suicide.

Taking up event sequences from *Iphigénie* (the use of marriage as a cover for Iphigénie's anticipated sacrifice) and *Andromaque* (the murder of Pyrrhus during his marriage), Racine has Hippolyte go to his death thinking that he is going to marry Aricie. He also takes up the supernatural elements introduced in *Iphigénie*. (There is a divine apparition at the time of Ériphile's death.) Specifically, Hippolyte is attacked by a monster that rises out of the sea. He fights bravely but is eventually dragged to his death by his own horses. The result recalls the death of other Racinian heroes in battle and the resulting condition of their beloveds. After these events, Phèdre kills herself. But, before she dies, she exonerates Hippolyte (a parametric variation on the exculpation of Xipharès at the end of *Mithridate*).

Since the play is so similar to other works by Racine, one might ask why it has been more successful. In part, this is the result of the quality of the verse, which is beyond the scope of this analysis (although this too is necessarily the product of Racine's authorial idiolect). However, it also has to do with the application of narrative development principles.

Perhaps most significantly for our purposes, there is a slight change in the principles of character development. Specifically, the destructive characters vividly express complex human emotions, making them more open to empathy, while the victims (Hippolyte and Aricie) are more emotionally opaque. Perhaps the most important factors here are emotional vulnerability and a sense of guilt. We have already noted both in the case of Oenone. Even more importantly, we find both in Phèdre. As to vulnerability, one could even argue that she is rather childlike. Certainly she seems much less adult than Aricie. This childlike character is most obviously evidenced in her dependent relation to Oenone, but it appears elsewhere as well. For example, when she meets Hippolyte early in the play, she tells him a rather silly story about how if he, rather than Thésée, had come to Crete, she would have helped him defeat the Minotaur. The story has the quality of a childhood fairy tale. In contrast, Hippolyte is all piety and moral rectitude, responding to the tale with horror. As to the feeling of guilt, the deaths of Oenone and Phèdre do not quite fit the pattern isolated earlier. They are the result of despair over a failed attachment. But they also suggest terrible feelings of remorse. In Phèdre's case, the childlike vulnerability only makes this remorse more poignant, since it partially mitigates, not the crime itself, but her responsibility for the crime (much as Oenone's maternal devotion to Phèdre partially mitigates her responsibility).

The thematic implications of the play are in keeping with these points as well. Despite common readings, the play seems in many ways deeply humanistic. It presents us with emotionally conflicted, morally uncertain people suffering – and causing others to suffer – because of an insistence on honor above compassion and too little willingness to forgive. In other words, we may understand the play as manifesting a deep sense of compassion for frailty – as Oenone puts it, "Weakness is only too natural for humans" (II: 242; my translation) – and an equally deep opposition to revenge. It is, in these respects, not only a great play but a fitting culmination of Racine's series of romantic tragedies.

Conclusion

Authors generate stories from their narrative idiolects. These idiolects include partially distinctive versions of universal story, character and scene prototypes; instances (exempla) of narratives, events, characters, and scenes (fictional, historical, biographical, etc.); and motifs separable from prototypes.

All these components figure in development principles, while some (esteemed or norm-defining) exempla are particularly consequential in evaluation principles.

Narrative idiolects may be modeled in terms of clusters of principles, which incorporate parameters that allow for various instantiations of the principles. For example, the heroic prototype involves a ruler and a usurper. Parameters would include the sex and relation of the two (e.g., if they are siblings). The principles are generalizations from enduring configurations of connection patterns in neural networks. The aggregation of principles may be generalized as character types, event types, and scene types. At each level, however, the patterns at issue are contingent on the underlying system of parallel, distributed processes of the neural network. Thus, for example, the principles generalized into character types are always separable from those types. Put differently, changing conditions partially reorganize the underlying neural network. One result of such reorganization may be a change in the interrelation of principles, thus a shift of principles from one character type or event type to another.

The production of individual works results in part from the systematic integration of principles and instances in simulation. The setting of parameters at one level has consequences at other levels. Most often, parameter settings for story prototypes derive first of all from character and, to a lesser extent, scene exempla. To put a finer point on it, prototypes may have default settings at the narrative level. These may guide the author's search for relevant exempla. When an exemplum diverges from a default parameter setting, then the change in setting may produce a cascade of alterations elsewhere in the story structure. For instance, the heroic prototype typically has a default setting for the ruler as male. This will most often lead authors to select character exempla who are male. In a particular case, however, the character integrated into that role may be female. That change in parameter has consequences elsewhere in the story structure, given a society in which female rule is exceptional and therefore more fragile than male rule.

Such processes of integration necessarily lead to changes in authors' idiolectal principles and the relations among those principles. More generally, there is a trajectory to an author's narrative idiolect. After some initial fluidity, an author develops partially fixed narrative principles and metaprinciples for given properties, such as gender. Following this early stabilization, an author's generation of particular stories may be somewhat mechanical with respect to those properties. Put differently, it may be constrained by tightly interrelated clusters of principles (e.g., those manifest in gender stereotypes). At the same time, the growth of an author's ability to operate with these principles is comparable to that found in any other skill. As the operation of the principles becomes more fluent, the integration of principles across clusters (or types) becomes increasingly possible. This results, at least in part, from enhanced parameterization – that is, the introduction of parametric variation into formerly fixed (or less variable) principles. We find this not only in story, character, and scene principles, but also in metaprinciples governing the integration of these basic level principles.

In addition, an author may benefit from periodic reconfigurations of his or her narrative idiolect – in effect, disruptions of the relations among idiolectal principles, disruptions that have systemwide consequences. Such reconfigurations may result from a change in the setting of some key parameter or in the coordination of parameters (e.g., changing the strict alignment of some parameters with one or another sex). Such a change may produce a cascade of alterations elsewhere. Those alterations may then serve to associate previously unrelated principles, thereby forming new clusters.[36] Such reconfigurations may play an important role in keeping an author from repeating himself or herself in subsequent works.

In the case of Racine, this evolution in narrative production was manifest most prominently in the following ways. First, he allowed for a fuller dissociation of principles from types. This permitted increased innovation in the creation of characters and, largely through characters, events and scenes. Second, he enhanced the parameterization of basic-level principles and metaprinciples, particularly those bearing on emotion or motivation. This enabled greater character ambivalence for a single target as well as a fuller integration of norms into characters' emotional response. Both of these changes increased dynamism in the use of development and evaluation principles. That dynamism then produced more frequent and complex shifts in variables within a single work. At least one fundamental alteration in Racine's narrative idiolect seems best understood as a systemic reconfiguration.[37] This was the shift in gender marked by *Bajazet*. This shift altered which principles could be integrated with one another. Specifically, it significantly reduced the segregation of principles by character sex. Finally, Racine developed greater sensitivity to complexities of audience response – perhaps particularly in relation to ambivalence – thereby achieving greater reliability in the evaluative component of simulation.

5

Argument and Metaphor in Brecht and Kafka

Up to this point, we have focused on the aspects of particularization that directly and literally develop structures and processes – such as character – that are internal to stories and we have been concerned with authorial idiolects that generate particular works, more than with the works themselves. In this chapter, our attention will shift in two ways. First, we will be examining some of the ways in which the particularization of story structures may operate indirectly or nonliterally, often drawing on elements external to the story (arguments and models). Second, we will more fully explore the individuality of specific texts.

Arguments and Metaphors

As a number of authors have noted, we may distinguish different varieties of simulation depending on the degree to which various conclusions are or are not determined beforehand. For example, speaking of goal-oriented planning, Faude-Koivisto, Wuerz, and Gollwitzer distinguish an "explorative mind-set associated with a more open-minded processing of information" from an "implemental mind-set associated with a more closed-minded processing of information" (74). Expanding on the insights of Faude-Koivisto and colleagues, we might further distinguish between implementation and argumentation. Consider the following example from Baumeister and Masicampo: "When one has a plane to catch tomorrow, one typically engages in a simulation that calculates backward from the plane's takeoff time" (955) to determine when one should leave for the airport. This is implemental in the sense that it involves reaching a fixed goal. However, it is exploratory in the sense that it does not determine any particular claim or contention about implementation (e.g., when one should leave) before the simulation takes place. In contrast, suppose Jones is being taken to the airport by Smith. Smith says, "We can leave at ten." Jones, however, knows that Smith is notoriously tardy. Thus he decides that, given Smith's judgment, he had better make a case for nine thirty. He then engages in simulation that not only works backward from takeoff time but also specifically aims at supporting the thesis that they should leave by nine thirty. We may refer to this as *argumentation-oriented* simulation since a simulation-guiding contention or claim is determined beforehand. Of course, all three sorts of simulation are integrated in practice. Indeed, there is an exploratory component even in argumentation as the evidence for the argument (e.g., possible construction delays) is not determined before the simulation.

The same points hold in literary particularization. It seems clear that authors do a great deal of exploratory simulation. Implemental and argumentative simulation are hardly absent, however. The former enters most obviously in evaluation. Negative evaluations may be particularly likely to foster simulation regarding how to achieve specific outcomes. For example, suppose an author feels that the work does not make clear the plight of the urban poor and the relationship of this plight to neoliberal economic policies. He or she is likely to engage in implemental simulation to rectify that thematic deficit. As this example suggests, implemental simulations bearing on themes are often argumentative as well. Moreover, authors may *begin* with some degree of argumentative simulation. Indeed, this is almost inevitable insofar as they set out to treat any political, social, or ethical issue. Given the importance of themes in most narratives, we would therefore expect argumentative simulation to play a role in the particularization of many literary works. It is likely to be especially important in works with a strong thematic orientation.

Thematic concerns operate most commonly at two levels. First, themes are likely to enter in the selection of particularizing elements at the start of exploratory simulation. For example, when Harriet Beecher Stowe thought about writing an antislavery novel, her choice of scenes and characters – as well as particular, historical, or biographical events – was undoubtedly in part guided by this thematic concern. Put simply, if one is going to write an antislavery novel, then one is likely to want to have a plantation as the scene for at least parts of that novel. One is also likely to have humanized or idealized slaves, despised slave traders, and so forth. The second level where the thematic concerns would most commonly enter is in evaluation principles. Having simulated a particular scene, an author might feel that it makes a slave trader too sympathetic or does not adequately communicate the suffering experienced by slaves.

Virtually every literary work involves some thematic interests, and these seem to be the usual ways in which those thematic interests enter into authorial simulation. However, some works go beyond minimal thematic concerns. For example, some authors develop works that are thesis driven, just as some authors develop works that are character driven. In these cases, not only the initial selection of elements (such as scene) but the simulation of story sequences is thematically guided. This may yield a relatively pure form of argumentative elaboration. Of course, if it is a narrative, it will not operate in the same way as an argument. An argument would commonly involve a fairly full elaboration of abstract principles (e.g., about the nature of an ideal society) punctuated by minimally elaborated instances (i.e., illustrative examples). In contrast, a thesis-driven narrative should involve a fairly full elaboration of the illustrative story, perhaps punctuated by minimally elaborated generalizations. Even in these circumstances, however, the illustrative portion of the narrative is almost certain to involve exploratory as well as argumentative simulation. Perhaps what is most interesting here is that such exploratory simulation may alter the argumentative conclusions and the associated argumentative simulations. This is the sort of thing that occurs when Smith begins with the idea that "Doe will never agree to endorse this book" but then concretely imagines the request and modifies his judgment ("Actually, now that I think about it, this might just be something Doe would consider doing").

A second type of simulation not explored in previous chapters is connected with a cognitive process that, although not precisely distinctive of verbal art, is widely recognized as crucial for verbal art and as particularly characteristic of it. This is metaphor and its various associates – more generally what is referred to as *modeling*. As writers such as Johnson-Laird have shown, one of the most important processes of human cognition is taking up one cognitive object and using it to think about another cognitive object. This can be a matter of using one particular to understand another particular or one general structure to understand another general structure. Often, the structures are drawn from very different domains – for example, when we understand the atom by reference to solar systems. In the case of particulars, however, we may be more inclined to draw from the same category; for example, in thinking about one narrative symposium in Germany, Jones is more likely to use another German narrative symposium as a model.

Clearly, modeling may be used for several purposes. Most important for our concerns, modeling may guide our simulation of likely trajectories of action or response – often through character modeling in particular. For example, Jones might hesitate to press an argumentative advantage over Smith if she thinks that Smith will "respond like a cornered animal." The metaphor implies a set of likely behaviors on Smith's part.

Although modeling is a ubiquitous feature of human thought, its verbal manifestation in metaphor is, again, widely seen as particularly character-istic of verbal art. Unsurprisingly, then, modeling in general, and metaphor in particular, are common sources of narrative specification. In keeping with the general operation of simulation, the initial manifestation of this may be in the determination of characters. But scenes and events are readily entailed by models as well. For example, in *Uncle Tom's Cabin*, Stowe to some extent modeled Simon Legree on Satan. However, this metaphorical assimilation was inseparable from the specifications of his plantation as hell and of his behavior toward his slaves as the infliction of the tortures of hell.

As this example suggests, there are cases where the elaboration of the model is more extensive and/or more explicit than others. Thus the model may be used only locally or it may be a primary source for characters, scenes, and events throughout a work. Similarly, the model may be foregrounded (e.g., through the use of metaphors or similes or through allusion, such as having a character use phrases from Satan in *Paradise Lost*). Moreover, the use of the model may be more or less literalized. Put differently, more or fewer literal properties of the target may be determined by the model.[1] For example, sup-pose Doe says, "Smith was a cornered rat at the department meeting." She may develop this simply by characterizing Smith's sense of threat and tendency to respond to threat with aggression rather than withdrawal. Alternatively, she may give Smith some further ratlike characteristics (e.g., little eyes, sharp teeth), while keeping him a human being. Finally, she may go all the way and tell the story of a rat named Smith, scurrying into a corner of the departmen-tal meeting room.

In modeling as elsewhere the primary purposes of particularizing and developing a plot are either emotional or thematic. As is well known, meta-phorical assimilation often has emotional consequences. In addition to what-ever feelings we may have about the target, we are likely to have feelings about the source as well, particularly if that source is highly concrete. Insofar as the source partially activates those emotions (through imagination or emotional memories), the emotions are almost certain to affect our response to the tar-get. The mere reference to a rat, plus the image or memory of a cornered rat (for those of us who have such memories), may serve to inspire a mild form of fear or disgust. That, in turn, is likely to affect our response to Smith. If any-thing, the point is clearer in the use of models to develop and particularize lit-erary narratives, as when Stowe uses the model of Jesus for Uncle Tom or that of Satan for Legree. As this example illustrates, the use of models for thematic purposes is no less evident. To assimilate a slave to Jesus and a slave-owner to Satan is to make a (fairly straightforward) thematic point about slavery.

Indeed, as we see here, the emotional effects of a literary work often serve the thematic purposes, and both may be inseparable from the models used to particularize the characters, scenes, and events.

In the following sections, we will consider particular cases of the two simulation techniques just outlined – argumentation and modeling. We will examine these both in general, theoretical terms and in exemplary literary works, specifically Bertolt Brecht's *Die Maßnahme* (*The Measures Taken*) and Franz Kafka's *Die Verwandlung* (*The Metamorphosis*).[2] The first is a fairly pure example of argumentative simulation. The second presents a partially literalized and thoroughly elaborated metaphor, integrated with other, more covert models.

Before going on to these works, however, it is important to remark on two things. First, we will be focusing on the elaboration of these techniques in particular works. However, this does not mean that there are no authorial continuities in the use of argument or modeling. Indeed, we have no reason to expect less continuity in these areas than in narrative principles and parameters. In other words, we would expect patterns across an author's works in these areas as well. We will touch on some of these continuities in the following pages, but only insofar as they bear on understanding the work at hand.

Second, these works manifest the usual preference for cross-culturally occurring narrative prototypes. Indeed, they make use of all the usual techniques that we have already considered, such as the integration of different prototypes and the insertion of motifs. Thus they continue the standard processes for the alteration, specification, and evaluation of universal structures. In this chapter, we are simply adding two new ways in which these processes operate.

Theater for Instruction: *Die Maßnahme* (*The Measures Taken*)

Bertolt Brecht's *Die Maßnahme* suggests its argumentative structure already in its subtitle, which names its genre: *Lehrstück* (*Teaching Piece*). As a first approximation, we may say that the work has at least two teaching purposes. The primary teaching concerns the means of changing reality, specifically altering the political and economic world, as the chorus exclaims in the final line of the play (268). These means are multiple and largely bear on the operation of the Communist Party.[3] This part of the play is directed, first of all, at activists who may commit one or another of the canonical errors isolated in Marxist theory. The other teaching purpose concerns the ways in which one may communicate an understanding of the means of changing the world – or, rather, one particular way, the way of greatest concern to Brecht: theater.

Theater is obviously a medium with tremendous potential for teaching people how they might engage in social, political, and economic change. Brecht had strong and articulate views on good and bad ways of doing this.

Die Maßnahme is a short play. Four agitators have been sent from Moscow to China to propagandize for the revolution. They ask a "young comrade" from the border to accompany them as a guide. The young comrade makes a series of blunders that harm the revolutionary efforts of the agitators. The nature of the errors and their deleterious consequences illustrate – or seem to illustrate – central tenets of Communist teaching about activism and Brecht's teaching about theater. A final error leads to the agitators' flight. In the course of the flight, they decide that escape is possible only if the young comrade is killed and his body defaced. The young comrade (apparently) agrees. After this, the agitators return to their political activities and have tremendous success – their "work" is marked by "good fortune" and "in this land too revolution is on the march" (257; my translation here and below).

The play begins with a brief preface that uses the standard device of establishing a frame for the rest of the play. The body of the play comprises a series of eight flashbacks, recounting the main actions of the story in as many scenes. The flashbacks are interrupted by returns to the frame structure, which is taken up again in a brief conclusion. The narrative frame is a criminal investigation into the actions of four agitators and the young comrade who is eventually executed. We will return to the thematic operation of the frame narrative later in this section. As it is somewhat more complex than the argumentative simulation of the embedded narrative, it is best to begin with the latter.

The first scene after the preface introduces the embedded narrative. It employs the cross-culturally common framing device of a journey. The four agitators are being sent from Moscow to engage in organization and propaganda work in China. As we will see, one of Brecht's main argumentative goals is to treat conflicts between romantic and emotional – particularly petit bourgeois – political activism, on the one hand, and orthodox Communist thought and party discipline, on the other. At least superficially, the argument guiding the elaboration and particularization of the story is an orthodox Communist criticism of several petit bourgeois revolutionary tendencies. It is therefore unsurprising that the simulation should involve a movement from the center of Communist orthodoxy (Moscow) to some area of political ferment. The complex reasons for and effects of selecting China are, however, less clear at this point.

In the second scene, the agitators join with the young comrade, who will help guide them in the unfamiliar land where they will be working. In preparing to begin their work, the agitators and the young comrade put on masks, concealing their faces. This is clearly an allegorical representation of underground activists taking on fabricated identities in order to protect themselves and their organization. The importance of such fabrication and concealment is stressed later in the play when the romantic young comrade removes his mask, thereby endangering all the agitators. That plot sequence is clearly designed to illustrate the argument that, when engaging in illegal propaganda work, concealment is necessary.

The introduction of the masks is important for another reason, however. The masks make salient the theatrical nature of their testimony. Indeed, the agitators explicitly act out the events, explaining that they will "repeat" what happened (e.g., 257, 258), rather than merely recounting or explaining it in testimonies. This is important because it introduces a second set of argumentative concerns in the play. These bear most directly on Brecht's theories of *epic theater*, but they also have consequences for the more overtly political themes just mentioned.

Specifically, Brecht saw *dramatic theater* as aiming to excite an emotional relation between the spectator and the characters. In Brecht's view, such an emotional response fosters the sense that the events presented onstage, with all their causes and consequences, are perfectly transparent – obvious, natural, self-evident – because they involve the same sort of feelings the spectator has himself or herself. This leads to the sense that such events are inevitable. In contrast, *epic theater* produces an "alienation process" (986) in which the spectator does not simply feel the emotions of the characters; rather, he or she is "surprised" (988) and sees the events as changeable, debatable (986). The latter is crucial for coming to understand the "laws of cause and effect" so as to "change the world" (986). More generally, Brecht sees feeling alone, unguided by an understanding of the regularities governing life, as "blurry," "ineffective" (994), and "vague" (995).

This opposition in types of theater is not confined to art. In one common view of socialist activism, this is precisely the difference between romantic revolutionaries, guided by feeling, and orthodox Marxists, who recognize the laws governing human social life. (On romantic anticapitalism, see, for example, Lukács *Essays* 47.) These laws are given in the "classics" of Marxism (such as *Capital*). Indeed, in the first scene, the agitators explain that they are not bringing material aid to the Chinese, they are, rather, bringing "the teachings of the classics" (257). The point, it seems, is to make the agitators parallel with Brecht himself, since Brecht is evidently bringing the teachings of the Marxist classics to his audience through this play. (We will see later in this section that this parallel is only apparent.)

The following scenes are in effect illustrations of the thematic claims just outlined – clear instances of argumentative elaboration and particularization. The third scene takes up the issue of emotion versus disciplined thought. Indeed, it addresses the particular sort of emotion that Brecht finds so untrustworthy in dramatic theater: empathy. Like the spectator of a dramatic play – and in keeping with his tendency toward political romanticism – the young comrade is driven by empathy with the oppressed rather than being guided by an understanding of their condition and a considered strategy for altering that condition. That understanding is provided by the agitators (thus the Communist Party), whom the young comrade ignores – with disastrous results. Specifically, the agitators send the young comrade to organize a particular group of workers. Filled with compassion, he tries to make an appeal to the human feelings of the overseer and physically aids the workers. In response, the workers mock him and the overseer denounces him. This results in the agitators being hunted for two days. Thus fellow feeling with the workers along with the humanistic appeals and charitable acts to which it gives rise do not help those workers. Rather, they hinder the political activities of the genuine activists. One suggestion of the scene is that dramatic theater has the same effects. Brecht has fairly clearly simulated the scene toward these argumentative implications.

In the fourth scene, Brecht reconsiders the same basic opposition with a change in the precise theoretical issue. The young agitator is sent to distribute flyers to workers at a factory where some of them are on strike. A police officer accuses one of the workers of distributing the flyers, and feeling compassion for the worker who is unjustly accused, the young comrade intervenes. Due to unpredictable events, the worker and a colleague both lose their jobs. This scene has the title "The Lesser and the Greater Injustice" (or, more literally, "The Small and the Big Injustice"). The idea is that the young comrade's compassion led him to try to avoid a small injustice and this resulted in a greater injustice, specifically the advance of strikebreaking (262). The argument guiding this scene's simulation is, roughly, that the individual must be sacrificed to the greater good. The greater good is class based – the good of the workers collectively rather than the good of an individual worker. The party recognizes that good through its superior knowledge. Thus individuals should be guided, not by their (individualistic, petit bourgeois) feelings, but by the analysis made by the party. This scene and its argument are particularly significant because they prepare us for the ending where the young comrade is killed in order to save the work of the agitators.

But there are complexities in this case – complexities bearing on the precise nature of the elaborative and particularizing simulation of this scene.

Specifically, it is clear that no science could have predicted the precise out-come of the young comrade's response to the police officer. The problem results from multiple accidental factors bearing on the precise way in which the police officer and the two workers act. It would have been just as easy to simulate a sequence in which the comrade intervened and the worker was freed. Moreover, the putatively "correct" action for the young comrade would seem to be a cowardly escape from the scene, allowing the innocent worker to be imprisoned. Even the most minimal simulation of this situation suggests that such behavior would be unlikely to win the confidence and support of the workers. In short, it would be very likely to inhibit the work of the agita-tors. At this point, it is difficult to say whether there is simply a flaw in Brecht's argument and associated simulation or if this ambiguity is part of a larger argumentative design. We will consider this issue further as we go on.

The fifth scene takes us to the issue of united front tactics in a colonial situation. The young comrade finds himself unable to overcome his disgust (again, an emotional response) with the national bourgeoisie. Thus he can-not engage in the sort of polite deference required to create a united front against imperialism. Here too there are complications, however. The united front is supposed to lead to the arming of the workers. But it is far from clear that the national bourgeoisie would have agreed to that tactic had the young comrade simply been more pliable. Indeed, the position of the agitators in this case becomes almost untenable when one takes into account actual events in the years just before the play – events that should presumably con-strain and orient our simulations. The Stalinist line in China had supported a united front between the Chinese Communist Party and the Nationalists (Guomindang). The united front greatly advanced the Nationalists in 1926 and 1927. However, when the Nationalists established control, "the commu-nists became hunted criminals" after 1928 (Zarrow 230). Indeed, having made use of the Communists to extend his domination of China, Chiang Kai-shek instituted "a massive 'White Terror' with the goal of exterminating all ... Communists" (237). Shortly before the 1930 premier of Brecht's play (and, of course, before Brecht's 1931 revisions of the play), the Nationalists began one of their "'extermination campaigns' designed to destroy the Chinese soviets, the Red Army, and the Chinese Communists" (Chai 16). In fact, as part of the united front cooperation, the Chinese Communist Party "itself disarmed Shanghai's workers after their successful takeover of the Chinese city." As a result, "when the Nationalists entered Shanghai," they "attacked the General Labor Union, killing and arresting workers" (239). In short, the united front policy in China is not what would have armed and protected workers, but what did in fact disarm them and put them in danger.[4]

In contrast, "Leon Trotsky had been urging the CCP to abandon" the united front, in favor of "a Communist-led armed uprising" (Chai 240). Indeed, some writers link Stalin's united front policy in this case directly to "his power struggle with Leon Trotsky" (227). This is one point in the play where the young comrade's actions seem to suggest Trotsky. This is not to say that the young comrade allegorically represents Trotsky. Rather, it is to say that here the play may suggest some political complexities by hinting at the conflicts between Stalin and Trotsky, perhaps as symptoms of deeper problems. In other words, Trotsky appears to have operated as one model for the young comrade at this point.

The sixth scene presents the young comrade as caught up in enthusiasm for a charismatic nonparty leader calling for immediate revolutionary action by the masses. When asked how they will fight against the massive weapons of the state and ruling class, the young comrade answers, "We will fight with teeth and nails" (264). It turns out that the nonparty leader is an imposter, bought and paid for by the merchants (264). The entire uprising is a trap. This incident leads to the flight of the agitators and their murder of the young comrade. It is certainly the young comrade's most extreme and most harmful mistake, leading as it does to the deaths of many workers.

The story in this scene follows orthodox Communist teaching in isolating a range of faults in romantic anticapitalism. The first and most obvious is that it shows the results of a lack of party discipline.[5] This is bound up with the romantic tendency toward spontaneism, the view that the spontaneous impulses of the workers should be followed by socialist intellectuals rather than being led by those intellectuals with their party doctrines.[6] This scene also reveals the dangers of factionalism, when the young comrade splits with the agitators. Perhaps most significantly, it reveals his tendency toward voluntarism, the view that the agents can simply join together and remake history.[7] This ignores precisely the social and historical constraints articulated in Marxist analyses, the knowledge pointed to by Brecht in his discussion of epic and teaching theater (see, for example, 994). In short, Brecht's simulation of these events was clearly guided by specific, argumentative purposes.

But, once again, there is ambiguity here, at least on one point. Brecht almost certainly did mean to present narrativized arguments against spontaneism and voluntarism. His depiction of personal enthusiasm for a leader and loyalty to the party, however, are more complex. There are some hints that we might connect the false leader, the agent of the merchants, with Fascism. The point is particularly striking given the very recent successes of the Nazi Party.[8] At the same time, it is difficult to see a Communist with great enthusiasm for a particular leader and not think of what later came to be called the *cult of personality* around Stalin. Undoubtedly, that cult was not as obvious in Germany at the time of the play as it is now. Nonetheless, the expulsion of Trotsky had occurred only very recently and the great concentration of Soviet power in the hands of a single leader should not have been difficult to discern. Thus, here too, the scene remains ambiguous. It is possible that Brecht's argument is not simply the orthodox Communist one, but a more complex presentation of different, even contradictory views manifest in a more ambiguous and ambivalent – thus more exploratory – simulation. [9]

In order to think about the precise nature of the argumentative simulation in this play, we might now return to the criminal investigation. Given that the play involves argumentative simulation, it is unsurprising that the narrative frame structure instantiates the criminal investigation prototype – the prototype most directly associated with argument. This genre undoubtedly received further activation from the topic of the argument as well – the methods of orthodox Soviet Marxism or Bolshevism. As a revolutionary movement, Bolshevism explicitly advocated violence. This violence eventually proceeded not only against the "class enemy," but against members of the Communist Party itself. Given the real and extensive possibilities for (and realities of) killing, it is not at all surprising that the criminal investigation genre received a high degree of activation for Brecht.

In keeping with the standard criminal investigation structure, there is a murder. The murder involves the violation of some bonds of association (here, comradeship rather than kinship or love), and the comrades left behind are the ones who demand an investigation. The investigation is conducted by an official with social and legal authority. It involves testimonies that reveal the conditions of the murder. Indeed, there is even the suggestion of a larger responsibility for the murder in those who set the policy followed by the murderers – that is, the Communist Party.[10] Recall that criminal investigation narratives often distinguish between the immediate agents of a crime and those ultimately responsible for that crime, who are less likely to be punished.[11] This distinction can contribute to ambivalence in the conclusion of such stories. It is at least arguable that the ending of Brecht's play has just this sort of ambivalence.

However, Brecht varies the criminal investigation format – in fact alters it drastically. First, we find a different distribution of characters. There is a Control Chorus, not unlike the chorus in a Greek tragedy, but in this case the chorus takes up particular genre roles – those of the judge and chief investigator. Moreover, it stands in for the Communist Party itself. This is important for several reasons. First, this follows the orientation of some Marxist literary and film theory of the period in creating mass or collective characters rather than individual heroes.[12] Second, it renders the governing authority impersonal. In connection with this, the "defendant" is also collectivized and rendered impersonal, comprising four largely indistinguishable "agitators." Another shift from the standard structure is that the characters demanding justice are the murderers. This is, of course, a familiar variant, most famously found in *Oedipus the King*. A difference from Sophocles's play, however, is that the agitators know that they are the murderers.

The fact that the agitators demand an "objective" or third-person judgment of their guilt or innocence may suggest that Communist activists are highly self-critical, that the violence of the Communist Party is under "control" and constantly scrutinized for any possible excess. Nonetheless, any reader sensitive to legal procedures cannot help but notice something peculiar about the legal proceedings here. The entire testimony comes from the defendants. Moreover, the defendants were sent to do their work by the Communist Party, the same Communist Party that governs the judicial process. In other words, within the cross-cultural scheme for the genre, the judges are inseparable from the unpunished figures of ultimate responsibility. In short, the Communist Party is in effect given the task of judging the guilt of the Communist Party with no outside voices allowed to intervene. For example, unlike in some Chinese theater, there is no ghost of the murdered young comrade to tell his version of the story. The agitators testify that, when they determined that they must execute him, the young comrade agreed completely with their decision.[13] However, that agreement is, again, simply reported by the agitators. We never have any separate, direct access to the views or words of the young comrade. Rather, we have only the murderers' claim that even the victim agreed he should be killed.

Indeed, this claim comes in the eighth scene of the play, given the title "Die Maßnahme," thus suggesting that it is the core of the work and, in some sense, a recapitulation of the entire play. In this scene, the agitators make their "judgment" (267) that they must kill the young comrade. The official justification is strategic. However, two scenes earlier, the young comrade had rejected the authority of the agitators and thus the party that they represent. Moreover, in the scene before that, we learned that he had "a great following among the unemployed" (264). Thus Brecht presents us a situation in which a popular leader defies Communist Party authority and the party representatives determine that he should be executed. Although early, the situation nonetheless recalls the conditions in the Soviet Union, particularly under Stalin.

The young comrade's agreement with the decision is also closely reminiscent of the coerced or fabricated confessions and self-criticisms that marked the trials of Stalin's opponents.[14] The connection is particularly clear given the clichéd manner in which the young comrade accepts his execution: "In the interest of Communism, in agreement with the forward march of the proletarian masses of all lands, saying yes to the revolutionizing of the world" (267). These words repeat verbatim what the local party leader had said before the agitators left for their mission in China. This direct repetition suggests a script written by the party rather than an individual's sincere expression of remorse.

To make matters worse, the agitators never actually show that there was any need to kill the young comrade. It is never clear how the movement would be harmed even if the young comrade were captured. In this sense, despite Esslin's phrasing and the discussions of other critics (e.g., Mittenzwei 53), it is never evident that there is a genuine "moral dilemma" here (Esslin 140). Rather, it is difficult to see how this is not simply murder rationalized by the agitators and the Control Chorus – again, very much in keeping with the Soviet model.

In terms of the preceding theoretical discussion, we might ask here whether the developments in this scene and elsewhere in the play resulted from argumentative or exploratory processes. One might reasonably conjecture that the answer is both. For example, historical precedents would almost certainly have guided Brecht's imagination of self-justifying trials even without explicit thematic purposes, thus in an exploratory way. At the same time, Brecht was clearly engaging in argumentative simulation throughout the play, at least with respect to canonical errors identified by Marxist theory.

The question, of course, is just what the relationship between exploration and argumentation might be. One possibility is that the argumentative simulations stand in an uneasy, even contradictory relation with more exploratory imaginations. In this interpretation, the play's tacit criticisms of Stalinism are the result of a relatively uncontrolled, exploratory simulation, whereas the more orthodox aspects of the play are the product of argumentative specification. My own inclination, however, is to see both aspects of the play as involving at least some argumentative specification. In his dramatic theory, Brecht stressed that a play should produce thought and discussion. He was opposed to a theater that led audience members to mere passive acceptance of inevitability, as we have already noted. Suppose Brecht's argumentative organization was solely a matter of advocating orthodox Communism. Then, if successful, the play should foster just the sort of passivity and acceptance he repudiated. It is more in keeping with his dramatic theory that he would argumentatively plot out apparently opposed positions and simulate clashing ideas and options in order to provoke reflection and dialogue. This is not to say, however, that exploratory simulation played no role in the work.

Brecht undoubtedly employed relatively free simulation extensively, and that affected his arguments and their conclusions, qualifying or even contradicting them, as occurs with any writer.

Further complications arise due to the embedding of a second cross-cultural genre in the narrative – sacrificial tragicomedy. The Marxist emplotment of history is a tragicomic emplotment in that it moves through a period of suffering to ultimate well-being. This emplotment may take different forms, depending on what aspects of the situation are stressed. In reference to China at the time, one obvious and pressing component of the tragic middle was hunger. Indeed, when the play was being written and performed, China was experiencing an extended famine (1928–1933; Roberts 246). In the course of the play, Brecht's characters make repeated reference to the Chinese peasants' and workers' lack of adequate food. When combined with willing death, this complex of scene and character is almost certain to activate the sacrificial prototype. This is precisely what we find in the play. The agitators seem to have little or no success in their operations, despite their work and the popularity of the young comrade. Once he is killed, however, things miraculously turn around. This is presented as a direct cause and effect sequence. The agitators explain that "we shot him" and "we returned to our work" (267). Then the Control Chorus announces again, just as they did at the outset, "And your work was fortunate" (268), although now the reason for the good fortune seems to be, precisely, the sacrifice.[15]

Of course, this too is not unequivocal.[16] The victim in sacrificial narratives may be the guilty party, but he or she is more typically innocent. Indeed, the transformational value of the sacrifice is often contingent on that innocence. Moreover, this is bound up with another complication. As we have already noted, both the Control Chorus and the agitators are impersonal and collective. In contrast, the young comrade has an individual personality, makes distinctive decisions, and appears fully human. Indeed, early in the play, when they are going into China, the agitators all agree to erase their own individual "faces" to become "nameless, motherless, blank pages on which the revolution writes [their] assignment" (258). In connection with this, they all wear masks for their work, as already noted. But the young comrade removes his mask, revealing an individual human face, just at his moment of defiance (266). All this is almost certain to foster a greater sense of identification between the audience and the young comrade, as opposed to the faceless agitators who kill him.

One might claim that the argument of the play – here understood as purely orthodox – should dissuade us from following through on our empathic impulses. But there are two problems with this. First, it is far from clear that didactic implications will override emotional preferences. Indeed, if they did, then there would be no need for epic theater. We would only require Brecht's instruction to resist the lure of traditional theater. In keeping with this, Brecht's plays themselves work – if they do – because they affect us emotionally in a way that logical arguments alone would not.

The second problem derives from the ways in which the play itself makes reference to the emotional effects of the legal proceedings as theater. As already noted, the agitators wear masks and explicitly act out their testimonies. This suggests that the trial constitutes a sort of play within the play, with the Control Chorus observing the performance in parallel with the actual audience. As the agitators come to the point where they are going to kill the young comrade – thus as they come to the point on which the party is to judge their behavior – the Control Chorus makes a revealing admission. To encourage the agitators to continue, they explain that they share the agitators' feelings, that they have "*Mitgefühl*" (267). Moreover, they go on to say that the agitators' "judgment" ("*Urteil*," the same word used for the legal decision of the Control Chorus [257]) was not made by the agitators but by "reality" (267). In short, the Control Chorus's sharing of the agitators' emotions leads them to the view that the outcome was absolutely necessary, that the agitators had "no way out" ("*keinen Ausweg*" 267). But that is precisely what Brecht criticizes in his account of dramatic theater, in opposition to epic theater. In dramatic theater, the spectator shares the feelings of the hero and feels that "there is no way out" ("*keinen Ausweg*") of his or her situation (986). The Control Chorus's sharing of the agitators' feelings is further connected with their lack of criticism (see 996 on this relation). Indeed, Brecht speaks specifically about the deleterious effects of "*Mitfühlen*" on the teaching purposes of theater (993; recall the Control Chorus's "*Mitgefühl*"). In contrast with the Control Chorus, the audience is in effect given a thematic instruction to be critical when in the final scene the agitators say, "Now you too think of a better possibility" (267).

All this in turn suggests that Brecht's specifications of both the criminal investigation and sacrificial prototypes were guided by argumentative simulation at two levels. There is, again, the obvious level at which Brecht is criticizing such standard revolutionary faults as voluntarism and spontaneism. However, there is, in addition, a complication of this initial, obvious argument. This is a further argument that develops the faults on the other side, the faults of the party.

Again, this is what one would expect from Brecht's encompassing program for theater. Specifically, he does not set out to "moralize" but to "study" (988). That study should not lead the audience to think that worldly events and conditions are natural and inevitable. Rather, the study should lead to "discussion" (see 996). Indeed, Brecht characterizes epic theater as defined by "an interest in the free discussion of life's questions toward the end of resolving them." Moreover, it "can defend this interest against all contrary tendencies" (989).

Picking up on the last comment, we may say that, in *Die Maßnahme*, Brecht faced two "contrary tendencies." One was the romantic politics of feeling; the other was Communist orthodoxy. His narrative specification of the two overarching prototypes (criminal investigation and sacrifice) was guided by an argumentative simulation designed not to support one of these tendencies over the other but rather to set them against one another. Thus the argument of the piece is not supposed to give an answer to the life question of how to make a classless society or to end oppression. It is, rather, designed to provoke productive debate on how those questions might best be answered.

The inclination of many literary analysts is probably to expect crude didacticism from argumentative simulation. In other words, many of us are likely to expect argumentatively elaborated and particularized works to present simplistic plots and characters. *Die Maßnahme* has been read as if it does just that. As the preceding analysis suggests, however, argumentative simulation can be highly complex. Specifically, Brecht's generation and evaluative revision of *Die Maßnahme* may be understood as manifesting two sets of argumentative principles. One set was fairly straightforward. These principles concerned representing, in a convincing manner, his vision of a new dramaturgy. This led, for example, to the "theatricalization" of the agitators' testimonies. The other set was less straightforward. These concerned generating thematically opposed elaborations and particularizations. Specifically, these principles required that the play present a case for and against both romantic socialism and orthodox Communism. Thus they required that the play communicate an understanding of the values and errors of both tendencies.

Again, this is not to say that exploratory simulation is missing from Brecht's play. For example, it is likely that the fuller and more individualized portrayal of the young comrade derived from Brecht's exploratory simulations. Moreover, these exploratory simulations may well have given force to the argumentative criticisms of the party and Stalin. This would, in turn, help balance the argumentative simulations of the work, if Brecht's critique of romantic anticapitalism was a more self-consciously elaborated argumentative goal, as seems likely.

Finally, Brecht's evaluation and revision of the play needed to reconcile these various argumentative and exploratory tensions aesthetically, as parts of a dramatic work. In Brecht's case, this was made possible by the goals of epic theater. In contrast with dramatic theater, Brecht's new dramaturgy aimed at producing discussion. It thus welcomed rather than rejected dialectical contradiction. Indeed, Brecht would undoubtedly claim that our intuitions about teaching theater get things backward. It is precisely the apparently "free" simulations of dramatic theater that are likely to produce thematically reductive conclusions – and to bind us to those conclusions with Mitgefühl.[17]

The Complexity of Models

The preceding discussion of argumentative elaboration and particularization suggests once again the complexity of shifting, interacting circuits of simulation. It should come as no surprise that we will find the same dynamism in the use of models. Indeed, the study of modeling in story production reveals further subtleties of simulation.

To consider this topic, we might begin by asking, given our understanding of simulation, how would we expect simulation of models to operate? First, models involve some source and some target.[18] In other words, there is something we are interested in explaining, describing, or characterizing emotionally. That is the target. There is also something that we are using to treat that target. That is the source. If Doe says that Jones was possessed by demons during the department meeting, Doe is probably trying to communicate something about Jones (the target) by reference to demonic possession (the source). Regardless of whether one is speaking literally or metaphorically, one uses the source to make inferences about properties and relations of the target, to formulate expectations about the target, and so on. The difference between a model or metaphor on the one hand, and literal categorization on the other, is the following. When literally categorizing a target, we assume that default properties of the source apply to the target unless we are given reason to believe otherwise. For example, if Smith says that Fifi was a lioness and means that literally, then we assume that Fifi had four legs (unless we are told that, say, one of her legs was blown off by a hunter). If he means the statement metaphorically, then we do not assume default properties. Rather, we assume simply that some salient property transfers from the source to the target in a contextually relevant way. For example, if we are speaking of how people respond to aggravation, then "Fifi is a lioness" may mean that she responds with dangerous aggression. If we are speaking of how people's hats make them look like animals, then we will draw different connections.

In some cases, we use metaphors or models simply to highlight information that we already have. In other cases, we use models to guide investigation, attentional orientation, or conjecture – including simulation. Moreover, as George Lakoff and others have shown,[19] in some cases our metaphors are explicit, whereas in other cases they are implicit. Thus, in some cases, our interpretation, inference, emotional response, and other aspects of simulation are guided by a self-consciously chosen model. In other cases, they are guided by a model of which we are not even aware. In a connectionist framework, we might say that a particular domain may be primed and thus influence our interpretation of a target without the domain name and the source/target mapping ever being directly stated. For example, it seems to occur with some frequency in racist discourse that white speakers think of blacks on the model of delinquent adolescent males (or, even worse, animals). Thus whites may speak of a group of blacks as arrogant, unruly, oversexed, irresponsible (or wild, vicious, bloody, dangerous). At the same time, they are likely to deny assimilating adult blacks to adolescent delinquents (or animals). Moreover, the denial is sincere in the sense that they do not realize they are using the model. (The point is obviously in keeping with the general limits on introspection, discussed in the Introduction and Chapter 1.)

In fact, in any given case of simulation, we would expect there to be several models at work, interacting with one another with different degrees of explicitness. For example, adolescent males are to some extent simulated in terms of animals. When whites simulate blacks in terms of adolescent males, that simulation often involves elements of a simulation in terms of animals. At the same time, the simulation in terms of animals has its own independent operation. We might expect these different models to have different degrees of activation, thus different degrees of consequence for simulation, in different contexts. If Jones is simulating a black man in a fight, the animal model might become more consequential. If he is simulating a black man in relation to trustworthiness, then the delinquent adolescent model may be activated more fully. Moreover, these models may themselves involve more transitory particularizations. In different contexts, Jones (a European American) might envision Doe (an African American) more in terms of an ape or a panther. Thus different sorts of animal (or adolescent) model may enter. Moreover, features of either the sources or the targets, or contextual features, may activate otherwise unrelated models as well. For example, Jones (obviously not a very open-minded person) may tacitly draw on a demonic model in simulating Jews (a common anti-Semitic development). Through, say, the Faust legend and some feature of a particular context, this may trigger an "amoral scientist" model as well. This may inflect simulation only briefly, it may recur in limited, parallel contexts within a simulation, or it may persist through the course of a simulation. In short, beyond being explicit or implicit, models may have localized, recurrent, or continuous consequences for simulation.

Note that in some of these cases, we would expect a degree of contradiction, as even related models are not always fully compatible with one another. Nevertheless, we would expect there to be some convergence across models as well. In other words, certain aspects of the models would reinforce one another. We would expect these aspects to become particularly prominent and determinative in a simulation. For example, if Jones is imagining blacks in terms of animals and delinquents, this will produce some discrepancies in the representation of blacks in different contexts. However, the two models will converge in contrasting blacks with adult humans. Thus we would expect some properties (e.g., lack of moral guidance) to be particularly salient and consequential due to the enhanced activation received from both models.

Again, the difference between models and literal categorizations is that the former do not involve the assumption that default properties of the source apply to the target. Typically, there are many default properties of a source that are clearly not applicable to the target. Earlier in this chapter, we spoke of some narratives as "literalizing" a metaphor. This is almost never strictly true. In other words, it is rarely (if ever) the case that all the properties of the source are taken over in the elaboration and particularization of a story. However, allegories and related works (e.g., some works of fantasy) do incorporate a broad range of default properties from the source, typically properties that are distinctive of the source. For example, as we will discuss in the following section, Kafka's Gregor Samsa is transformed into a dung beetle. This does not mean that the source (dung beetle) is fully literalized. For example, Gregor continues to understand German, which is well beyond the capacities of dung beetles. However, Gregor does have the hard back, the soft underbelly, the multiple legs, and other physical properties of a dung beetle. In other words, he has distinctive default properties of a dung beetle. In effect, partial literalization involves the transfer of some default properties that we would ordinarily not count as applicable from the source to the target. Put differently, it involves properties that are not part of the thematic significance of the metaphor. For example, Kafka's story does not suggest that the sort of life lived by Gregor would lead someone to have extra legs.

Die Verwandlung (*The Metamorphosis*)

This obviously leads us to Kafka's story. Moreover, it does so in such a way as to highlight one of the main questions that arises in connection with this story – what does it mean that we are to understand Gregor in terms of an insect model (if it does not mean that he has extra legs)? Margaret Breen has presented an affecting account of how she read the story as an adolescent.

Finishing the narrative, she felt that Gregor's condition expressed her own dilemma as a lesbian in a world that saw her desires as wrong and even disgusting. Breen's purpose in this treatment of the story is less a matter of explication than of application, as scholars of hermeneutics would put it. But it suggests a key part of Gregor's experience – his sense that other people, even the members of his own family, find him disgusting. This is undoubtedly a crucial part of the Gregor's characterization, and one that is directly relevant to his metamorphosis. Specifically, Kafka has envisioned a main character who (roughly) believes that people find him repulsive and thus develops a deep feeling of shame (e.g., due to "shame," Gregor hides from his sister and "could no longer lift his head" [71; my translation here and below]).[20]

That fundamental sense of other people's disgust is probably what activated the (explicit) model of the insect initially.[21] Kafka then chose to partially literalize the model. The effect is both emotional and thematic (as well as narrative). Emotionally, it does three things. First, by creating novelty, it enhances interest. Second, it makes it possible to intensify the family's rejection of Gregor without thereby making them entirely unsympathetic. Here it is particularly important that Gregor retains his human consciousness but cannot communicate it, thus making him appear more inhuman to the other characters. Finally, it allows for some comic distancing of at least certain aspects of the narrative – although that comic distancing may, in turn, intensify the pathos of Gregor's suffering when we return to Gregor's internal experiences.

A sense of disgust, however, is not the only fundamental generative component of the story. In order to consider the metaphorical simulation of the story more fully, we need to isolate both the overarching genre and the basic causal sequence of events that defines the story. Given that disgust relates most fundamentally to food and hunger, it is perhaps unsurprising that the main cross-cultural genre of the narrative is sacrificial. This is clearest at the end. Gregor dies and his family finally feels freed from their burdens. They are suddenly happy and optimistic about the future. The scene of the story changes from the interior of the apartment to the outside. In keeping with standard images of renewal after sacrifice, it is springtime (97), and Gregor's sister stretches her young and beautiful body before her proud parents, who contemplate her marriage, thus suggesting sexual as well as natural fertility being restored by Gregor's sacrifice (99). In short, the family's condition of distress has been ended by Gregor's death, in the usual sacrificial manner.[22]

At a literal level, the family sees itself as freed of a financial burden. Indeed, they had just blamed Gregor for their problems and suggested that they would only recover if they were rid of him. But, literally, this does not make a great deal of sense. Gregor in fact costs them nothing, even in food. What little he does eat would only have been fit for the garbage anyway. This literal senselessness suggests the operation of an implicit model along with the explicit one. Explicitly, Gregor is an insect. Implicitly, however, he is someone who is sick (cf. von Wiese), thus a burden for the family in terms of both care and expense.[23] The feeling of disgust is common to both, and undoubtedly helps make the two models mutually reinforcing. We see glimpses of this second model from the start of the story when Gregor is late for work. He cannot get out of bed – more typically a result of illness than of being transformed into an insect. He thinks to himself that he has fallen ill (59, 64); his mother asserts that he is ill (61); he himself states that he was ill but is now feeling better (63); and they send for a doctor to examine him (64). Initially the family shows great concern for avoiding contamination when cleaning the room. Moreover, the cleaning is entrusted to one member of the family only. This is reminiscent of cases where it is necessary to reduce the risk of spreading contamination or infection. Put differently, the simulation seems to have its source in such cases. The mother in particular is kept from the room. Literally, this is to prevent the shock of seeing her insectiform son, but she also suffers from fragile health. The care taken to keep her away from Gregor is more appropriate for someone who has a communicable disease than someone who has a shocking appearance. In keeping with this, when his sister, Grete, once catches a glimpse of Gregor, she responds "as if she were with someone seriously ill" (72).[24] This model does not always involve infection, however. The family's view that Gregor does not understand what they say (73, 94) suggests a model drawn from brain damage or degeneration, such as that produced by a stroke. The underlying presence of a model of sickness is also suggested by the setting in which Kafka locates the story. Of the many sorts of building Kafka could have made visible from Gregor's window, he chooses one that was, it seems, prominently activated in the course of his simulation of the story. That building is a hospital (66).[25]

Thus we have a sacrificial narrative in which Gregor's death liberates his family. Prior to this death, he is viewed as disgusting and burdensome. The disgust is associated with an explicit, partially literalized model of turning into an insect. It is also connected with a largely implicit model of sickness, which is in turn linked with the characterization of Gregor as a drain on the family's financial and emotional resources. That model of sickness itself includes more transient particularizations of either infectious disease or brain damage.[26]

This leaves many things about the story obscure, however – including the importance of the guiding, explicit model. Moreover, in terms of narrative, it primarily treats the end of the story. To understand the reasons for the central insect metaphor and other aspects of the elaboration of the story, we need to turn to the beginning of the story. The narrative starts with Gregor awakening to find himself transformed into a bug. We subsequently learn the crucial facts about what occurred before this event. The family had been prosperous. Then, due to the "collapse" of his father's business (74), they had been financially ruined. The result of this was a heavy burden of "*Schuld*" laid on the family ("the Schuld of the parents" [57]). In this case, *Schuld* refers to debt. However, the word also means "guilt," and Kafka employs the word in this sense elsewhere in the story – specifically, in reference to Gregor's feelings of responsibility for his mother (82).[27] This change in the family's status had a profound impact on Gregor. While Mr. Samsa sank into despair and Mrs. Samsa became enfeebled with asthma, Gregor tried to redeem the family.

Specifically, Gregor took a job traveling for a business (75). It is clear that this job consumed his entire life. Thus his mother recounts how he is at home every night, often studying train schedules and the like in order to plan his travels for the company (62). She explains that "the boy has nothing in his head except the business" (62). The ludicrous extent of this is made clear by the fact that Gregor has awoken to find himself transformed into "a monstrous vermin" (56), but his main worry is that he is late for work. One result of the job is that he no longer has any normal friendships or significant social ties; "enduring and sincerely developing human associations" (57) are denied him. The point seems to extend even to his own family, for he sits with them at night, not in conversation, but planning for future work. One of the most touching images of Gregor's extreme isolation is found in his attention to a magazine photograph of a "lady" (56). He actually takes several evenings in order to make a frame for this photograph of a woman he does not know and never will know (62). It is a substitute for someone he might have known, a correlate for the memory of a chambermaid in the provinces or the failed courtship with a cashier (87).

In connection with this, we may say that *Die Verwandlung* presents us with two sacrificial narratives – one in which the story is realistic and only metaphorically sacrificial; the other in which the story is fantastic and literally sacrificial. The former is the story of Gregor taking responsibility for the debt and shame of his family and (metaphorically) sacrificing his life through work to relieve them of that debt and end that shame. The second is Gregor physically manifesting his family's guilt and shame through his bodily transformation, then (literally) sacrificing his life, thereby freeing them from their guilt and shame. In keeping with the sacrificial prototype, the family's salvation occurs only after the second story, which is to say, after the real self-sacrifice, the literal death. Nonetheless, the conditions of devastation found in the earlier parts of the sacrificial prototype are manifest more clearly in the chronologically prior, more realistic story. There it is the father whose *Schuld* has caused the family to suffer, and it is the innocent Gregor who sacrifices himself to restore the family.[28] This is a fairly prototypical version of the sacrificial plot, except for the nature of the sacrifice itself.

Many elements of the first sacrificial story recur in the second. Gregor's taciturn presence, studying train schedules at night with his family, becomes his inability to speak with them at all. The "bad food" (57) to which he must accustom himself due to the sacrifices of his job becomes the literally rotting food that he eats as an insect. The photograph, a pathetic substitute for human contact, becomes the last hint of human contact left to him when his sister and mother decide to empty his room.

The emptying of Gregor's room brings out another important model for simulation and, with it, another aspect of Gregor's alienation from his family. Specifically, Gregor's sister and mother undertake this task in order to give Gregor more room to crawl (80). Although consistent with his condition as an insect, this reference to room for crawling strongly suggests the model of infancy, as people rarely are worried that bugs do not have adequate room to crawl. Unsurprisingly, the model is suggested elsewhere as well. For instance, Gregor's initial struggle to turn himself over (when he is stuck on his back) is not only the struggle of an insect. It equally recalls the struggle of an infant – who also lies on his or her back with flailing limbs, like Gregor at the start of the story (56). Moreover, his need to eat without teeth (90) is the sort of issue that arises for infants rather than for insects.

The modeling relation here is peculiar, however. Whereas babies inspire strong feelings of attachment, Gregor inspires strong feelings of repulsion. Whereas family members genuinely try to prevent crawling children from harming themselves, Gregor's family continually harms him and puts him in a position to harm himself. For example, early in the story, he is made to crawl through an overly narrow passage, thereby wounding his side. In this way, it is misleading to say that there is an implicit model of infancy. There is such a model. But it is not used in the same way as the insect model.

Specifically, a model or metaphor may be used either positively or negatively. For example, in order to clarify what it means to be distinctively human, Smith might contrast humans with beasts. In saying, "Man is not a baboon," Smith is using a model. He is drawing on the source, "baboon," to understand the target, "man." He is asking us to use the model to orient our attention, guide our inference, and so on. However, he is doing so negatively. Rather than being asked to draw properties and relations from the source, we are being asked to negate properties and relations and use the negations to guide our attention. The same positive versus negative division may be found in both explicit and implicit metaphorical guidance of narrative simulation.

In this particular case, we may infer that the explicit, positive model of the insect and the implicit, negative model of the infant were mutually enhancing in Kafka's simulation. Specifically, Gregor is a crawling insect precisely insofar as he is not a crawling baby. In keeping with this, as an object of disgust, he is precisely opposed to the darling of the family that everyone wants to pick up and hold. Also in keeping with this contrast, he loses his ability to communicate with his family, rather than gradually acquiring it. There are several points where this opposition is brought out particularly. For example, the family's inability to leave the house with Gregor there recalls the situation with a child (as its simulation was presumably guided by that model). But the reason is, in a way, the reverse (since the model is used negatively) – rather than lacking a competent babysitter, they find that no one is willing to be left alone with Gregor (74). In an even more straightforward case, after his transformation into an insect, Grete tries to serve Gregor food. Her idea is to give him milk (70), thus the food one gives to an infant. But he finds that he cannot drink milk. As we have already noted, Gregor's insect-like taste preference is bound up with his job and the necessity of eating bad food. The suggestion here is that at some point Gregor was a baby, crawling (but learning how to walk), drinking milk, learning language. Later, after the family's fall into *Schuld*, he became an insect, also crawling (but having lost the ability to walk), now rejecting milk for garbage and losing language. More importantly, in the first case, he was loved and cherished by his family. In the second case, relations of attachment have been replaced by relations of shame and disgust. For example, when he overhears his family discussing financial needs that he cannot fulfill, he becomes "all hot from shame" (76).

Finally, we may add that the difference in simulation between the two versions of the sacrificial story is itself also guided by a contrastive model – that between waking life and dreams.[29] Again, the insect model is literalized within the story world. That literalization is itself guided by a model – the model of a dream. In other words, Kafka implicitly develops Gregor's transformation as if he were recounting a dream. Of course, right at the outset of the narrative we are told that Gregor's transformation "was no dream" (56), but the use of a dream model is entirely consistent with this assertion. Indeed, the explicit reference to a dream is part of what one would expect from such guidance. Specifically, the model is necessarily activated to some degree and thus likely to be explicitly mentioned, even if that mention involves a denial that the story literally recounts a dream.

The simulation of literary works is often guided by explicit and implicit, positive and negative models – often a number of models that interact in complex ways. Many readers find Kafka's story deeply affecting, despite its superficial absurdity. The guiding metaphor in the story is not only explicit, but obtrusive. As such, it offers itself to the reader and critic as an explanation for the story's artistic impact as well as its thematic implications. But, understood on its own, this metaphor (roughly, "Gregor is an insect") yields a somewhat overly simple account of the aesthetic or emotional organization of the work and of its thematic implications. To understand its emotional resonances and thematic nuances, we need to recognize the relations between the explicit and implicit simulative models as well as their interconnection with encompassing narrative structures.

Conclusion

In previous chapters, we considered what might be called *internal* simulation in narrative. This is simulation guided by principles bearing on characters, scenes, and sequences of events. These principles are internal in the sense that they apply to components of the narrative (e.g., characters). In addition, there are important forms of external simulation. These forms of simulation shape narrative development by reference to something that is not a component of the narrative. There are two prominent forms of such external simulation. The first orients a simulation to instantiate an argument.

Argumentative simulation is contrasted with exploratory simulation and implemental simulation. Exploratory simulation does not involve a predetermined conclusion, but rather allows the integration of character and scene to proceed where it will. Implemental simulation involves a goal. The simulations we considered in previous chapters are partially exploratory and partially implemental. (The implemental component comes, for example, in the tailoring of story simulation to the outcomes defined by genres.) Argumentative simulation constrains exploratory simulation by reference to some claim or contention – thus, in literature, a theme. Argumentative simulation may or may not include explicit statements of the argument's conclusions, premises, or inferences. It may simply illustrate the claims narratively. In most literary works, there is some degree of argumentative simulation, along with exploratory and implemental simulation. Clearly, argumentative simulation constrains exploratory simulation. Exploratory simulation, however, often modifies and redirects argumentative simulation as well. Thus we would expect an author's precise conclusions to change in the course of writing a work – at least developing greater specificity, perhaps greater nuance. Nonetheless, argumentative and exploratory simulations may come into conflict with one another. That sometimes leads to inconsistencies in the work – inconsistencies that the author may ultimately accept (e.g., as components of a dialectic).

Bertolt Brecht's *Die Maßnahme*, a "teaching piece," integrates exploratory simulation with a high degree of complex argumentative simulation. It begins with a standard criminal investigation frame narrative in which it embeds a sacrificial narrative. The individual episodes are guided largely by Communist criticisms of what is often termed romantic anticapitalism. However, what is most interesting here is not this manifestation of doctrine, which is fairly straightforward. Rather, the most interesting points concern two things. First, there is a complex interaction of the argument-based simulation with the narrative prototypes. In the case of both the criminal investigation prototype and the sacrificial prototype, this tends to foster ambivalence and intellectual complexity in the (at first, apparently straightforward) presentation of Communist doctrine. Second, there may be a difference between Brecht's spontaneous, exploratory simulations and his more explicit, argumentative simulations. Specifically, it seems that Brecht's spontaneous imaginations are more sympathetic to romantic anticapitalism than his more regulated and self-conscious developments. However, Brecht was undoubtedly willing to accept the ambiguity and ambivalence of his work in his processes of evaluation because this fit his larger argumentative purpose of fostering dialogue and debate on such issues. Indeed, this is precisely how he believed theater should operate. Moreover, this conception of theater is a central thematic concern in the work itself and inseparable from its argumentative simulations. Finally, in addition to his argument against certain aspects of romantic anticapitalism, Brecht also suggested – through argumentative simulation – a case against certain aspects of Stalinism.

The second sort of external simulation involves the use of models to guide narrative alteration, specification, and evaluation. Models are sources of understanding that apply metaphorically to targets. When a source applies literally to a target, that means that we assume default properties of the source apply to the target unless we are given reason to believe otherwise. When a source applies metaphorically to a target, we simply do not assume this. In both cases, we interpret the relation of the source to the target in terms of current communicative interests. The narrative representation of a metaphor may involve some degree of literalization of the metaphor. Literalization of a metaphor is the transfer of some default properties from the source to the target, including properties that are otherwise communicatively (e.g., thematically) irrelevant.

We tend to imagine that model-derived simulation involves a single, explicit metaphor. However, simulation is often guided by implicit modeling. Moreover, it may be affected by multiple models, not only serially but also simultaneously. These models may contradict one another in certain respects, thus inhibiting one another's effects in those respects. At the same time, they may also coincide at points, thus enhancing activations at those points and increasing their narrative effects in the usual manner of parallel distributed processing. In the process of narrative simulation, one model may be purely local in its consequences. Others may recur, but only in limited contexts. Still others may be more or less pervasive. In this way, the precise configuration of models operating in simulation may be highly dynamic in the course of the development, evaluation, and redevelopment of a literary work.

Franz Kafka's *Die Verwandlung* involves both obvious and implicit model-based simulations. In this work, Kafka created two versions of the sacrificial narrative. One involves the literal guilt and debt of Gregor's father, the Samsas' financial ruin, and Gregor's metaphorical self-sacrifice in work. The other involves Gregor becoming the cause of his family's shame and financial distress; it is resolved by Gregor's literal death. The former is the backstory to the latter, which provides the main narrative of the work. Kafka elaborated and particularized these sacrificial narratives and their relation to one another via three interacting models: one explicit and positive (the insect), one implicit and negative (the infant), one implicit and positive (the sick). (A model is used positively when it guides our understanding of what a target is. It is used negatively if it guides our understanding of what a target is not.) Finally, Kafka's use of these models, particularly the literalized and explicit insect model, was itself guided by an implicit model of the story as a dream. This, then, served as a second-order model or metamodel in Kafka's simulation. Recognition of these multiple models and their hierarchical relations complicates how we understand Kafka's simulation of this work, and how we understand the work itself.

6

Emplotment

Selection, Organization, and Construal in Hamlet

In the preceding chapters, we have been concerned almost exclusively with the story part of narrative. In this chapter and the Afterword, we turn to discourse. Again, story is the "what" of narrative – what happened, as it happened. Discourse is the "how" – how the story is presented. Thus discourse includes what aspects of the story are recounted, when they are revealed, who reports them from what perspective, and so on. Discourse itself has two components. One, narration, concerns (roughly) who is speaking. We will turn to that in the Afterword. The other concerns what the speaker tells, what is called *plot*. That is the topic of the present chapter. Clearly, we cannot explore either topic in detail. It is important, however, to gain at least some preliminary understanding of how both plot and narration are particularized and how simulation operates in such particularization.

Emplotment – the creation of a plot from a story or story world – comprises selection, organization, and construal. Selection is what story world information is presented in the narrative. For example, suppose Smith tells a story about being taken to a room for special security screening at the airport. He may or may not recount how many guards were involved, precisely what they said, and so on. Organization is the placement of information – when it is presented (thus timing), what it is presented with (thus collocation), the degree to which it is highlighted (thus foregrounding and backgrounding), and so on. To take an instance of timing, Smith may begin his airport security story with the phrase, "Fortunately, I got to the airport early, because I needed nearly an hour for security," or he may wait until the end of the narration, leaving the audience uncertain as to whether he made his flight. Construal is the precise verbal characterization or sensory depiction of the selected story information. For example, roughly the same physical information is given in the following phrases: "Surrounding me, the three guards moved me to a security office," and, "The three guards walked with me to a private room." However, the event is characterized, thus construed, differently in the two cases.

The following analyses examine some key discourse features of *Hamlet*. Specifically, this chapter sets out to isolate recurring techniques that transform the story world of *Hamlet* into the plot as we encounter it in the play. These techniques are to a certain extent characteristic of the play and of its author. Thus, extending Chapter 3, the following pages further the analysis of Shakespeare's narrative idiolect, now addressing the set of principles that generated emplotment in his works. At the same time, these principles are not confined to Shakespeare. They are found, in different configurations, in a range of authors and thus form part of a more general account of emplotment. Finally, if successful, the following discussion should illustrate how a careful analysis of emplotment may reveal significant but otherwise ignored aspects of a literary work – aspects with both thematic and emotional significance – even when that work has been the object of extensive critical scrutiny.[1] In all these respects, *Hamlet* provides a particularly valuable case for the study of emplotment, because of its great literary success – not only in English but also in translation. (Its success in translation suggests that its appeal is not solely a matter of language.)

Indeed, *Hamlet* is also fitting because it is a work of drama. There is a common view that drama is mimetic rather than diegetic or narrated (see Richardson "Drama" 151). In the sense intended by Plato and Aristotle, this is certainly true.[2] With limited exceptions, there is no overt narrator in drama, no speaker of the entire piece.[3] However, given a more complex notion of narration, one may argue that drama does have a narrator, as several authors have pointed out.[4] More generally, drama involves not only a story world – thus *what* is represented – but also a discourse, a means of representing the story world – thus *how* that story world is represented. As Hühn and Sommer write, drama involves "selection, segmentation, combination, and focus." Similarly, Fludernik points to "anachronies, selection and juxtaposition" ("Narrative" 359). As these examples suggest, the "how" aspect of dramatic representation is perhaps more evident in emplotment than in narration. In any event, the common understanding of drama as mimetic makes it a particularly apt (as unexpected) object of narrative discourse analysis.

The Emplotment of *Hamlet*: Some General Principles

The emplotment of Hamlet is marked by several recurring devices. Two of the most prominent are trajectory interruption and intensified parallelism.[5]

Trajectory interruption occurs when one emotionally significant causal sequence remains incomplete because another such sequence is initiated. Intensified parallelism involves the repetition of more or less isomorphic sequences, thus structurally similar complexes of characters, actions, and/ or situations.

Intensified parallelism is the more complicated of the two. Plot parallels may be spread out across the story (as in the homologies relating Prince Hamlet and King Hamlet to Laertes and Polonius as well as Prince Fortinbras and King Fortinbras). Shakespeare, however, often develops parallels across scenes, which is to say, across sets of characters confined to a particular place and time in the story world and presented in a single, continuous part of the narrative discourse.[6] (Note that a scene in this technical sense will not always correspond to what is marked as a scene in a play.) This point extends from explicit to implicit scenes – that is, scenes recounted by characters or even scenes that the reader must reconstruct. In some cases, Shakespeare develops the parallel with the same point of view; in other cases, he shifts the point of view. These varieties produce sometimes extremely complex cases.

For example, in Act I, scene iv, Hamlet and Horatio are outside the castle awaiting the appearance of the ghost. They hear trumpets and firing. Hamlet explains that this is the king drinking. Obviously, we do not see this "rouse" (I.iv.8), although we know by the sounds that it occurs. In the final scene of the play, Claudius announces that he will drink and have "the battlements their ordnance fire" (V.ii.271) if Hamlet does well in his contest with Laertes. Here, we are inside the castle, thus the perspective has changed. Moreover, there is also a change in modality. In the first instance, the rouse actually occurs. In the second, it is only a possibility. Nonetheless, there is a clear parallel between the two.

Parallelisms and interruptions in *Hamlet* are often guided by what might be called a *selection model*. When selecting information for emplotment, an author may draw on a particular model that orients his or her attention to specific aspects of the simulated story world. In both productive story generation and discourse selection, authors often rely on models that are salient in the context of writing. These models include that of an author, who plans out the actions and experiences of his or her characters. In this case, the writer takes authorship as a source domain and uses the idea of authorial creative control as a model for imagining some character. The resulting character is a schemer, who tries to script the actions and experiences of other characters as if he or she were, in effect, an author creating a story with those characters. In the case of plays, the relevant models also include the audience, the unobserved observers of events. The audience-based model fosters spy characters and overhearers.[7] The spy character combines an audience model with another model salient for a dramatist – the actor. This leads to a character who systematically misrepresents his or her identity, interests, knowledge, and so on.

Shakespeare makes almost obsessive use of these models in both story world creation and emplotment.[8] As such, these models have consequences for the work's causal and emotional structures. They also have important narrational consequences in that the author- and audience-like characters become embedded narrators within the work.[9] Some of the key consequences, however, appear to be thematic. These derive from the fact that the schemes and spying, engaged in by powerful figures in the government, routinely fail, often with tragic consequences.[10]

Shakespeare also makes use of complex techniques of construal. In drama, without a general narrator's voice, direct construal – thus the explicit, verbal characterization of events, characters, or scenes – is usually confined to embedded narrators (e.g., a character recounting an event). However, there may be indirect or suggested construals. One way of indirectly construing events, characters, or situations is through genre categorization. For example, a young woman walking down a street at night is implicitly construed one way in a romantic comedy and a different way in a horror film (a point stressed in Noël Carroll's idea of "criterial prefocusing"). Such genre categorization may occur overtly (e.g., when the genre is named in a work's title) or implicitly (when it is suggested by the ongoing development of the work). In *Hamlet*, changing indirect suggestions of genre may repeatedly shift the spectator's genre evaluations and expectations, thus providing variable, indirect construals of events, characters, and scenes.

To be more precise, there are four genres at issue in *Hamlet*. The main plot, involving Hamlet, Claudius, the ghost, and Gertrude is ambiguous between heroic and revenge genres. The secondary plot, involving Hamlet, Ophelia, and Polonius is ambiguous between the romantic and seduction genres. As explained in Chapter 2, the heroic prototype involves two story sequences, one bearing on usurpation of the rightful leader of a group, the other concerning threats to the group from some external enemy, commonly an invading army. The revenge genre prototypically concerns the hero's attempt to kill the murderer of some family member. As in *Hamlet*, this attempt often results in the death of innocents and even the death of the revenger himself or herself. The heroic plot most often strongly favors the usurped ruler, presenting his or her restoration as just and even utopian. In contrast, the revenge genre is often highly ambivalent, sympathizing with the hero's grief and anger but condemning his or her violence. The romantic plot involves lovers being separated by some social representatives, such as parents, then (in the full, comic version) being reunited in an idealized union. The seduction plot involves deception and abandonment, often with the woman pregnant. The seduction plot may lead to the deaths of those involved. However, even when it leads to marriage, it tends to be highly ambivalent.

Again, *Hamlet* is often ambiguous between the heroic and revenge genres (for one part of the play) and the romantic and seduction genres (for another part of the play). At times, these ambiguities serve to intensify the emotional impact of the play. At other times, they seem to have primarily thematic consequences. Note that, in both cases, the genre changes mean that the play ambiguously shifts between more and less ambivalent construals. This greatly increases the emotional and evaluative complexity of the work.

Finally, Shakespeare also takes up discourse features at the intersection of narration and emplotment. The discourse largely confines depiction of inner psychological states to the title character. At points, however, Shakespeare strategically violates this restriction, revealing the inner thoughts of other characters.[11] He does this, first of all, to produce understanding of the main causal sequences. However, he also does this to extend thematic concerns and to enhance the emotional impact of the work, in part through intensifying our empathic response to characters.

In connection with the last point, it is worth briefly recalling the varieties of emotional impact in literature. The most obvious variety comprises those feelings provoked by the story. However, other sorts of emotional effect enter with discourse manipulation. Somewhat reformulating the valuable analysis of Ed Tan (see 65 and 82), we may distinguish three sorts of affect in narrative.[12] These are story emotion, plot interest, and artifact emotion. Story emotion concerns response to the events, characters, and scenes in the story world.[13] Plot interest is a function of the selection, organization, and construal of the story world in emplotment. For example, it includes our curiosity about past, unreported events and our suspense regarding future events (to use Sternberg's terms). Artifact emotion bears most importantly on the aesthetic features of the narrative as a human creation. This includes matters such as style. Commonly, our aesthetic artifact emotion seems to result from one of two factors. It may derive from our isolation of unusual patterning, thus patterning – perhaps temporal patterning in particular – that goes beyond some expected norm to which we are habituated (e.g., rhythm in meter, which goes beyond the patterning of ordinary speech, or rhythmic variations in meter, when the metrical pattern is itself expected). This is suggested by some research in music.[14] Alternatively, aesthetic emotion may be the result of unusual prototype approximation, particularly for spatial (rather than temporal) targets. This is suggested by some research on beauty in visual arts as well as human beauty.[15] Plot construction is obviously most relevant to plot interest, but it bears on the other varieties of emotion as well. For example, it often serves to create a sense of large structural patterns in the work (e.g., through scene parallelism), thus fostering artifact emotion.

The Emplotment of *Hamlet*: Textual Particulars

Any reader unfamiliar with *Hamlet* may be surprised to find that, despite its wealth of story concerns, the play begins with two minor, indeed wholly insignificant characters – Barnardo and Francisco. In doing so, it is quite revealing about the nature and function of emplotment. Specifically, Francisco is on watch. Barnardo comes to replace him. He is to be joined by Horatio and Marcellus. In terms of story understanding, there is no clear reason to begin the play here rather than with Horatio, Marcellus, and Barnardo waiting for the reappearance of the ghost. Note that this point does not concern the story but rather the plot. In the story world, there would be regular changes of the guard, thus a guard on duty before Barnardo. The question is, why did Shakespeare select this part of the story world for presentation, since it appears irrelevant for understanding the main causal sequences of the play? The reasons seem primarily emotional. The opening presents us with Francisco's isolation and establishes a degree of wariness with the question, "Who's there?" (I.i.1). This is significant primarily due to Hamlet's subsequent isolation. But why connect Francisco with Hamlet? Before leaving, Francisco remarks that he is "sick at heart" (I.i.9). We are never told the reasons for this. But Francisco's unease is echoed in the final scene of the play when Hamlet remarks to Horatio on "how ill all's here about my heart" (V.ii.213–214). The parallelism suggests the pervasiveness of melancholy and foreboding in Denmark, making these feelings more broadly social, less specific to Hamlet. The parallelism also serves to tie the opening scene with the end, thus contributing to a pattern of circularity. This is significant because circularity is often an aesthetically consequential artifact feature of a narrative.

After Francisco leaves, Marcellus introduces the topic of one main story sequence, briefly recounting the appearance of the ghost on two previous nights. The ghost then reappears. This is a manipulation of organization such that we learn about the three appearances of the ghost in quick succession, the first and second presented in abbreviated form. Clearly, this serves emotional intensification. In contrast, imagine an emplotment that actually depicted the first watch with the ghost on stage, then had the characters return for the second watch with the ghost, and then reassembled them for the third watch with the ghost. This would almost certainly dissipate the audience's response through habituation, perhaps even producing comic effects. At the same time, this tripling of the ghost's appearance reinforces our sense of his reality (in contrast with a single representation).

The dialogue of the watchers serves to introduce not only the identity of the ghost but also the story of his combat with Fortinbras. This selection of information has a story function in providing us background for a separate story sequence (the conflict with Norway). It also provokes interest (curiosity, to use Sternberg's term) regarding the details of this story.

As already noted, a recurring emplotment technique in *Hamlet* is trajectory interruption. Just as a story sequence is moving toward some point of intensity, Shakespeare breaks off and presents us with part of another story sequence. This aspect of emplotment is clearly designed to maintain interest in much the way that cliff-hangers sustain interest in television serials. Often, Shakespeare does this by shifting scenes. (This is a version of the "meanwhile, back at the ranch" technique.) Thus, after the meeting with the ghost, the next scene takes us to the inside of the castle and the relationships among Hamlet, Gertrude, and Claudius. Before this, however, there is an interruption within the opening scene itself.

Specifically, after the ghost has appeared, we are not immediately given his purposes or the consequences of the appearance. Rather, once he leaves, Marcellus speaks of preparations for war. Horatio then proceeds to explain the nature and development of young Fortinbras's actions to regain the lands lost by his father. Realistically speaking, the scene is bizarre. The three men have just seen a ghost. Horatio "tremble[s] and look[s] pale" at the sight (I.i.53). But now they shift to a leisurely conversation about contemporary politics. Evidently, audiences do not question the transition, however. This is presumably related to the fact that it coheres with other aspects of the scene. First, the enhanced watch is due to preparations for war. Second, Horatio's speech elaborates on the story of King Hamlet and Fortinbras, briefly introduced a moment earlier. Finally, this political situation is used to explain the appearance of the ghost. In connection with this, the political dialogue develops plot interest, even as it violates story plausibility.

Yet it is still peculiar. It would not be peculiar, however, if it were narrated rather than enacted. This may be the key point. We in effect treat this sequence as if it were narrated by someone outside the main action, a narrator who recounts the ghost's appearance, then, unperturbed, shifts to political background. This sort of *narrational disjunction*, as we might call it, is more common than one might imagine. It happens with some frequency that a narrative has one overt narrational form but operates as if it had another narrational form. We may refer to these as the *apparent* and *functional* forms respectively. We find this, for example, in the first section of Faulkner's *The Sound and the Fury*, which is apparently first-person (autodiegetic) but often operates as third-person narration. Consider the sentence, "I got undressed and I looked at myself, and I began to cry" (56). It seems directly parallel to "Caddy unbuttoned Jason. He began to cry" (56), particularly in its apparent distance from the emotions recounted. In other words, it seems to express, "Benjy got undressed and he looked at himself, and he began to cry." The shift to a superficial autodiegetic form operates primarily to indicate that the narrator is reporting only facts of the story world that were experienced by Benjy. In a sense, it is a sort of shorthand. The opening scene of *Hamlet* has a different type of narrational disjunction. The apparent form is continuous and contemporaneous representation, but the scene operates as if it were recounted from a different time and place. Nonetheless, both cases illustrate how narrational disjunction may produce anomalies, particularly in the emotional responses of characters.

Following the discussion of politics, in keeping with the play's recurring emplotment devices, the interruption we have been considering is itself interrupted by the return of the ghost. Horatio links and justifies the two interruptions by taking up the political theme in relation to the ghostly visitation. Specifically, he asks the ghost about the "country's fate" (I.i.133). But before the ghost can answer, the cock crows and he must return to confinement. Here again, we have an instance of the interruption technique serving to intensify emotional response.

The crowing of the cock brings up an interesting aspect of the scene's timing. There is a common, if usually implicit expectation that mimetic works present actual occurrences in (roughly) their actual duration, except in unusual circumstances (e.g., when film speed is altered). In other words, the idea is that in mimetic works plot duration and story duration must be about the same if there is no deletion of story elements in the plot. This scene suggests something very different, however. Shortly after Barnardo arrives, he remarks on the time, "Tis now struck twelve" (I.i.7). A mere thirty-two lines later, the ghost enters. The suggestion is that the ghost is entering at one o'clock (see I.i.36–39). Only about 100 lines later, it is dawn. Clearly, Shakespeare has drastically reduced the story time in the narration time.[16] This is another instance of disjunction – in this case, emplotment disjunction – and may suggest a further reason why we are able to accept the quick transition to ordinary conversation after the appearance of the ghost, We may tacitly adjust the timing so that it is not as quick as it appears. More generally, it seems that audience members are able to accommodate themselves

unselfconsciously to discrepancies between apparent and functional discourse properties. Here, it means that we may implicitly sense that discourse
time is a radically condensed version of the story time, despite apparently
continuous representation.

The scene ends with a plan. They will discuss what they have seen with
Hamlet. This leads nicely to the second scene, where Hamlet is introduced.
However, it does not lead to the colloquy between Hamlet and Horatio. That
plan is interrupted, and we are introduced instead to Claudius. Just as Horatio
provided the backstory to the appearance of the ghost, Claudius now provides some of the backstory on the death of King Hamlet – thus the backstory
to there being a ghost in the first place. This clearly is connected with plot
interest in that we are first introduced to the emotionally intense appearance
of the ghost, which leads to a range of questions. Those questions are partially
answered by Claudius – but they are only partially answered, since we still
do not know the nature of King Hamlet's death. Nor do we understand the
precise relationship between Claudius and Gertrude that led to their quick
marriage. Here, we might expect further treatment of the king's demise, but
that is interrupted by reference to Fortinbras – the movement from the dead
King Hamlet to Fortinbras precisely paralleling the sequence in the preceding
scene. The danger posed by Fortinbras is, of course, the danger of invasion.
This is, again, a definitive part of the heroic prototype. This may give at least
some viewers the sense that they are witnessing a heroic plot, orienting their
expectations accordingly. (Needless to say, they need not self-consciously
and explicitly formulate such expectations.) This topic is then deferred (in
another interruption) until there is further communication with the present
king of Norway, Fortinbras's uncle.

At this point, one might expect a return to King Hamlet. But now Laertes
is introduced. He is given permission to return to France. The point of this
plot selection seems to lie merely in contrasting this decision with Claudius's
wish that Hamlet not return to his studies at Wittenberg (thus yielding an
inverse parallel). Now Prince Hamlet finally enters the play. He does so first
in an aside, revealing the nonpersonified, encompassing narrator's internal
access that will recur later in the play. Claudius says that Hamlet's departure
is "retrograde to our desire," and he wishes Hamlet to remain in "our eye"
(I.ii.114, 116). The reasons are putatively a matter of affection. However, insofar as we have hints that this is a heroic narrative, it is not too difficult to infer
that Claudius may worry about possibly subversive actions undertaken by an
unobserved Hamlet. Again, this is all a matter of emplotment, selection from
the story world. We know from elsewhere in the play that the nonpersonified narrator is not strictly limited to Hamlet's thoughts. Rather, the narrator

conveys Claudius's thoughts when needed. He or she does not do so here, although such access to the story world would confirm or disconfirm our suspicions.

Subsequently, we are presented with Hamlet's first soliloquy. This again indicates the narrator's internal access. It also fosters the audience's alignment with Hamlet (to use Murray Smith's term) and, indeed, a sort of trust. Specifically, our introduction to Hamlet is strongly and directly an introduction to his internal states of thought and feeling. This is particularly important in a work so concerned with playacting or strategic deceit. Indeed, in Hamlet's first speech to his mother, he contends that "a man might play" (I.ii.89) the role of a grief-stricken son, but, Hamlet goes on, he himself has "that within which passeth show" (I.ii.90). In contrast with our very limited access to the minds of other characters, we are repeatedly exposed to Hamlet's internal feelings. Thus we can, sometimes, tell when he is sincere, as he is with respect to his grief. Here we see a clear case where plot selection affects story emotion.

The first soliloquy also has consequences for our understanding of other characters and our sense of genre. Specifically, Hamlet explains that Gertrude has married Claudius "within a month" of King Hamlet's death (I.ii.145). Today, audience members have become so accustomed to the play that they may hardly even notice this. But it is, indeed, shocking. It strongly suggests a prior relationship between the two that went beyond that of sister-in-law and brother-in-law. In the genre context of the revenge prototype, this may hint at a crime in which the queen was complicit – or even active. Put differently, the genre categorization may suggest a particular construal of the relationship between Claudius and Gertrude as well as their joint responsibility for King Hamlet's death. (Subsequently, other aspects of the play suggest that the queen was innocent of the murder, although not of adultery. For example, the ghost exempts Gertrude from punishment [I.v.93], which would seem less likely if she were guilty of the murder. Moreover, Gertrude reacts with apparent surprise and incomprehension when Hamlet suggests that she is guilty of killing King Hamlet [III.iv.34–36].)

At this juncture, with its hints of a revenge narrative, Horatio enters and explains the ghost's appearance to Hamlet. Three points are important for our purposes. First, Hamlet immediately swears Horatio, Marcellus, and Barnardo to silence on this topic. This suggests a strong mistrust of the other royals and perhaps the beginnings of a strategic plan. Second, this plan may hint at the use of an author model. Finally, there would be no reason for a plan if Hamlet did not already suspect a particular motive for the ghost's appearance. Horatio describes the ghost as expressing "sorrow" rather than "anger" (I.ii.232). Nonetheless, Hamlet immediately infers that there has been "foul play" (I.ii.256). It seems very unlikely that someone would jump to this conclusion (on the basis of a sorrowful ghost) if he or she did not already have suspicions – a possibility that fosters plot interest. All this discourse information is carefully selected to suggest but not confirm the existence of such suspicions. The point is even more striking here than in the case of Claudius, since Shakespeare could easily have had Hamlet spell out these suspicions in an aside or soliloquy.

The next scene again interrupts the development of the King Hamlet story. It begins with Laertes, but the topic is the romantic involvement of Hamlet and Ophelia. This introduces a further story – or, rather, two further stories. In the course of the play, Hamlet presents his wooing of Ophelia as part of a romantic narrative. However, Laertes and Polonius both construe it as a seduction narrative. Moreover, they do so by explicitly projecting possibilities for the future "loss" of "honor" (I.iii.29) and pregnancy (I.iii.109).

The use of plot parallelism is almost obtrusive here. In this scene, Laertes advises Ophelia; then Polonius advises Laertes; then Polonius advises Ophelia. We may also recall that, in the preceding scene, Horatio told Hamlet about the ghost, as earlier Barnardo told Marcellus, Horatio, and us – and as, even before that (we are informed), Marcellus told Horatio.

The intensified parallelism continues with the following two scenes in which Hamlet, Horatio, and Marcellus wait for and encounter the ghost, just as Horatio, Marcellus, and Barnardo did earlier. Indeed, these scenes end the first act, giving it a circular formal structure. The link between Hamlet and Francisco is established here initially, for Hamlet introduces the scene by observing that "it is very cold" (I.iv.i), as Francisco earlier observed, "'Tis bitter cold" (I.i.8), just before explaining that he is "sick at heart" (I.i.9).

Because this is only a single chapter, we cannot go through all plot elements in these scenes; however, a few further points are worth noting. Hamlet's initial worry about the ghost is whether he is real or a demonic impersonator (I.iv.40). This straightforwardly introduces a question into the minds of the audience, who now can envision two possible outcomes. These outcomes have great consequences for everything that follows, most obviously in suggesting that the ghost may be an unreliable (embedded) narrator. The point is elaborated by Horatio, who specifically worries that the ghost will lead Hamlet to suicide (I.iv.69). This prepares us for Hamlet's subsequent thoughts of suicide. At the same time, it makes those thoughts ambiguous. Is his apparent death wish part of his scheme? Is it a spontaneous emotional tendency? Is it evidence that the ghost is indeed tempting him? All these possibilities result from the selection of information presented in the discourse and the construal of that information by the characters (here, Horatio's worry over the ghost's intentions). The answers should be readily available in the story world – and to the narrator who, again, has access to Hamlet's thoughts. These elements of emplotment clearly have emotional consequences, but they also may have thematic resonances relating to questions of satanic temptation.

A scene change occurs when Hamlet follows the ghost to a place where the others cannot observe them. Here, the ghost explains that he has been killed by Claudius and calls for "revenge" (I.v.7). This clearly connects the play with the revenge genre. Subsequently, this genre is probably more salient than the heroic genre. However, the play remains ambiguous between the two. No less important, when the ghost explains who committed the murder, Hamlet exclaims, "O my prophetic soul!" (I.v.40), indicating that he did indeed suspect that his uncle had committed murder (or, in terms of the heroic narrative, usurpation). Moreover, the phrasing of the ghost's subsequent speech allows the possibility that Claudius seduced Gertrude before the murder (hence the reference to adultery [I.v.42]).

Finally, there is Hamlet's surprising announcement that he may "put an antic disposition on" (I.v.172). This again suggests the author model, with Hamlet manipulating a story. As he has not had time to formulate a scheme since speaking with the ghost, we must conclude that he had this scheme in mind already. Again, our omniscient narrator could certainly have presented this information to us (e.g., in the form of a soliloquy). But the selection of information is more likely to provoke our interest by eliciting curiosity over what the purpose of an antic disposition could be and just how this (author-modeled) scheme might operate.[17]

The second act begins like the first, with something – in this case, a plan rather than a character – that is largely irrelevant to the causal development of the story. It does, however, bear on the audience's attentional orientation and on some thematic concerns of the play. Again, the first act ends with the hint of Hamlet's schemes. The second begins by extending the author model to Polonius. Drawing on the closely related audience model, Polonius has plotted out a scheme of espionage. Indeed, it is espionage that is not mere eavesdropping, but playacting to produce intelligence. Specifically, Polonius explains how Reynaldo can take up a role in order to learn the truth about Laertes's activities in France. This scene calls out for an analysis in terms of emplotment because it is so clearly outside any significant causal sequence in the story world. It is entirely superfluous in terms of story information. We therefore infer that it has other functions. Among other things, it enhances our sensitivity to acting and espionage.

This is followed by Ophelia's distressed account of Hamlet's madness. Polonius construes this as the madness of love. Here we may recall Hamlet's statement that he will perform the role of madman, especially as strategic playacting has been made salient. At the same time, however, implications of the romantic genre (with its frequently distracted lovers) may lead us to wonder about the degree to which Hamlet is acting and the degree to which Polonius is correct about Hamlet's lovesickness. Thus the audience is likely to remain uncertain about Hamlet's true condition.

Once one becomes aware of patterns in the work's emplotment, the second scene is almost shockingly predictable. Here, we learn that the king has brought Rosencrantz and Guildenstern to spy on Hamlet in order to discover the nature of his madness. In short, we have a third instance of playacting to produce intelligence through espionage (the others being the schemes of Hamlet and Polonius). However, this is not simply aesthetic parallelism bearing on the work as an artifact. The fact that Claudius has done this suggests again that he finds Hamlet's behavior worrisome and his intentions potentially dangerous, in the manner of either a heroic or revenge narrative.

In short, Hamlet's idea of acting to produce intelligence is interrupted by Polonius's espionage scheme, which is not developed as we turn to the Rosencrantz and Guildenstern scheme of espionage. This is in turn interrupted by Polonius's report that he has discovered the cause of Hamlet's madness. Before this can be developed, however, there is yet another interruption. Specifically, we return to the invasion sequence of the heroic plot. Just as the threat of Fortinbras had interrupted Claudius's speech in the second scene of the first act, it now interrupts his speech in the second scene of the second act. The interest of the audience should be rather intense at this point, given the multiple layering of uncertain futures for the action – all intensified not only by selection and construal but by the clear manipulation of timing as well. At this point, the Fortinbras issue is supposedly resolved. But the resolution is insane. Denmark is supposed to allow Fortinbras's army free passage to go and fight against Poland. In effect, Norway says, "This army was put together to invade you. If you just let the army enter your territory, however, it won't attack." This situation too is likely to provoke plot interest. Claudius does not actually decide at this point, which leaves that issue up in the air as well when we return to Polonius.

As already indicated, Polonius has changed his view and believes that Hamlet's approach to Ophelia is part of a romantic narrative rather than a seduction narrative. (Of course, he would not phrase it this way.) In connection with this – and in keeping with the romantic prototype – he presumably fears that Claudius and Gertrude will not only reject the marriage as beneath

Hamlet but will be outraged by Polonius even suggesting the possibility. This accounts for his nervous attempts to delay introducing the topic (often performed – erroneously, I believe – as if they simply show Polonius's foolishness). Once he arrives at the point, however, Polonius proposes the one solution that has become obvious in the development of these events – espionage. This spying, like all other schemes in the play, fails. The thematic suggestion throughout is that intelligence gathering tends to be self-confirming. Polonius, like other spies, finds only what he expects or wants to find.

Indeed, the point is particularly striking in the context of the relation to the Norway plot. We may divide the narrative sequences of the play into three large groups. There is the revenge or usurpation sequence involving Prince Hamlet, Claudius, and King Hamlet; there is the seduction or romantic sequence involving Hamlet and Ophelia; and there is the (abortive) invasion plot involving Denmark and Norway. The first and second narratives involve deceitful playacting and espionage, which clearly fail. The third narrative could have involved espionage, but, instead, it involves more straightforward negotiation. Although the outcome is still not entirely clear at this point, eventually we see that the process of negotiation works. Or, rather, negotiation would have worked in this case, but the deceit of the revenge/usurpation plot leads to the self-destruction of Denmark's government.

After introducing the possibility of espionage in the seduction/romantic plot, Polonius approaches Hamlet. Hamlet indicates that he is aware of Polonius's purposes when he says that Polonius is not "honest" (II.ii.176). In this scene, Hamlet's "antic disposition" suggests equivocation, the play with language that Jesuits used to conceal subversive schemes and actions. This gives us some hint – but only a hint – as to the nature of Hamlet's own scheme, perhaps relating it to the heroic more than the revenge prototype (given the purposes of Jesuitical equivocation).

Once again, it is important to stress that this is not simply story world simulation but also emplotment. Given that Shakespeare tacitly simulated Hamlet as having plans, he could have presented us with those plans. Moreover, he could have given us greater access to Hamlet away from court observation, so that we could have a more definitive sense of his madness or sanity. These are all matters of selection and organization. Similarly, he could have been less equivocal about the play's genre. Again, this may be a usurpation/restoration plot, aimed at enthroning Hamlet, the rightful heir and a popular leader ("loved of the distracted multitude" [IV.iii.4]). Alternatively, it may be a revenge plot. At least for the original audience, the former would be likely to provoke less ambivalence, in keeping with the usual operation of these genres. In terms of our particular interests, these discourse manipulations (e.g., development of genre/construal ambiguity and withholding of disambiguating psychological information, intensified parallelism, and so on) are the recurring products of Shakespeare's narrative idiolect – the way his mind made plots. In production and revision, they are inseparable from his tacit, evaluative simulation of audience response to the selection, organization, and construal of the story.

After Polonius leaves, Hamlet turns to the next set of spies. Here, the suspicions of Claudius are indicated indirectly by Rosencrantz's suggestion that Hamlet's distress is caused by "ambition" (II.ii.256). Moreover, "ambition" suggests the heroic usurpation sequence rather than revenge. Hamlet's own knowledge of the espionage comes out when he says, "I know the good King and Queen have sent for you" (II.ii.288–289), evidently implying that he has his own spies.

After these multiple instances of acting and espionage, the play introduces real actors. Literalizing the model that has been so fruitful to this point, Hamlet determines to use the real actors for intelligence gathering – specifically, to test the ghost's statements about Claudius. Before this, however, we have another parallel in which the actors recite the story of the murder of a king – a story taken from a heroic narrative. The connections here are so straightforward that they do not require explication.

The act ends with Hamlet reaffirming his commitment to right past wrongs, in parallel with the conclusion of the preceding act. Or, rather, it ends with a reaffirmation that is contingent on establishing the reliability of the ghost. The scheme involving the acting troupe will supposedly give Hamlet the confirmation he needs. As discussed in Chapter 3 (and as recognized by critics [see, for example, Foakes, Hawkes, and Kastan]), this is hardly true. The problem with this plan is that Hamlet makes the play within the play too overt. The queen character explicitly says that a widow does not remarry unless she "killed" her first husband (III.ii.186). Virtually any king in Claudius's situation would interpret the play as seditious. Hamlet learns nothing from the fact that Claudius objects to the play. Once again, playacting fails as espionage, or espionage fails to produce intelligence. It serves only to confirm the spy in his earlier opinion. In this case, it happens that Hamlet's opinion is correct, as we know from our brief access to Claudius's thoughts. But Hamlet himself has no reason to know this. Put differently, what we find here is a case of self-confirming construal. Hamlet construes Claudius's response to the play in accordance with his own prior theory; he simulates the events in a certain way. But there are other, initially more plausible alternatives.[18]

Of course, before moving from Hamlet's scheme to its enactment in the play within the play, we have an interruption. The third act begins with Claudius

consulting Rosencrantz and Guildenstern about the results of their espionage. This directly parallels the beginning of Act II, scene ii. As in the earlier
scene, Polonius enters, shifting the espionage from one based on a heroic
plot and suspicions of rebellion to one based on a romantic plot. Claudius
and Polonius stage a little play scene, with Ophelia reading. They then spy on
the couple. This scene is curious in part because Hamlet seems to respond
with sincere feeling to Ophelia's rejection. In other words, there are suggestions here of romantic attachment. At the same time, however, he virtually
confesses his intentions regarding Claudius. First he says that he is "revenge-
ful" and "ambitious" (III.i.125, alluding to both the revenge and heroic prototypes). Then he says that "those that are married already – all but one – shall
live" (III.i.150–151), which to Claudius's mind must closely approach a threat.
This is perhaps the one point in the play where espionage might reveal something. But even that is unclear. Claudius does become convinced of Hamlet's
murderous intent, but that is primarily because he was convinced of it before.
In any case, this leads to Claudius's elaborate scheme to send Hamlet away to
be killed. Unsurprisingly, Polonius suggests more espionage. In this case, he
recommends setting up Hamlet and Gertrude to be observed, as he had just
set up Hamlet and Ophelia. Again, the multiplication of parallels is clear.

But before this further repeated staging and observation can be put into
motion, there is an interruption. Specifically, we now return to Hamlet's
scheme. We have already seen the problems with this scheme of an actual
play used to produce intelligence. Hamlet becomes convinced of Claudius's
guilt, however, even if this is primarily because he was already convinced.
This directly parallels him with Claudius in the preceding scene.

The focus on Hamlet has to this point undoubtedly oriented our sympathies toward him. Nonetheless, in actual questions of guilt and innocence,
things are far from clear. In a social context where regicide is perhaps the
most heinous crime, Hamlet's plans to kill Claudius cannot appear wholly
admirable. Moreover, when Rosencrantz and Guildenstern come to Hamlet
after the play, he explains his distemper by saying that he "lack[s] advancement" (III.ii.347). In short, he covets the kingship. This could suggest that, in
a heroic narrative, Hamlet, not Claudius, is taking up the role of (potential)
usurper.

At this point, Shakespeare breaks his usual practice of giving us only
Hamlet's thoughts.[19] He reveals Claudius's thoughts in order to inform us
that, in fact, Claudius did commit fratricide. This is a striking interruption
in the middle of the play that reorients our questions, interest, and attention.
This is obviously a matter of emplotment – most important, timing. In the
story world, Claudius must have thought about his murder almost constantly.

Thus Shakespeare could have revealed this information to the audience at any time. He presumably chooses this moment for emotional reasons. To a certain point, we are intrigued by the uncertainties of the plot. But, as Hamlet's plans potentially advance, it may become more difficult for the audience to sustain its sympathy with him, if his actions are a matter of usurpation rather than restoration, or murder rather than revenge.[20] One of the remarkable narrative qualities of *Hamlet* is undoubtedly the sense of timing, a sense derived from the idiolectal principles and the simulations of audience reception that produced the play's emplotment.

The following scene takes up the audience model once again, now making Polonius the unobserved observer in Gertrude's meeting with Hamlet. The romantic, heroic, and revenge genres interact such that the object of Hamlet's antagonism in the heroic revenge story is replaced by the interfering father from the romantic story (i.e., Polonius). In a mixing of the genres, Hamlet revenges himself on Polonius, strangely mistaking him for Claudius (although presumably their voices are adequately distinguishable). After the murder, Shakespeare gives us another bizarre interruption. Specifically, Hamlet simply ignores the dead body and determines to chastise Gertrude. No less strangely, Gertrude goes along with this. This is parallel to the first scene when Horatio sees a ghost, then proceeds to have a conversation about foreign policy. Here too it seems that the events are nonetheless effective with audiences. In this case as well the effectiveness is connected with the cultivation and partial satisfaction of plot interest in the following dialogue. At the same time, the continual presence of the corpse provides a sense of urgency and some degree of horror to the entire scene, intensifying emotional response. A key point for our purposes is that the scene is not only parallel to the opening, it also involves the same sort of discourse-production principle. We may consider this a case of emplotment disjunction, although we have no separate evidence of timing discrepancies (as we do in the opening scene). In any case, we do have the same swift conjunction of events in which the time for recovery from shock (a murder in one instance, the appearance of a ghost in the other) is simply eliminated. This aspect of Shakespeare's narrative idiolect has fairly straightforward emotional effects.

At the end of the act, Hamlet announces that Rosencrantz and Guildenstern are "adders fanged" whom he will "hoist with [their] own petar, and ... blow them at the moon" (III.iv.204, 208, 210). Thus he in effect announces that he knows the content of their "mandate" (which is "knavery" [III.iv.206, 207]). This more or less contradicts Hamlet's later account of the events. From his conversation with Horatio in Act V, scene ii, it appears that Hamlet did not know about the danger in the mandate until he saw it on the ship. In any event, it seems clear that he already had the plan against Rosencrantz and Guildenstern before leaving. This is consistent with the highly selective nature of the information we are presented about Hamlet's schemes. It seems that the narrator has communicated just enough information to sustain interest ("How will he hoist them with their own petar?") and just enough information to suspect Hamlet ("Did he determine to kill Rosencrantz and Guildenstern on the basis of suspicion alone?"), without fully condemning (or exonerating) him. The discourse selection principle here seems to be something like, "Enhance moral ambiguity without losing audience sympathy for the hero."

The opening of the fourth act includes further instances of consultation after spying. Beginning in scene iii, the heroic plot is recalled as Claudius worries over the popularity of Hamlet with the ordinary people (IV.iii.4). This heroic connection is developed as Hamlet encounters Fortinbras's army Although they are not invading Denmark, the choice to bring Fortinbras and his army on stage clearly serves to remind the audience of the earlier threat, thereby suggesting the genre that involves such an invasion.

After Hamlet's murder of Polonius, there has been relatively little reference to the consequences of the act, other than the concern to recover the body. In the fifth scene, we learn that, in the interim, Polonius has been interred unceremoniously, leading to rumors and popular suspicions (IV.v.81–84). The emplotment choice here is to report the concealed interment rather than represent it. This choice contributes to the audience's sense of the burial's secrecy. It also allows for a manipulation of organization, bringing the report of the secretive burial in close proximity to Laertes's return and pursuit of revenge against Claudius. Both discourse decisions bear on the emotional impact of the sequence and our clear sense of the causal relation between the two – contrast a fully represented scene of the interment, followed at some distance by the entrance of Laertes.

These emplotment decisions recall the opening narration of appearances by the ghost followed by the ghost's actual appearance. This suggests a discourse principle along the following lines: "Use embedded narration to bring causally, emotionally, or thematically related events together if they are otherwise separated in the story." This is particularly interesting because it is closely related to the use of unmarked ellipsis following shock or trauma (in emplotment disjunction). Together, these suggest a larger principle in Shakespeare's narrative idiolect: "Reduce plot time relative to story time, even in continuous presentation, when this serves emotional or thematic purposes."

A curious aspect of the Laertes emplotment involves Laertes's claim that the "drop of blood that's calm" in the face of Polonius's death "proclaims me bastard,/Cries cuckold to my father, brands the harlot/Even here between the chaste unsmirchèd brow/Of my true mother" (IV.v.117–120). Reporting this speech in such full detail is clearly a decision of selection, construal, and fore-grounding (through duration). The development over four lines makes the claims particularly salient. The issue then is the degree to which we should take this as an appropriate construal of tardiness in a son's revenge. If taken as such a construal, it may serve to suggest again Gertrude's prior involvement with Claudius, now extending back to Hamlet's conception. Of course, there is not particularly strong evidence for this – although Claudius does refer to Hamlet as his son (I.ii.63). But there is enough of a hint in the emplotment to make the work at least to some degree ambiguous on this point. The ambiguity about Hamlet's paternity could have moral consequences if we view parricide as more objectionable than other sorts of murder. Thus this appears to be another instance of the "enhance moral ambiguity" principle. It would also have the effect of emotional intensification.

Prior to the section with Laertes, there is a segment with Ophelia, who has gone mad. Here too the timing of the emplotment is clearly important. In this case, it bears on the emotional impact of Ophelia's transformation, which faces us as sudden and complete rather than developing gradually. This is clearly a version of the "reduce plot time" principle. Here, however, it intensifies the impact by excluding preparatory information, thus steepening the gradient of change from normalcy to sorrow.[21] (This is, of course, a fairly common principle, far from unique to Shakespeare.)

The problem with such an elliptical presentation is that it may make the final event appear anomalous. Thus we are rather starkly faced with the question of why Ophelia has gone mad. Claudius attributes this development to her father's death (IV.v.41). Her madness, however, manifests itself in songs that seem to have greater application to Hamlet than to Polonius and to be linked with the seduction genre. Thus she begins by singing of her "true-love" (IV.v.25) and his "cockle hat." The cockle hat marked "a pilgrim who had journeyed ... overseas" (Barnet's note at IV.v.26). This recalls Hamlet's journey overseas (even if he did not undertake it as a pilgrim). A subsequent song concerns St. Valentine's Day and a maid being deflowered. Her final song before Laertes's entrance treats a young woman who sleeps with a man who promises to marry her but abandons her after the consummation. These songs seem to suggest despair over the loss of Hamlet and a worry over her own condition, perhaps even with a hint of pregnancy. Her subsequent death is perhaps a suicide, which would be consistent with these suggestions of the seduction genre.

The act ends with Claudius and Laertes setting out their elaborate scheme to murder Hamlet. Thus the actions of the characters once more mimic those of an author scripting a drama. This scheme has a triple safeguard – an unbated rapier, poison on the rapier, and poison in a drink. It would seem foolproof. Like all other schemes in the play, however, it fails, largely because there are countless chance elements that schemers cannot control.

The fifth act begins, like the first (and the second), with a largely irrelevant scene and largely irrelevant characters – a grave and gravediggers. The grave of course bears on Ophelia's death. But it is a normal fact that a grave would be dug for a funeral, so it is entirely unnecessary to select this information for communication in the emplotment. The scene is primarily comic. Thus, through contrast, it may serve to intensify the grief Hamlet feels and we feel for him when he later discovers that the grave is for his beloved Ophelia. In other words, it follows the principle, which we have already encountered, of steepening the gradient of emotional change. At the same time, the scene includes some hints of sorrow, when Hamlet is reminded of an attachment figure from his youth, Yorick. This selection too may serve a function of emotion intensification as it concerns attachment vulnerabilities, stirring emotional memories that bear on the new attachment loss that Hamlet is about to experience (that of Ophelia). It also recalls the context of the entire play – Hamlet's loss of his father. In short, we have an initially unlikely plot selection that serves to enhance emotional impact. The emotional function of the subsequent burial scene is straightforward.

The play culminates in the scheme already mentioned. Unsurprisingly, it involves spectatorship and performance – a fencing match between Hamlet and Laertes. Before this occurs, we find Hamlet explaining how he has had Rosencrantz and Guildenstern murdered. Since he has now killed three people, it is difficult to maintain that he is superior to Claudius, who is responsible for only one death (although he has sought a second).[22] Moreover, Claudius evidences feelings of guilt over that murder, whereas Hamlet merely passes off the killings by saying that the victims were of "baser nature" (V.ii.60; cf. Hawkes 183 and Foakes 93). Once again, we are faced with Shakespeare's idiolectal principle of enhancing moral ambiguity. Nonetheless, one might wonder if he has gone too far in this case. Here genre considerations enter and perhaps help Hamlet to some degree (at least for the original audience). Specifically, Hamlet complains to Horatio that Claudius "popped in between th'election and my hopes" (V.ii.65). This suggests again a usurpation sequence of the heroic plot, which might partially mitigate Hamlet's treatment of anyone who collaborates with the usurper – thus Rosencrantz and Guildenstern or even Polonius. But Hamlet's reference to his own ambition also suggests that he is not personally superior to Claudius. These points, then, do not seem to contribute to intensification of the usual heroic emotions. Rather, they seem likely to promote ambivalence along with moral ambiguity. This leads to the question of just what function is served by enhancing moral ambiguity and ambivalence. One possibility is that it may contribute to a theme of the moral (or immoral) equivalence of the ruling class, whether they are "legitimate" rulers (such as Hamlet) or usurpers (such as Claudius). If so, this is a somewhat obscured theme in the play. Given the circumstances in which Shakespeare's plays were performed, however, it is the sort of theme we would expect to be obscured. (Technically, Shakespeare's evaluation principles would include prudential considerations bearing on political themes. These would lead him to make potentially dangerous themes plausibly deniable.)

Before we get to the fencing match, Shakespeare introduces another largely irrelevant character, Osric. The scene is particularly noteworthy for duration. Shakespeare includes more than 100 lines that, in terms of the main story sequences, do little more than invite Hamlet to the fencing match. The scene is, in a sense, the inverse parallel of that with the gravedigger. Both characters speak in an idiom that is distinctively different from that of the other main characters. Both provide comic relief, which is to say, serve to establish a lighter mood that may intensify the distress felt subsequently by the audience. In this sense, they suggest a development subprinciple involving comic intensification of grief. There is, however, a significant difference in the two cases as well. The gravedigger largely outwits Hamlet in verbal play (even in Hamlet's own field of "equivocation" [V.i.140]). In contrast, Hamlet mocks and confuses Osric. At least in part, this is related to the thematic concerns of the work in which the conditions of courtly life – unlike manual labor – seem to push people toward pretense and decadence. This point in turn defines a possible development principle for character.

We have already noted that the play's culmination follows the author and audience selection models so prominent elsewhere in the play. A few further points are worth considering in conclusion. First, Laertes has insisted that any scanting of revenge would suggest that he was a bastard. But when actually faced with the possibility of killing Hamlet, he balks. Here the non-personified, encompassing narrator communicates the inner thoughts of Laertes through an aside in which Laertes says that killing Hamlet "is almost against my conscience" (V.ii.297). This has consequences for our understanding of the story world. It returns us to the issue of Gertrude's possible infidelity, indicating that Laertes's earlier claim about revenge and parentage was wrong. Thematically, it contributes to the play's general opposition to revenge. This opposition is made clear by the carnage that ends the play, with Laertes, Claudius, Gertrude, and Hamlet all killed within a few moments. In terms of discourse, it is another case of what we might call Shakespeare's selective violation of restrictions on representing the characters' private mental life.

The emotional function of the multiple killings hardly requires comment. The horror of this concluding spectacle is only intensified by the subsequent announcement that Rosencrantz and Guildenstern have been executed. The timing here – specifically, the minimization of plot time – is important not only in terms of the conjunction of deaths. It is important also because it is only some ten lines after Horatio's wish that "flights of angels" will "sing" Hamlet to his "rest" (V.ii.361). Horatio's wish means something precise, that Hamlet will go to heaven, rather than having flights of demons convey his soul to hell. The audience can envision this happy possibility. Hamlet killed Laertes and Polonius unwittingly. He and Laertes have exchanged mutual forgiveness. His murder of Claudius was in heated response to Claudius's role in Hamlet's own death and in the death of his mother. But the appearance of the messenger and the announcement of the deaths of Rosencrantz and Guildenstern remind us that he has engaged in premeditated murder. It is difficult to imagine that act fitting with an afterlife of angels. Moreover, in political and familial relations (thus in heroic and revenge genres), all this devastation was for nothing. The final material result is that the fanatical Fortinbras will take the throne. Now, rather than being ruled by his brother or his own son, King Hamlet's kingdom will be ruled by the son of his enemy. Thus everything has been lost, both what is temporal, and, it seems, what is immortal as well. By the end of the play, it is no longer clear that the ghost was not a devil. The fact that he – the work's most important embedded narrator – spoke truly does not mean he did not do so for demonic ends. (Recall Watts's comment that "the Devil can tell the truth to suit his purposes" ["Where" 18].) If his ends were demonic, he becomes the one author-like character to have succeeded with his scripted scheme.

Conclusion

In the course of *Hamlet*, Shakespeare has elaborated and particularized the emplotment of his story using idiolectal discourse principles bearing on selection, organization, and construal. These principles include systematic trajectory interruption and intensified parallelism across represented and recounted, actual and hypothetical scenes. They often involve selection models as well. These lead to author-like "plotting" as well as espionage understood in terms of playacting and audience observation, all of which give rise to embedded narration. Shakespeare also makes tacit use of shifting genre categories, with the different, indirect construals they entail. In addition, he takes up narrational and emplotment disjunction – collectively, "discourse disjunction." In discourse disjunction, the apparent narrational or emplotment devices of a work may be at variance with the functional devices (e.g., a work may be in first person, but operate as if it were in third person). This may produce apparent emotional, temporal, or other anomalies in the discourse, although those anomalies may go unnoticed by readers or audience members. A related principle of Shakespeare's idiolect involves enhancing causal, emotional, or thematic connections by closely conjoining elements in plot that are more distant in the story. This may be done by ellipsis (particularly following shock or trauma) or by embedded narration. Considered individually, these principles are undoubtedly found in a wide range of literary works, including dramas and other mimetic forms. In contrast, the complex of principles may be more distinctively characteristic of Shakespeare's narrative idiolect.

Isolating this complex of principles contributes to our understanding of the patterned particularity of *Hamlet*. These principles are most obviously relevant to plot interest and story emotion, but they also bear on artifact emotion (in revealing some aesthetic features of the structure of the work) as well as theme. For example, recognizing the selection model of espionage helps sensitize us to possible political implications of the work. Collectively, these points may suggest some of the discourse-based reasons for the success of *Hamlet* with readers and audiences. More generally, they illustrate the theoretical point that, like the story, the plot results from idiolectal processes in an author's productive and receptive simulations.

Afterword

"If on a Winter's Night a Narrator ..."

You are about to begin reading "If on a Winter's Night a Narrator...." Don't relax. Don't put up your feet. Find an uncomfortable position. (It will help discourage drowsiness.) Prepare yourself for the worst. Then whatever you encounter will be a pleasant surprise.

THE MURDERED MAN: What I'm tryin' to tell all of you now, if you don't mind hushin' up for a spell, is that narration, I reckon, it's just a sort of a story.[1] I'll be dog if it ain't the same darn thing we been talking about for about five thousand pages now – what them fancy brain folks call *simulation*.

THE GHOST OF MR. COMPSON: Yes, it starts out preponderantly identical – abstract and Platonistic, generalized as water. It goes on the same as well, multiplying itself outward to the visible form of the concrete thing, what you read, there on the page, growing in the mind like an expansion of crystals, following out an inner precept that no sentient mind can precisely divine or control.

MM: Only difference, I reckon, is it ain't about some lover boy with his britches shot off him from them feuding Montagues or Capulets – whichever one of them two he ain't.

GMC: There is, indeed, the simulacrum – the imagining of mind and sensation aggregated into the visible knots that we see without seeing, when we read what some man or woman has written for us to hear without hearing.[2] Thus it is both the same and not the same. It repeats what we have said before. But it changes the self-identical item, so now the condition is a voice, with all its illocutions and perlocutions, and there it is sounding away in its utter and irrevocable silence to that other also invisible and inaudible party, striving like the rest of us with his own enfeebled means to utter and articulate the dulce and the utile, so that he can look up, after the whole and complete telling, into the unseen eyes of his interlocutor and read in them that approbation he had sought in telling the story *ab origine*.

161

A VOICE FROM THE CROWD [TO HIS NEIGHBOR]: What the Sam Hill aborigines got to do with anything?

THE NEIGHBOR: What's a auberigine?

THE THIRD MAN: It's a kind of a purply sort of a [he gestures vaguely with cupped hands].... I et one once, fried up and in a samich.

MM: Now, now, you all quiet down a piece or we ain't never gonna finish, or even get started proper.... Okay, then, professor, we're all ears.

Simulating Narrative Minds

Once upon a time, and a very good time it was, there was a storyteller coming down along the road, and the storyteller coming down along the road met a nicens little girl named "Baby Tuckoo."

Gentlemen and ladies, allow me, if you would be so kind, to refer to this here piece of prose writing as "Exhibit A," which I have altered from its original source (that may or may not be familiar to you that are present here today).

A CAD WITH A PIPE: I ain't never heard nothing like it.

Well, never you mind then. 'T'ain't important. You know plenty from what you heard just now. What I am proposing to this august assembly is that this "once upon a time" establishes a *pro-to-typical* "situation of telling," as we might nominate it.[3] That is to say, it is itself a species of the genus, story. In particular, it is a phenomenon seemingly strange and rarefied – but in reality all too common (like mortal sin or halitosis). I am speaking of a story that itself concerns the telling of another story. Like that second story that it circles in the manner of a vine of morning glories on the post of your front porch, it has people who want things, desire things, long for things, and who want those things so deeply in the very sense and possibility of their being itself that they set themselves perhaps against tremendous odds. Or perhaps the odds are not so tremendous and are, it may be, even in their favor. But here the task they set themselves is just the telling of the second story. So, there you have it, the two of them, two storytellers and two stories, like twins looking in a curved mirror and not knowing who is who, or like those dolls the Chinese make, each one just a smaller version of the last, as you open them, one by one, as if the book itself had another book inside it. I will now turn over the podium to my esteemed and venerable colleague.

Many thanks. Let us cast our minds back to the opening of this most educative lecture, where we were introduced, by the ghost of Professor Compson, to a storyteller who is coming down the road. Suppose now that this here storyteller, who is coming down the road, is a former slave who has learned of his emancipation and is going to join the Yankees. Now, what kind of a tale will this fellow relate to our good mistress Tuckoo? Imagine it for yourselves. Suppose Tuckoo is a black child. Her calico frock is clean, but badly worn, hair a little frazzly. There she is, looking up at the man, all suspicious, as if she was thinking in her little mind of a child some big thought, like, "Who this strange ol' man staring at me with his mouthful of teeth?" Then the man pokes her in the belly, soft-like, not hurting her none, and makes a funny noise with his mouth, like air coming out of a balloon when you pull the neck tight, a kind of a squeak. Then he says, "Why, you mus' be li'l Baby Tuckoo! Why I ain't seen you since you mouth was all gums like a old woman, like somebody granny done forgot her teeth that day. Now you all big – gonna be a woman soon." Tuckoo keeps giving him the one-eyed stare, still all suspicious-like. "You know, you a free girl now – free! You looking back for your mammy – yeah, she free too. White folk don't know it yet though. We going right now to learn 'em 'bout freedom. Yes, ma'am! We makin' sure they get the point this here time." Then he's setting down his satchel and raising the girl up in his two arms like she was something he needed to lift up into the light to see better or to look through, like you might hold up a unopened envelope to see if it's got money in it; you almost expecting him to hold the girl to his ear and give her a little shake too. But no. He cranes back his head, squinting agin' the sun, telling her, "You don' worry none. Uncle Isaiah gonna teach 'em good!" As Isaiah is leaving down along the road, little Baby Tuckoo's turning her face to follow him leaving and that twisted up li'l face of hers ain't change no more than if it was painted on the side of a store or like a photograph in a magazine, and she thinking *that man got some big teeth* and how, if only she knew how to talk, she'd tell her ma all about it.

THE VOICE: Whatchoo tellin' us, professor? I ain't made head nor tails of nothing you been saying.

THE THIRD MAN: Who's Isaiah, and who on God's green earth's got a name like "Baby Tuckoo?"

THE CAD: Sure and I don't know if it's fish or foul he's feeding us this day.

Friends, friends, allow me to elucidate. You see with what ease and facility we all proceeded to fabricate and to reciprocate the fabrication, the optimism, and the illumination of that fantastical meeting between Ol' Isaiah and Baby Tuckoo – though you never met nor even heard about them until this very day, nor could you have done so, since they are as unreal as the element of ether and the ethereal chimera. So, you can go on and on, fancying to yourself what story Isaiah'd tell to Tuckoo, and what Tuckoo might have told her mama, if only she had the gift of tongues and could speak without yet knowing language. You could even imagine my esteemed colleague – solid here as the earth that's holding us all up from falling into Hades or Gehenna like into quicksand – you can even imagine that he too is a mere will-o'-the-wisp, a idea we all excogitate when we think up someone tellin' us a tale about somebody else by the name of Isaiah and his little niece, Baby Tuckoo.

This, I can't say it enough times, is simulation.

Let us follow the lead of my esteemed colleague and consider the sequelae, as my colleagues in the medical college would say. Now – just keep on imagining with me – or even fancy to yourself that you are imagining me, that I'm not standing here before you, like the preacher on a Easter Sunday, brought in from St. Louie, to tell you the fire and the Lamb and the abomination. May be that I'm a story told by my esteemed colleague, who is himself but a phantasm of wavering thought and a trick of light in the mind's eye.

It's a few years later, and Isaiah is returning by the same road, but the opposite way, and he sees Baby Tuckoo and she knows him now (she's seen him in the interim, perhaps he bivouacked in her cabin once, when the white folks had left and the Yankees were there, the cavalry pouring in from the hills like blue and brown waves of the sea). She pleads with him to tell her what has happened – to the waves of blue, to the land that they have still been planting while the white folks were gone with their bonnets and their carriages, to the words of the language itself, both beautiful and terrifying as dreams.

There, my friends, we have it. The same simulation shaped by character and situation, but here *for the narration* – the simulation of the narration[4] – as Isaiah begins to tell what there is to say to a still tiny girl whose old suspicion of a child was (as she looked at the changes on her mother's face and limbs during those months and years) replaced by a sort of tortured hope, then by hunger, and now by a desperate confusion that alternates between images of paradise and a blank futureless dark that is neither desire nor despair.

This is, as all of you must by now have recognized, the selfsame simulation – the same agents with their emotions and aims, the same scenes, the same motions and complexities of causes and consequences, the same chains of action, the same movements of the heart and of the God-given mind – interest and feeling, morals and policy.[5] The one self-evident and incontestable difference comes in the fact that the narrator's story is all about talk, not action. It's about telling something to somebody. Yet its most profound and consequential element is not the author's imagination of the speaker. There is something stuck even down in that: the imagination of the speaker's imagination. And even more: the imagination of the speaker's imagination of the person he or she is speaking or writing to – for that's who the narrator aims to please and teach. And even that is inside something wider, more encompassing, like rings in a stump. That narrator and narratee are imagined by some implied author in the imagined mind of an imagining reader.[6]

And that ain't the whole of it, neither. If we took the thing further still, we'd find arguments too, chains of logic selecting out from the possibilities of event or person or place just those that fit that author's purposes.[7] Most times, these are adjunct to the story itself, a story inseparable from the thematic import dramatized in the cupidity and the hate, the abomination and the purgatorial passage through, and everything else that makes for the story as it opens into the mind of the author, and the reader, and the author as a reader. But narration too may have its own argumentative and exploratory simulations, its own conclusions and enthymemes. When it does, these might circle like buzzards around a single center, may be the authority of the narrator himself, the nature and eternal falsity of the speaker who pretends to know a tale, when he has merely fabricated everything from the stories to the syllables – or, if not fabricated, then so jumbled up and modified it to his own purposes as to make all talk of knowledge or veracity or even realism both sad and laughable, like a dead man whose burying clothes don't quite fit.

And don't some of you begin to suspect that *models* are missing from this grand – one could almost say providential – scheme, in which the small reflects the great, in which the container itself is one great mirror for the contained and its multitudinous processes.[8] These models of course include those of writing itself: the audience and the performer, the creator and the character, the author and the reader – not the real reader, mind you, but the imagined one, the one who guides the author, who himself fades to hazy implicitness through that guidance.

Now, you may say, "But Professor, ain't that there simulated reader, ain't that just the same old thing anyhow – the narratee 'nominated to a more diversified appellation,' as you might say?" Leaving aside the snipperiness of such a question, and focusing our attention solely on its substance, we would have to say no. Among other facets and developments, in the usual run of things, a narratee is a person or some group of persons, and persons are, by their nature, particular – specified, unique. But the reader – imagined, implied – can be a most generalized and abstract idea or, indeed, even less than an idea, a sort of inclination, an inarticulate sense on the part of an author that something is or is not quite right, a sense that this right here must be modified, and that over there excised like a noxious growth, and this third kept as it is.

Indeed, there is a point to be made here about simulation and other minds and, if you are so kind as to allow me, I will venture to make it. There are two types of simulation. In one, I imagine *any*one, anyone at all, in the particular situation at hand, a mere formalism, without the individuating substance that grants that form its incidental properties, a simple idea or eidos, as the

Platonists amongst you would have it. This is when I say the like of, "Well, who wouldn't be scared silly in the middle of the night with the water moccasins all around, their fangs dripping poison you can almost smell, and the yapping of the bloodhounds coming closer and closer?" The other kind of simulacrum is *some*one, someone I know in his or her unique speciality and strangeness. That's when you let out with, "That's just the sort damn-fool, hidebound nonsense of abominable mule-headed persistence you'd expect from Buckwell!" In between, there are the cases where I fix a property or two, a parameter – like when I say, "Any man with a sore foot won't be volunteering to walk all the way to Jefferson just out of the kindness of his heart to hand deliver a letter unless he plans on having a look-see at the contents."

And this, my friends, is where the problem lies. For the narrator addresses a narratee specified in one manner and one degree, whereas the author invisible behind that narrator is speaking to and writing for an imaginary reader both different and more general. The trick is to preserve the smooth artifice of narration while driving the reader on to the knowledge and the feeling and the desire – not least of all, the desire to keep on being driven. That is the falsity of narration, and its genius.

Here's the simplest of cases – why does that very covert narrator of *Hamlet*, hidden as he is, like Polonius behind the arras, why does he not get on with telling us what he knows about Claudius and the murder right at the get-go?[9] Well, we all know – it's on account of how it would weaken the play and make us all less likely to purchase it for our classes and devote books and articles to its explication. But it's perfectly clear that he could have revealed that information at any time it pleased him to do so. Once you get thinking about it, it's curious.

Authors facing this crisis and dilemma usually set to it in one of two ways. The most obvious is by trying to hide the artifice, while hoping we don't notice – and, usually, we don't. The other is to bring the artifice right out there on the stage, then deal with it. Here too we may engage in that much derided nomination to diverse appellations, and make a further division. The artificiality may be *explained* or it may be *flaunted*. Just as a for instance, one of the main purposes of limiting what a narrator knows is to explain emplotment and make it natural-like. In contradistinction, the flaunting of narrative manipulation is a signal characteristic of what our esteemed colleagues nominate and appellate "the postmodern."

Narration Occluded or Explained: Faulkner's *Light in August*

What precisely brought Miss Lena Grove all the way to Jefferson, Mississippi, walking alone for weeks from Alabama? And what consequences did it have, for her, for Lucas Burch, and for Byron Bunch? In fine, what fancy frames Faulkner's fiction?

Marry, it was a fine, saucy tale of seduction and abandonment, with a soupçon of the Don Juan variety. Let us summarize the events:

The dear orphan, Lena, with no mother to counsel her and provide her a store of wisdom and prudence, succumbs to the enchanting endearments of Mr. Burch, who should have inspired the trust of a used snake oil dealer. Hearing that the proverbial bun is in the oven, Burch absconds, leaving Lena in lonely anticipation of his missive calling her to join him in the states of Mississippi and matrimony. Literally fed up to here [*imagine appropriate gesture*] with waiting, Lena heads out on her own, planning to reach at least Mississippi. Through a confusion of names, she gets herself all mixed up with some Mr. Bunch, a clinging, insignificant sort of a fellow that meant well and even took to the manly art of fisticuffs in defense of his lady love, but who, when faced with said lady love, evidenced all the backbone of a pudding. Aided by the moony Bunch, Lena does find out the elusive Burch, only to be abandoned once again – now with the babe in arms.

Bunch Bumbles, Lena Leery

So, once the little fellow (that is, Burch, Jr., that is, the babe in arms) saw the light of day, the only thing left for her to do, I suppose, was to set out in search of the profligate progenitor, with the ever-faithful Bunch trotting along behind like a drugged puppy.

To this extremity, neutral observers would doubtless agree that we are witnessing a quite ordinary version of the seduction prototype. And we might expect lovely languishing Lena to abandon her ill-fated pursuit of the perfidious Burch and join herself in wedded bliss with the pertinacious Bunch. That is, indeed, what the ending suggests.

What devices, of narration or emplotment, of discourse or diegesis, did Faulkner choose to extend and qualify in the ultimate particule of this particular parcel of prose? What circumambulations and circumscriptions and even circumlocutions did this entail? What narrative beginnings did it belabor and what narrative endings did it elaborate? In short, what conclusions may be concluded about this conclusion?

If you'd be so kind as to allow me to answer, I'd be much obliged. Mr. Faulkner introduces a new narrator in this here last chapter. Carolyn Porter says, "It is as if a whole new story is about to begin" (92). And she's right. It is a new story – exceptin' that the new story is just about the new fella telling the story – the rest is just the old story stretching itself out a bit. So, now we got ourselves two narrators. The first one is faceless and nameless; that is, he ain't a character – or she ain't. I'll just simplify and say "he," though. So, this faceless narrator introduces "a furniture repairer" in Tennessee (368) who was taking a little trip into Mississippi. On his way back, he happens on a woman, a infant, and a man – that would be our Lena, her little ankle-biter, and her fidus Achates, her Patroclus, her good Horatio. Then he tells the story of their trip together. The story itself isn't so much the point – we've seen plenty of them before, even if this one does have its ironical twistings and turnings. But what is of significant import here is – yes, of course, the narration, just what the good professors were jawing about and none of us understanding a god-dam thing coming outta their mouths.

Now, we all know stories where the main man or the woman might recount the events, or some other person involved in the actions, reactions, and inter-actions. But Faulkner does not have Lena or Burch or Bunch tell us about it, not to mind the mewling and puking infant.

Does any of them focalize it, like them fancy-pants narratologists say?

No, not that neither – and that's part of the queerness of it. He just intro-duces this irrelevant fellow with no other part in the novel but to hint us at what doesn't happen to Lena and Bunch, but that probably will happen or might happen, 'cause all they do with him is ride along, with Bunch renewing his overtures and Lena refusing him calmly but firmly, though the furniture repairer thinks she'll eventually give in – and, of course, so do I and my guess is you do too.

Anyway, everything we've been saying about simulation appears right here as if Faulkner had read all about it in that book by that fella – I plum forgot his name, Logan or Hoban or maybe Hogan, like that wrestler fella what had the program on the TV. Anyways, it's like Faulkner read the whole book, includ-ing of course this part here (that I ain't finish yet), then set down to write out his novel as a illustration. 'Cause, first, he starts out by telling us about this furniture repairer. Then he tells us about the furniture repairer's wife, who's gonna be there listening to him tell his story. Faulkner (We can just call the big narrator "Faulkner"; that'll make things a heap easier, don't you think? Good.), Faulkner even tells us that the man found the events "amusing" and thinks "he could make it interesting in the retelling" (368). So Faulkner right out up and explains it to us how this narrator is doing what any storyteller aims to do – what with the emotion and the interest – like Faulkner himself.

So, this here furniture repairer starts off on his story and, what do you know, but the big narrator (the one without a face, what we're calling "Faulkner") has to step in and tell the reader this information and that information about the husband and wife being in the dark, cause otherwise we won't understand why the man can't see if his wife is or is not blushing (though we all figure she ain't). Now, we all know that the narrator could have told us this on page one. So we have all this artifice. And it's hard to miss it. Why take us all the way into a bedroom in Tennessee to let us know about Lena and Bunch – and who is it that's observing the furniture repairer and his wife? And why can't he give us the information we need at the start, like I said before? Sure, that big narrator that we nicknamed "Faulkner," sure he must know everything the furniture repairer knows, and more.

It's not that the artifice is forcing itself on our attention, like the pimple-face boy trying to woo the pretty girl at the spring dance. It's not like that at all and lots of folks probably miss out on it entirely. But it's there, and Faulkner (the real one, the author), he's counting on some of us noticing. Yes, siree, he is. So, the wife, why she starts playing the role of the implied reader. Other words, Faulkner done modeled this here part of the narration on the implied reader, who should start asking hisself questions, just like the wife starts asking the husband. So, when the furniture repairer says that Bunch was desperating himself up for something, the wife asks, "What was it he aimed to do?" (371) – just the question the implied reader might ask at that point. The husband holds her off by appealing to his own lack of knowledge at that time in the story – even though he could surely tell her now, because he learnt it later. That's what I was getting at before about how an author might bring out the artifice only to explain it – or try to explain it or make some sort of show and pretense of explaining it – and that's what Faulkner's gone and done here.

That'd be alright, I suppose, but things get curiouser and curiouser, as somebody once said. The furniture repairer starts filling in what Lena and Byron know and what they don't know. He qualifies it ("It was like they didn't even know themselves" [370]), but he's still telling his wife and us about it, like a omniscient narrator, which he can't be, seeing as he's a character and he ain't God the Father or Jesus Our Savior or the Holy Spirit.

Like I said, Faulkner was using this model of a implied reader to guide his particularization of the narratee, what with the wife asking the questions we might be expected to ask. Now he goes and takes up that model again, but the purposes 's differnt 'cause now the narrator explains that he learned what he knows by overhearing Lena and Byron when they didn't know they was being overheard. Again, he's got this knowledge that he shouldn't have. So he tells us why. All well and good. But then he hears more and more, and he sees things in the dark – and he sees things from a distance that poor Byron can't see even close-up (373). What he knows, and what he tells, ain't just what that furniture repairer would know and tell if he was real. Sure, that's there. That's part of it. You can't take that out of the simulating. But there's the model too – the unseen, seeing audience – 'cause it seems this furniture repairer was almost at a picture show with what he was seeing in the dark, and hearing too, cause this wasn't no silent movie.

So, what we got here is a fine piece of narrating and simulating. We got the simulating of the events themselves – what Byron Bunch done desperated himself up to do and never did and how Lena Grove fixed herself to hold out just a piece, with that stand-in loping along after her like old Custer, the family dog; then we got the second simulating – that's our furniture repairer and his wife and him all playful-like because the two of them "are not old either" (368). More to the point, in that second narrating and simulating the big narrator keeps sticking his nose into things and telling us what we don't know but should and the whole process of who's telling what to who is conducted like they been thinking the whole time about the novelist himself and the way he's imagining a reader – not a particular reader, like you and me, of course, but some general kind of a reader, just asking questions to himself like, or watching a picture show.

So, it's all condoned with explication, giving the ifs and the whys and the wherefores. Or it's papered over with obfuscations and vague talk. Or we get all distracted and keep looking off somewhere else, the whole time taken in by the sleight of hand and the fast-talking. But all the while artifice hovers over the story – or, more like, it hovers below the story, underlies it, undergirds and props it up as its necessary fakery.

Not entirely unlike me talking to you right now, is it?

Celebrating Artifice: Calvino's *Se una Notte d'Inverno un Viaggiatore* (*If on a Winter's Night a Traveler*)

I'm afraid I have a confession to make. Perhaps you will be surprised to hear that I am not William Faulkner, nor a dead southern professor from one of his novels. On second thought, that won't surprise you. I must botch the dialect here and there. Okay, more than here and there. Perhaps it's so bad that you found yourself holding your ears closed and saying, "Good Lord spare me this abomination and putrefaction of the English language!" But, in fairness, you must admit that I warned you at the beginning to expect the worst.

In any case, as I say, I have a confession to make – and I believe it will give you some sympathy with my inadequacies in articulating different voices. I am, of course, the "big" narrator here – the "embedding" and (up to now) nonpersonified narrator. You may say, "Well, so, how does that mitigate your rather embarrassing overreaching (thinking you could imitate Faulkner! My God – Faulkner! It's perfectly scandalous!)? My prediction is that no self-respecting university press will ever publish this book now." Well, as the song says, "Call me unreliable." But you are imagining that I'm a person, someone with his or her faculties intact, someone who really can choose to desist from pretending that he or she is Faulkner. But, you see, there's the rub. I'm not a person. I'm just a character. Indeed, I'm a specific character. I'm the character called *I* in Italo Calvino's *Se una Notte* (yada, yada, yada – you know the title; if you don't, just look back at the section heading; it's printed there).

So, can you forgive me now?

But the complications don't end there. No, not by a long chalk. In fact, the strangest difficulty is not the narrator, but the narratee. It's you – yes, you, sitting there, right now, with the book in front of you.

I know, set it down, close it up, look away, turn your back – try to make a liar out of me. But it won't do. You're still the person I'm addressing.

So, there you have it. This whole narrative – and I hope you recognize how much it is guided by an argument and, indeed, by models of narration! – this whole business about narration and particularity is being articulated by a fictional entity, a nothing, the merest suggestion of words, prompts for simulation. It is, however, addressed to and actualized by a real person – you. So just where does that mean the bad Faulkner imitation exists? Tell me that, smarty pants! The point is that there is only one person here who even can be guilty of botching this pastiche – and that is *you*! Yes, you. It certainly can't be me; I don't even exist.

Enter the ghost of Italo Calvino.

CALVINO: Abjure, thou naught without a digit, thou scraped peasecod, thou eggshell!

Isn't that a bit bloated diction for Calvino? you ask. He's a ghost; that changes things.

CALVINO: If ever thou didst love thy author well, forswear thy falsehoods; pour not thy poison in the porches of thy readers' ears!

Hey, I already said I'm unreliable.

Okay, so, there's this idea that sometimes "second person narration" is really addressed to the real reader.[10]

GHOST: Forswear!

Peace, sweet mole! I broach the matter presently. Well, this is a bit silly. When do we address an individual? In part, it's a matter of how we define "address." But a reasonable definition might be something along the following lines: An utterer addresses an individual when he or she has either perceptually or conceptually isolated that individual uniquely. For example, suppose I look at Calvino's ghost and say, "Art thou a spirit damned or have flights of angels sung thee to thy rest?" In that case, I am addressing the individual that I perceive. Alternatively, suppose I organize a séance and, through some credentialed medium, cry out to the spirit world, "Oh, most splendid author of the incomparable *Le Città Invisibili*, pour the sweet nectar of thy heavenly speech into the longing portals of my anxious ears!" I am addressing some-one picked out conceptually – roughly, the author of *Le Città Invisibili*.

So, do authors ever address actual readers? Yes, they do – but it's pretty rare. The obvious case is love poetry. Shakespeare addressed his sonnets simultaneously to an anonymous readership (including you and me) and to a particular beloved (or, rather, two beloveds, depending on the sonnet). But that's it. My author, Calvino, wasn't addressing any real reader any more than I am. I'm so sorry if that disappoints you. I suppose it might make you feel special to have a nonexistent being really talk to you, and only to you, with every other reader only overhearing things, like the furniture repairer with Lena and Byron. It would make me feel special. Perhaps you could convince a love poet to write sonnets to you. That might help some.

But if I'm not really addressing you personally, why does it seem that I am? Well, that's where modeling comes in. I'm simply modeling my narratee on a generalized idea of the reader. It's just what Faulkner does with the furniture repairer's wife. The difference is that, in this case, I'm flaunting the artifice, rather than obscuring or explaining it.

So, that leads us back to my creator. Surely he is addressing you, isn't he? I'm sorry to say – no, he's not addressing you any more than I am. Take the first chapter of *Se una Notte*. There he merely imagines what a reader in general is likely to be doing – for example, how he or she bought the book. But even a mere moment's reflection should have told you that this imagi-nary reader is not *you*. It's just *some* reader, a generalized reader, an abstract simulacrum. Indeed, even careful attention to the language shows this. "*Stai per cominciare*" (3) tells us that we are on the verge of beginning the novel; it goes on to instruct us in preliminaries – settling ourselves in the chair and so on. But as soon as you read "*stai*," you have already begun the novel and are already settled. The first chapter simply cannot address what you are doing. It addresses, rather, what some reader might already have done. Of course, it wouldn't matter if you were really doing it (perhaps you hadn't thought to put up your feet and, as you read the words, you do just that – a perfectly sensible decision, although why didn't it strike you before?). It's still an artifice, a coincidence between the generally imagined narratee and you as a real reader.

Indeed, that is presumably part of the thematic point. If Calvino is flaunt-ing the artifice of the fiction, he is surely *not* saying that he directly addresses me or you or the fellow over in the corner of the Starbucks who seems to be reading – yes, what a coincidence … it's a copy of … Italo Calvino's *Se una*

Notte d'Inverno un Viaggiatore! He's right at the beginning. Let's wait – yes, now he's putting up his feet. But you lose interest in observing him before you see whether he tries the yoga position mentioned in the novel. It's time to leave Starbucks anyway. Perhaps you have to go to a session at the Modern Language Association convention. Perhaps you are delivering a paper yourself. There you are, listening to everyone go on and on about how we must interrogate the site of the binary in the conjunctural moment of hybrid historical constructedness.

But eventually you return to Calvino. You are now finishing up the first chapter. Here, you are told that you expect to "recognize" the characteristic "accent" of the author – and, of course, you do expect that. But then you are told that it is absent from this book, that the only constant characteristic of this author is that he changes so much from book to book (10)! But, surely, that is not true. Could anyone other than Calvino have written this book?[11] (Okay, perhaps Pirandello – but we know he didn't.) That, again, dear reader, is a flaunting of simulation and a flouting of the convention that authors should use art to conceal art.

Of course, the narration here is not entirely wrong. The beginning of the novel proper (the first interchapter), while not wholly different from what you expect from Calvino, is also not wholly the same. There is novelty in it, and it does therefore provoke your curiosity (10). But, even here, in stating the function of the novelty, as Calvino does, he to some degree makes the artifice itself salient. (Wait, am I beginning to sound like that MLA speaker? If I say anything about the text inviting you into the conjunctural space of dialogic performativity, you should immediately close the book and send it back to amazon.com for a refund – well, I mean anything other than this sentence here, of course; this sentence itself doesn't count.)

But now you see something strange and wonderful. The interchapter begins the book within the book. It is "Se una Notte d'Inverno un Viaggiatore." Does that mean that the novel itself is embedded within an interchapter that is itself embedded within the novel? What fun! That Calvino is really something (you say to yourself). The thrill of paradox – especially a paradox of recursion! That's why he refers to Zeno (18, 26), best known for just these sorts of paradox. (If Zeno and a turtle are both trying to finish reading a novel, the turtle will win because Zeno must finish half of the novel before he finishes all of it, and he must finish half of the remaining half, and half of the remaining quarter, and so on, to no end point. I think we have all read novels like that.)

"Excuse me – excuse me – could I say something here?"

Well, it's rather unorthodox for a real person to insert himself into a discussion with someone who is only a fictional character.

"Oh, I'm just a simulation myself. Indeed, I'm not even sure who my author is. I've been going to Mr. Pirandello's salon, but he leaves me alone in the corner while he talks with that harlot and her father."

In that case, be my guest.

"Thanks so much. Here is what I'm thinking. Perhaps this fascination of ours results from adaptation. For example, recursion is a key feature of language. Thus children need to take an interest in recursive processes, to focus on them and imitate them. And they do. But we tend to dwell only on things that have some hedonic element. (Sorry to talk so much like a psychologist. It's against my nature. But one has to keep up with the times! Especially those of us who have been orphaned by our creators.) It's at least imaginable that children attracted by recursion were more successful in assimilating recursive practices. That, then, would be one adaptive mechanism that spread interest in recursion throughout the population."

Just so!

"But, like all mechanisms, it has nonadaptive consequences as well. Our strange delight in paradoxes of recursion might be one case of this."

So true. Yet your delectable ecstasy – well, at least amusement – in seeing the novel you are reading contained in a part of that novel that is itself printed in the novel you are currently holding in your hands (and that you will never actually finish reading because you always have at least half of the rest left to read) – is not all that strikes you. There are other emotions. There are themes – why, there is the flaunting of artificiality itself, what you just heard about at the MLA convention as "an invitation into the heteroglot space." (No, you don't get to return the book yet. I just cited the phrase; I didn't actually use it! There's a difference.)

But then again the interchapter does not really reproduce the novel. It presents me – a character from the novel – describing the novel. For example, it does not begin with the first words of the novel (whatever those might be). It begins with me explaining to you how the novel begins. In doing this, I continually refer to features of both the story world (e.g., the train station) and the book itself (the pages, the paragraphs, the sentences). The purpose of this is clear. It makes salient the multiple levels of embedment. Our inclination is always to forget, to put out of our minds, the fact that the book we are reading is a book. This happens again with a book within a book. By repeatedly referring to the physical object as well as the story, I keep the book itself salient. (Or perhaps my author does that. I'm not sure. It certainly feels to me as if I'm doing it.)

Other instances concern the asking of questions, which, as you know, is so important for reading. For example, at one point, I infer that you, dear reader, might be wondering about the exact historical setting of the events. Is this a station today (i.e., in 1979 – that once was today, even if you are so young that it seems as if 1979 must have been a time when only dinosaurs roamed the earth)? Or is it a station from the past? But, I explain, the author hasn't actually told us. Indeed, perhaps he hasn't simply withheld the information, "perhaps the author is still undecided" (13). "How strange! How … *interesting!*" you say to yourself. "I must read further. Why, this is turning out to be a real page-turner!"

Here (I think you've probably noticed this by now), my beloved progenitor, I. C. ("I." for short), simply does what Faulkner did – although, of course, I. created a much more fascinating and, if I may say so, better-looking character than that furniture repairer. But Faulkner partially conceals the artifice by putting your questions into the mouth of that furniture repairer's wife. I. obtrusively links the question with you yourself – right there at the library, with your mouth half open, almost asking things out loud and disturbing the other patrons in the reading room – and with the author himself. This is that postmodern purpose of flaunting artificiality. Or perhaps I am doing that. Yes, I think it's me – not that author, who thinks he is some sort of little god. Or maybe not. In any case, it's one of the three of us. This all has the rather banal thematic purpose that all you literary critics recognize (pardon me for lumping you all together like this; the author of the present book, himself a literary critic, is now strenuously objecting to this stereotype – look at him over there, fussing and cursing and getting all red in the face. But I'm sticking to my guns!). I know, I'm the one who introduced that theme a few paragraphs ago. (I realize it seems longer.) But I'm already beginning to get bored with it. It's fine once or twice, but its interest fades quickly. Alright, alright – enough already! We get it! Narration is artificial. Well, aren't we all so clever!

But what truly fascinates you about Calvino's book (beyond its utterly enchanting central character and narrator) is that, after making artifice salient, it then goes on to show that making artifice salient is itself artificial. Moreover, it indicates that the apparently artificial quality of narration and emplotment are also real. That's what makes the book more than some undergraduate exercise in postmodern narratology.

So, let's begin with the story world. Up to this point, we have only looked at works that follow some cross-cultural prototype. The fragment of *Se una Notte* suggests a more localized genre – one focusing on espionage. Although not a cross-cultural genre per se, it does derive in part from recurring motifs of espionage in cross-cultural genres. These prominently include the heroic plot and the revenge plot, as I showed you in *Hamlet*. (I should perhaps confess here that I have been narrating this book all along, even though I embedded

a fictionalized version of the author – I believe his name is Ohman[n?] – in
my narration. In consequence –

"Excuse me, sir! Excuse me!"

"What is it now?"

"My name is Hogan!"

Very well, then – in consequence, it should be clear that I am solely responsible for the content of these arguments and analyses while the admirable
"My name is Grogan!" over there deserves neither praise nor blame for them,
despite the fact that his name appears on the cover of the book, and on the
contract with the press, although this is due only to the fact that the law does
not recognize property rights for fictional characters, a form of blatant dis-
crimination that I must leave aside for the present.) These recurring motifs
are strongly affected by their usual generic contexts, and also by the authorial
model that they commonly involve. Specifically (just in case you've forgotten
this from Chapter 5 – well, I know *you* haven't forgotten, but some other readers, you see, they are getting old and forgetful; they remember when it was
1979; it's sad, really; one has to be kind to them), they often include a version of
the unseen audience that is quietly overhearing all us characters speak to one
another. Not only in plays, mind you. For all my self-confident assertions, I
can't actually see you. You can see me – well, hear me; well, read what I've written – well, something, but I actually have no idea what you are doing. Perhaps
you are smiling benevolently. Perhaps you are laughing derisively – well, no;
I'm sure you are not doing that. Perhaps you are weeping because we will never
have the opportunity to meet in person (which is certainly very sad, for you
especially). Perhaps you are reading this passage aloud to another audience at
the MLA annual convention and praising my brave challenge to the discourse
of truth and the apparatus of power. In any case, the point is that espionage –
based as it is on unobserved observation and the concealment of a fictional
artifice – is a very fitting means for rendering salient the artifice of fiction.

And – as you might figure from the reference to genres – espionage has not
remained confined to motifs. It has become a genre as well. It is a very diverse
genre, with multiple concerns and stories. Indeed, it has its own recurring
motifs. These include secret meetings between people who do not know one
another and recognize one another only by a sign or token, anonymity and
multiplication of identities, intentional or unintentional switches of properties or people (e.g., mix-ups of luggage in which sensitive and incriminating
materials are lost), misrecognitions (e.g., in which a random passerby happens to say the password for the secret meeting).

Such motifs recur not only in narratives that seek to cover their tracks (so
to speak) – thus more "traditional" narratives, as one might say. They also

appear in experimental fiction. A prominent case is Alain Robbe-Grillet's *Dans le Labyrinthe*. Although not a spy story, Robbe-Grillet's famous novel takes up these motifs in the context of a (broadly) postmodern work. Indeed, it is just the sort of work that is often taken to have many of the standard postmodern thematic concerns. Thus a common view of the novel is that it is not about warfare and clandestine operations at all. It is, rather, a fiction about fiction, a text about producing the text (see, for example, Leki 78–79 and Morrissette 184).

This is relevant to our purposes because Calvino suggests at the beginning of the second chapter that his embedded novel is actually a work by Robbe-Grillet. Specifically, perhaps Robbe-Grillet's most famous stylistic feature is the cyclical repetition of phrases, images, and events with only slight variations. The second chapter of *Se una Notte* begins with me explaining something to you. (If you think back on your experience of the novel embedded within the interchapter embedded within the novel, you'll remember this – or, rather, you would if "you" here actually did address *you*, rather than some implicit narratee.) Specifically, recall how "at a certain point you observe[d]" that this or that sentence "does not appear to be new." Indeed, you thought – "This entire passage … it seems to me I've read it before" (28). After a time you concluded that this is one of those literary virtuosi who repeat a paragraph now and again – or an entire page, or – hold your horses! This is the same book. Look at the page numbers – once you come to page thirty-two, you advance again to … page seventeen! It's a printer's error.

Well, needless to say, the virtuoso here is Alain Robbe-Grillet. The joke is that readers of Robbe-Grillet have exactly the opposite experience. One doesn't imagine that the repetition is a literary technique only to find that it is a printer's error. Rather, a reader is likely to wonder if there is a printer's error – only to find that it is a literary technique! In short, Calvino (through my voice, thank you) is parodying the entire postmodern approach that we just claimed his novel was exemplifying!

Well, this leaves us in a pickle. What is going on thematically here? Is this novel teaching us about the arbitrariness of narration? Or is it a great take-off on those techniques that pretend to teach us about the arbitrariness of narration? I suppose it could even be both. The novel makes artifice salient but then goes on to show that making artifice salient is itself artificial. (Oh, I said that already. Well, I'll just make out that the repetition was intentional. *Note to copy editor*: Leave this in. It will make readers think I'm parodying Robbe-Grillet.)

Or am I (or is Calvino) even making the initial thematic point at all (that narration is artificial)? The story concerns a man (that's me) with a suitcase, at a train station in a provincial town. I am supposed to meet someone else from the organization. We will inadvertently exchange suitcases. I will leave. It does not take much commitment to biographical criticism to see in this story elements of Calvino's own time in the anti-Fascist resistance, even if I (and Calvino) never bother to tell you that.

This leads us in an entirely different direction. The disruptions and inconsistencies of the narrative may not tell us how artificial fiction is with respect to life. They may suggest something about how life itself operates, at least its most intense and difficult moments. In a letter discussing his brief time as a partisan, Calvino wrote that it was "a series of reversals" involving "dangers" that were "unnarratable" (he didn't send the letter to me, but it is quoted by some fellows named Barenghi and Falcetto on page xxiii; I can't vouch for their reliability; perhaps they are just making it up and there is no such letter, but we can only go with the evidence we have before us). He seems to have included literary representations in the scope of this statement. Not only are the dangers "*inenarrabile*." Moreover, the "reversals" are *peripezie*, which commonly translates Aristotle's term for a narrative "reversal," *peripeteia*.[12]

This suggests that the thematic focus of this part of the work is perhaps not so much writing or the novel but rather such terrible events of life as comprise the struggle against Fascism. Indeed, it is easy to understand the entire section in terms of simulations that would necessarily pass through the mind of a partisan given such an assignment. He is told the plan, or part of it – the commander does not tell him everything; he does not identify everyone or explain all the details. The commander is, then, like an author who does not tell everything to the reader, or inhibits the narrator from telling everything to the narratee, like the furniture repairer does not tell everything to his wife. But now the partisan begins the ordinary process of simulation. He is told that it is "a perfect plan" (18) – but, he wonders, what if the train is simply late? Here, then, it seems that Calvino is using a fictional simulation to help clarify the nature of ordinary, practical simulation. It is almost the opposite of foregrounding artificiality.

Indeed, the connections go further. My worries about being an obtrusive presence for the people in the station are the worries of a partisan faced with a mission to an unfamiliar place to meet an unknown contact, risking arrest at any moment; they are perhaps the worries of Calvino himself who could not help but "place in this 'I' a little of himself," of what "he imagines feeling" (17). I am also like that partisan, whether Calvino or someone else, in my envy of the normalcy in ordinary lives ("Yes, envy. I'm looking from afar at life on an ordinary evening in an ordinary town ... who knows how long I will be far from such ordinary evenings" [19]). Such normalcy is not the stuff of fiction and – this is the crucial point of connection here – it is not the stuff of a partisan's life for, like a reader, a spy does not know from moment to moment what peripeteia will follow ("In an existence like mine, one cannot anticipate" even "the next half-hour" [22]). Normalcy, after all, defines precisely what is *not* part of fiction, or what is there only as background – like the "bits of conversation that seem to have no other function than to represent the life of a provincial city" (20).

That normalcy itself is complex, however; it is a composite of its own banalities and its own consequences. Anything could provide the spy with a hint as to a threat or opportunity, just as anything said in a novel could provide the reader with a clue as to who is the murderer and who is innocent. Thus, "to read well," whether in literature or espionage, "you must register" both what is noise and what reveals "hidden intention" (20–21).

In short, the thematic significance of *Se una Notte*, at least in this section, is not primarily a matter of foregrounding and flaunting the artificiality of fiction; nor is it centrally a matter of parodying such postmodern disruption (although there are undoubtedly elements of both in the novel). The main thematic orientation here does not seem to be toward writing but rather toward life. Nor does it seem to be a matter of life generally – our now clichéd "postmodern condition" of disorientation and uncertainty. Or, rather, this section does focus on disorientation and uncertainty, but of a different sort. Specifically, this part of the novel faces us with the discontinuities and uncertainties of real simulation, the places where simulation is unreliable – the points where it must change rapidly and where the stakes are high. In connection with this, it is no coincidence that the people in the bar are gambling, betting on small, possibly cumulative, chance events.

Of course, these thematic concerns should not occlude the emotional function of Calvino's flaunting of ordinary practices of narration and emplotment. This is not simply a matter of delight in paradox, just as the themes of the novel are not simply a reflex of postmodern self-consciousness. Rather, just as the novel draws your attention to the anti-Fascist resistance, it draws your interest and engagement toward the plight of our hero – that is, me. I hope it is clear by now that being a spy is no bed of roses. The tension only rises at the end of the chapter. Jan has been caught. You don't know Jan. But now you know me a little, and the prospects don't look good. Gorin warns me and I have to rush to the train, an express that is not scheduled for a stop – and I don't even know whether I can trust Gorin. He works for the police. Is he one of us? Is this all a trap? Am I being seduced into belief and acceptance like any narratee of a romance?

This sort of simulation is necessary for us in the resistance (remember, I'm still fixed at the time of the novel, so it's still current for me, despite my anachronistic references to the MLA and evolutionary psychology). But it is highly disturbing – nightmarish, in fact – until the escape. Flaunting the techniques of narration gives an element of comedy to a situation that is anything but comic.

"Sure, it does make you laugh, don't it now? Yes, siree. Take that furniture repairer, what with him turning to his wife all in the dark and her asking, *Well what did Bunch want to do? And him telling her right back, Why I just done showed once; should I do it again?* Which one of you all ain't laughing at that?"

Yes, you are entirely right. It's the same in both novels. Of course, in *Se una Notte*, this relieves some of the anxiety – yours, and I.'s too, since he is the one with the traumatic memory of those reversals. That comedy allows you to go on with the reading – and even leads you to expect a positive outcome. Once you are absorbed in the danger, you stop laughing. But it helps sustain your confidence in an escape.

"Why, it's the same with them other folks. There's no risk of them being hauled off for prison. But Byron seems desperated up to force himself on the poor gal. That would not only make the whole kit 'n' caboodle all worrisome. It wouldn't make us care much for Byron – which would be a pity after all he done for Lena. Agin that, we might worry too that he'd leave, like he almost done. But, then, I wonder if you got it back-to-front. The way I reckon, it's not the comic mood that makes us go on to the happy ending – well, at least what ain't a awful, drag-through-the-mud, downright miserable ending. Instead, it's that the comic shenanigans with the narrators and narratees and what have you all mixed up like a load of wash – it's that what allows you to accept the happy ending as the right and sensible outcome of it all, and even to see it as a happy ending.

"But, anyways, if you's anything like me, you been reading this here book way too long. Your husband or wife keeps begging you – 'Sweetie pie, why don't you just turn out that light and go to sleep. It's already three A.M. Can't you just finish that darn book in the morning?' But you can tell her that there ain't much more to go. Now you have only eight more sentences. Now seven. Now, you are just about to finish. You're on the edge, about to cross over. First you get through half of what's left. That leaves jus' a tiny bit. Then you finish half of that. Now there ain't hardly nothing left and you don't even notice your wife or husband reaching to turn out the light, ready to click the switch right as your eyes come to the final, undividable moment of.

Conclusion

"How in the Sam Hill am I supposed to read this thing in the dark?"

But there is nothing more to read. Now you simply think back on what you have finished reading, mulling it over, letting it sink in. Suddenly, you realize that you are in complete agreement with the author (Peter something – Holbein, perhaps? Or Hoyden?) about the particularization of narration. It *is* identical with the simulation of story, including development and evaluation principles, prototypes (although of course they are prototypes for narration now), even the use of arguments and models – prominently including models drawn from the production and reception of literature itself. Moreover, the simulation of narration is motivated by the same emotional and thematic goals. You are also utterly delighted by the innovative and illuminating analyses of Faulkner and Calvino. "Yes, yes," you mutter to yourself. "Rather than concealing the artificiality of narration, both authors expose it. But Calvino flaunts this artificiality, whereas Faulkner seeks to explain it!" You very nearly exclaim the final point, much to the dismay of your partner, who had finally begun to anticipate the possibility of sleep. The treatment of Calvino you found particularly enlightening because it overturned the usual reading of the novel as postmodernly self-referential, demonstrating its commentary on real-life conditions of simulation – but you considerately keep this observation to yourself. "What a truly magnificent book! The finest work of literary theory since …" Closing your eyes, you sink slowly into another world of stories and simulations.

Notes

Introduction

1. See chapter 3 of *A Room of One's Own*.
2. It is important in this context that prototypes are not innate archetypes. Their recurrence derives in part from the common genetic structures of our emotion systems. However, they are also the product of common patterns in group dynamics, childhood development, and other factors. (For a discussion of some factors that can contribute to recurring literary patterns, see States.) The resulting cognitive structures are not entirely uniform across individuals – a key point for the differentiation of literary works. However, they do tend toward considerable convergence – the key point for commonality across literary works.
3. On the general idea of priming, see Baddeley "What" 12; on priming and literature, see Oatley *Passionate* 98.
4. On this prototype, see Hogan *Affective* 199–209.
5. In the simulation literature, "counterfactual" is commonly used to refer to something that might have happened in the past but did not; in contrast, "hypothetical" is used to refer to something that might happen in the future. There are some significant differences between the two (see Van Boven, Kane, and McGraw). For the most part, however, those differences do not bear on fictional works. For this reason, the following discussions will largely pass over the distinction, using the terms more or less interchangeably to refer to nonfactual trajectories.
6. This idea of intertranslatability may seem to set aside the arguments of writers such as Fodor (9–26). The most significant point is that Fodor's arguments apply to general laws. His contention is that regularities may be captured by generalizations at one level of description (e.g., in economic theory) but not at another (e.g., in physics). I entirely agree with Fodor on this point. Fodor accepts that particulars can be explained at more basic levels even when laws cannot be captured at more basic levels. For example, Jones's economic actions today may be explained by Jones's psychology, even if the larger economic laws his actions instantiate cannot be captured by psychological laws. This token-to-token (i.e., particular) intertranslatability is all that the present analysis claims. Indeed, the value of incorporating reference to rules is bound up with Fodor's point about the difficulty of type/type reducibility (thus translatability of generalities). The preceding discussion simply makes a

weaker claim – one still consistent with Fodor – that rules are more perspicuous than the detailed, particularistic analyses of neural networks. Nonetheless, important issues remain. Most significantly, we would expect there to be a tighter correlation between more proximate levels of causal analysis. Thus we would expect there to be a closer relationship between neurology and psychology than between physics and economics. One might expect proximity to lead to some type/type reducibility. It should at least lead to a greater degree of theoretically consequential constraint from one level to the next. Of course, there is always constraint. Economics cannot violate the laws of physics, but that constraint probably does not tell us much of significance about economics. In contrast, we would expect psychology to be more consequentially constrained by neurology. Put differently, we would expect contiguous levels to have more relevance to the formulation of generalities in both directions. Neurology may not tell us everything about psychology. Nonetheless, our understanding of the brain should be consequential for our understanding of the mind (and vice versa) – for example, in distinguishing types of memory.

7. The point is familiar in the western critical tradition. On some of the basic principles of Middle Eastern, South Asian, Chinese, and Japanese traditions, see Hogan and Pandit. The following analyses will often refer to normative goals as *themes*. It is important to note this, given the broad range of uses of the term in narrative study (see Pyrhönen "Thematic").

8. Genres are not confined to the class of universal prototypes. One can make a story from any causal trajectory of goal pursuit, and recurring patterns may arise within narrow cultural and historical limits. It appears, however, that the majority of literary stories treat a limited number of goals, and the trajectories of literary stories are far more likely to have some forms than others. (For the evidence of universal prototypes, see Hogan *The Mind* and *Affective*.) It is particularly important – for our understanding of literature and the human mind – to examine these prominent, cross-cultural patterns.

1. Simulation

1. See, for example, the discussions of deictic shift in Herman *Story Logic* and Stockwell; for an overview of the idea in narrative study, see Hanks.

2. This is commonly discussed under the label of "immersion" (see Schaeffer and Vultur) or "transportation" (see Green and Donahue) and is often treated in terms of simulation.

3. On our sensitivity to differences in "deictic centre," see, for example, Jeffries 149.

4. The following analysis of simulation, however, departs from Oatley's view as presented in some recent work. Specifically, the following analysis views fiction as simulation in the sense of counterfactual or hypothetical imagination. The point is that fictional experience is continuous with ordinary processes of imagination. In some of his work, Oatley takes up a different notion of simulation. In that account, simulation is a sort of practice, as with a flight simulator (see "The Mind's"). There may be ways in which reading fiction involves something like practice. But this is a different sense of the word "simulation," and it is important to keep these different senses distinct. (On the sense related to computer games and the like, as this bears on narrative study, see McMahan.)

5. More exactly, simulation is a variety of imagination in the ordinary language sense. In the next section, we will see that it may be distinguished from fantasy, another variety of imagination.

6. Taylor, Shawber, and Mannering note a parallel between this character autonomy and children's attitudes toward their imaginary friends (215). This nicely illustrates the process and suggests its cognitive breadth.

7. On the importance of preferred outcomes for readers' or viewers responses to stories, see Tan 98

8. For a lucid overview of some such discussions, see Gorman.

9. The evolutionary value of simulation is widely recognized, sometimes under different names ("imagination," "off-line processing," and so on). For discussions of this topic with particular relevance to literature, see Tooby and Cosmides, Mithen, and Hernadi. On the basic relations between fictional simulation and emotion, see particularly Tooby and Cosmides 8–9.

10. On the relation of Abhinavagupta's work to recent research on emotion and cognition, see Oatley "Suggestion" and citations.

11. Alternatively, in Klinger's terms, we might say that, in simulation, one at least attempts to be realistic rather than fanciful (see 226).

12. Character autonomy is perhaps clearest when one author takes up an earlier author's characters. For instance, Huisman notes that, when a new head writer is brought in to a soap opera, he or she faces the problem that "many of the show's viewers have a better sense of who the show's characters are and what is plausible to happen to them" ("Soap Operas" 184). In an amusing instance of this, Nikolai Gogol wrote in his preface to *Dead Souls* that "it would be an excellent thing if someone who is endowed with the faculty of imagining and vividly picturing to himself the various situations wherein a character may be placed, and of mentally following up a character's career ... would scan each character herein portrayed, and tell me how each character ought to have acted at a given juncture." This is, of course, ironic, as few readers have simulative capacities equal to Gogol's, thus their "corrections" are likely to be misguided. Nevertheless, the crucial point for our purposes is that corrections can in principle be perfectly reasonable. This is because simulation is normatively constrained by properties of the characters (and situations) simulated, whether in real, practical simulation or literary imagination.

13. The particularity of experience, and the resulting individuality of human brains and minds, has been stressed especially by Edelman.

14. Recently, neuroscientists have become very enthusiastic about the idea that episodic memories are recruited for our anticipation of the future (see Schacter and Addis; Addis and colleagues; Schacter, Addis, and Buckner; Szpunar and McDermott). Work on this topic is certainly important. However, it should not come as a great surprise, despite the claims of researchers such as Schacter and Addis that "a function of memory that has been overlooked until recently concerns its role in allowing individuals to imagine or simulate possible future events" (S108). In fact, in general terms, nothing could be more commonplace than the idea that we rely on the past to imagine the future. This is, after all, the basis of inductive reasoning, our primary way of anticipating the future. On the other hand, research by Schacter and others makes the connections of memory with simulation precise and rigorous, and that is the crucial point. One part of this precision and rigor involves

the observation that people may take past experiences and modify them in limited ways to simulate the future (see Gamboz and colleagues). This is particularly true for near future events. Something along these lines is undoubtedly a frequent occurrence in literary simulation. The idea is in keeping with the view, developed in the following pages, that broad goals are largely defined by prototypes, whereas particular, ongoing (thus "near future") details are a function of simulation that relies on episodic (and emotional) memories.

15. On this distinction, see for example Gazzaniga 173–178. In fact, many accounts of theory of mind assumed that simulation itself was effortful and even inferential, if not precisely theoretical. Wojciehowski and Gallese point this out and develop an account of spontaneous simulative response based on bodily mirroring, crucially including bodily mirroring derived from literary imagination.

16. The general model here involves task conflict interrupting spontaneous or default processes and leading to effortful processing. This is in keeping with neurological research suggesting that anterior cingulate cortex monitors for such conflict and activates a working memory response (see MacDonald and colleagues, Lieberman and Eisenberger, and Kondo and colleagues).

17. The general point is made by a number of writers. See, for example, Myers and Hodges (289).

18. In keeping with both points, according to research reported by Stein and Kissel, "Both children and adults use their knowledge of stories to create fantasies … and plan for future interaction" (569). Although I am developing the idea differently, I draw the basic notion of a fantasy structure from Norman Holland's valuable *Dynamics of Literary Response*.

19. We will consider the nature of these particular prototypes in Chapter 2.

20. For a fuller, but still accessible example, see Goldblum 79–82.

21. Technically, in a PDP account, ideas themselves are distributed across units. However, adhering strictly to the distributive requirement here would complicate the exposition without enhancing the analysis.

22. In the larger context of the work as a whole, such guidance should not be surprising. The novel includes many biblical references, as even a quick look at Minter's annotations shows (see Mintner 38, 51, 56, 60, 64, 65, 74, 108, 109, 110, 111, 112, 139, 154, 184, 185). In a rather broad way, critics have noted "the Christian symbolism of the Passion Week … in the church service" (Porter 49) but with little recognition of the relevance of the resurrection to Quentin and her flight from home.

23. Lisa Zunshine established Austen as a figure of particular genius in portraying the operation of theory of mind. More recently, Kay Young has explored details of character imagination in Austen. Young's reading of Emma's imagination is particularly germane here (see 29–50). Young takes up some of the very broad issues that I have set aside in favor of a more detailed analysis of particular mechanisms. She also does a valuable job of relating earlier critical views of *Emma* to a neuroscientifically inflected approach.

24. The point applies most obviously to remembering the gist of a conversation, as opposed to the exact words. But it also bears on the inclusion of associated extrinsic information (which may, of course, be false) in relation to supposed memories of exact words. See, for example, Baddeley ("Episodic" 94–95) on the interference of schematic knowledge with recall of what one has read.

25. Mirroring is, roughly, the implicit, neurological imitation of other people's actions or expressions. It often involves a spontaneous, parallel emotional response to another person's emotion expressions, perceived or imagined – for example, feeling sad on seeing a sorrowful face. On mirroring and theory of mind simulation for literature, see Wojciehowski and Gallese.

2. Story Development, Literary Evaluation, and the Place of Character

1. For example, certain scripts for activity types (such as going on a date) will enter locally as the story develops. (On activity types, see Culpeper and McIntyre.) Although we will not be examining such scripts, they play a significant role throughout narrative particularization.
2. Here, as elsewhere, this is a stipulative definition, a statement of how the term will be used in the following pages. The use of the word *motif* in narrative study is quite diverse (see Würzbach).
3. The point is in keeping with empirical research on creative processes. See, for example, Locher on sketching as "a cyclical, dialectic process that results in the continuous emergence of ... reinterpretations of a potential design" (139).
4. For a fuller discussion of these points, see Hogan *The Mind* and *Affective Narratology*.
5. The greater variability of the minor genres may be connected with their less frequent repetition as the main story structure, particularly in canonical works (as opposed to more ephemeral and less continuously familiar works). Frequency of retelling tends to promote at least some degree of convergence. We see this most clearly in the case of particular stories in the oral tradition (see Phillips 31 on variation and convergence in more or less frequently told parts of a west Sumatran oral epic).
6. This division is not intended to isolate some absolute essences, but merely to clarify in a practical way the main sorts of development that contribute to the particularizing simulation of stories.
7. See Rubin 30 and citations for examples.
8. For example, Propp 79–83.
9. Circumstances are usually a matter of other characters.
10. The points here most importantly concern hypothetical stories. The situation is different with stories that we see as already determined by facts (e.g., when we know what policy decisions were made and we are trying to infer the agents' motives).
11. For some relevant research, see Mitchell and colleagues 77; Ito and colleagues 193, 196; and Kunda 324–325.
12. See, for example, John Holland and colleagues 223–224.
13. For example, in romantic plots, the first category commonly includes the lovers' forbidding parents or other blocking characters, while the lovers themselves commonly fall into the second category. On this distinction, see Hogan *The Mind* 205–217.
14. This leads to the recurring tendency to undermine villainy (see Hogan *The Mind* 144–147).
15. For a discussion of these concepts, see Hogan *Colonialism* 9–17.
16. On the extent and depth of readers' fascination with Hamlet, see for example Lamont.

17. For a detailed discussion of authorial receptive intent, see Chapter 1 of Hogan *Narrative*.

18. Proust expresses the point well when he presents one of his characters as hearing her own speech "with the mind" of those to whom she was speaking (139). The sensitivity of this particular character is only a more intensified version of a generally shared property.

19. Of course, it can be self-conscious. However, in those cases, it may be more likely to become mechanical and imitative. This is at least in part because unselfconscious cases usually involve complexes of evaluative instances, whereas self-conscious cases may be singular. An unusually explicit – and mechanical/imitative – case may be found in Marcel's relation to Bergotte (Proust 118).

3. A Narrative Idiolect

1. This is one difference between cognitive science and certain forms of structuralism. The sorts of examination undertaken by Claude Lévi-Strauss in his *Introduction to a Science of Mythology* (e.g., in volume one, *The Raw and the Cooked*) are an important influence on the literary analyses undertaken here and in Chapter 4. However, the analyses of Shakespeare and Racine explore the particularity of specific authors. In addition, the mental architectures of cognitive science are very different from those assumed by structuralists.

2. Part of the reason for this judgment is that the critic in question is searching for "a formula which fits every one of Shakespeare's tragedies and distinguishes them collectively from those of other dramatists" (1). That is different from the present concern for isolating idiolectal, generative principles, the use of which need not be entirely identical from work to work.

3. Critics do sometimes depart from the standard genres, particularly in discussing individual plays. For example, Miyashita insightfully discusses the combination of romantic and familial structures in *Twelfth Night*. Moreover, critics are often aware of the arbitrariness of the division, particularly in exploring thematic concerns, such as the relation to authority (see, for example, Hattaway 104). The traditional genres nonetheless persist as the fundamental way of organizing Shakespeare's canon.

4. Here the example of linguistics is instructive. If we analyze English grammar in isolation, it is likely to appear much more complex, much more a matter of arbitrary and diverse rules, than if we analyze it in the context of universal grammar, specified through the setting of parameters (on the Chomskyan idea of parameters in universal grammar, see Belletti and Rizzi). We simply miss things about particulars – especially the patterns into which they fall – when we fail to recognize their relation to universals.

5. This is not to say that it is impossible to make significant observations about tragedy as such. McAlindon notes that "Shakespeare seeks to render the brutal actions of the noble hero ... potentially forgivable" by "often" making "the fatal act ... unpremeditated and rash" (11). This almost certainly constituted a generative principle in Shakespeare's narrative idiolect. So too was "the final restoration of the protagonist's nobility ... by the manner in which he meets death" (15).

6. Moreover, the phrasing here almost suggests a sense of trajectory of the sort we will consider in the Chapter 4 with respect to Racine.

7.   For examples and further analysis, see Hogan *Understanding Nationalism*.

8.   The general point has not been lost on Shakespeareans. For example, it bears on Ebihara's contention that criticism of Tudor political doctrine is central to Shakespeare's dramas (Ebihara). More recently, Stephen Greenblatt has argued that "in Shakespeare *no* character with a clear moral vision has a will to power and, conversely, no character with a strong desire to rule over others has an ethically adequate object" (*Shakespeare's Freedom* 78). However, as far as I am able to ascertain, this thematic recognition has not been linked to the details of Shakespeare's idiolectal heroic prototype and development principles, thus the specific recurring patterns in his story structures.

9.   Although speaking more generally, and in a different analytic context, Bill Rosen made a related point about "opposing values" in Shakespeare's works (147; see also Kiernan 206 and 219).

10. This is not to say that they do not produce unequivocal preferences in individual readers. They often do. This is true for two reasons. First, it is part of our emotional makeup that ambivalent inputs tend to produce singular emotional outputs (see Ito and Cacioppo 69). More important, many readers are simply not emotionally sensitive to some of the complexities in Shakespeare's works. For example, when reading *King Lear*, my (American) students seem to have no sense of the horror of a foreign invasion. They do not feel a sense of conflict between England and France. They are numb to the fact that talk of a French invasion was so threatening at Shakespeare's time, it probably gave rise to censorship of the play (see Weis 28).

11. The difference of this play has been noticed by critics. For example, Greenblatt comments that "*Henry V* is probably the closest Shakespeare ever came to representing the authority of the ruler as divinely sanctioned" (*Shakespeare's Freedom* 79). He qualifies this by reference to subsequent history, cited in the play's epilogue. But the misfortunes of Henry VI's rule do not suggest any serious questioning of the nationalism presented in this play itself.

12. Despite this, even writers who look for ambiguity and irony often do not come up with much. For example, Khan focuses on "ambivalence" in the play (51) but only finds brief moments of uncertainty in a work that, as he puts it, "unashamedly undertakes to be simple and naïve" (64). Mason makes a more extended case, but it is difficult to imagine audience members taking the play to show "the brutal reality of war" (185) in a way that does not simply blame the enemy for the brutality. For example, she writes that the audience is invited "to note the terrible inappropriateness of the position of a child in war" (188). But it seems much more likely that the French killing of the boys would be viewed as evidence of French perfidy, at least by Shakespeare's own audience. Finally, some critics have focused on the fact that we learn about Henry's killing of the French prisoners a few seconds before we learn about the French killing of the boys. But this is not really a problem. One only needs to assume, quite reasonably, that Henry knew about the boys before we did.

13. Although treated in very different contexts, the ambivalence of the play has been recognized for quite some time. As early as 1968, René Fortin argued that the "focal point of recent studies of *Julius Caesar* has been the very ambivalence of a play which has allowed for such contradictory responses" (341).

14. In Berys Gaut's terminology, our alignment leads to something like "epistemic identification," which "has a tendency to foster empathy" (210).

15. In keeping with this, Miles sees Brutus as "Caesar's mirror-image" (134). Along the same lines, Girard discusses the ways in which "Brutus unconsciously turns into a second Caesar" (109). More generally, Rebhorn argues that the assassination of Caesar "is carried out by individuals whose actions are presented in the play in exactly the same way" as those of Caesar (29). Rebhorn convincingly ties Shakespeare's development of this point to the historical condition of English political economy at the time.

16. Kiernan rightly emphasizes the rhetorical function of the scene as impugning the characters of the triumvirs (see 59).

17. As the preceding comments suggest, the crucial matter determining tragic outcomes in Shakespeare's heroic plays is violence. These outcomes are more commonly understood in terms of Renaissance ideas concerning ambition. For example, Watson writes that "the desire to transcend oneself, to become something greater than one was born to be, is a natural and seemingly noble human tendency; yet it becomes a means of self-destruction, a betrayal of nature and origins that invites primal punishment" (162). It is undeniable that issues of ambition are of central importance in Shakespeare's works. However, what generates heroic tragedy is not, it seems, ambition per se but violence – specifically, murder. This view is supported by the fact that the terrible, cyclic effects of violence are apparent in both of Watson's types of tragedies (those of ambition and those of revenge). Perhaps more important, it is supported by the existence of a late heroic comedy, *The Tempest*. In this play, it appears that tragic outcomes are avoided not by the absence of ambition (which is ubiquitous in the play) but by the eschewal of violence in favor of forgiveness and empathy, and by the absence of murder. We will consider these points below in the section on *The Tempest*.

18. The accusation against Richard is unproven in the play. Although it may be historically accurate, its uncertainty in the text itself is what is most crucial here. For discussion, see Watts "Who."

19. Given that a conflict of values is explicit in the play, it is unsurprising that this has been recognized by critics. For example, Siemon, in a Bakhtinian context, writes that the play involves "multiple and overlapping commitments that are not easily ... ranked on any single ladder of hierarchy" (220).

20. Critics have remarked generally on the split in Catholic and Protestant ideas on this topic, drawing various conclusions (see, for example, Pearlman 81–82). Watts's treatment is lucid and thorough (see "Where"). Of course, the most developed and influential treatment of the issue of purgatory in *Hamlet* is Greenblatt's (*Hamlet*).

21. A number of critics have commented on the parallel between Hamlet and Claudius in this regard. See, for example, Westlund 246. Kastan applies the point to the perennial dilemma of Hamlet's inaction, explaining that revenge "makes action problematic" for "it duplicates the crime" ("His Semblable" 199).

22. For example, as critics such as Foakes have pointed out, Claudius's reaction to *The Mousetrap* is open to different explanations and hardly provides the definitive proof claimed by Hamlet. As Hawkes puts it, "*The Mousetrap* doesn't work very effectively" (183). See also Kastan "His Semblable" 204.

23. For a discussion of this topic, see Kiernan 68–69.

24. As Levin points out, even "maintaining ... positive feelings for Hamlet is no simple task" (218).

25. As Ferguson indicates, this murder, which substitutes for Claudius's planned murder of Hamlet, furthers the parallel between Hamlet and Claudius. This is particularly true as it is based on "the power to kill and … the tendency to justify killing with lines of argument unavailable to lesser men" (Ferguson 146).

26. Hamlet praises Fortinbras for his military violence. However, as Westlund points out, he does so "in such a way as to stress the emptiness and horror" of Fortinbras's actions (246).

27. In a cross-culturally common pattern, Shakespeare frequently combines heroic and romantic plots, not only in the plays just mentioned but also in more consistently heroic dramas, such as *Hamlet*.

28. The political and social value of not killing may seem uncontroversial, but it is not. For example, Machiavelli downplayed the significance of murder relative to property crimes, claiming that "men are quicker to forget the death of a father than the loss of a patrimony" (66).

29. See, for example, the essays in Graff and Phelan 202–322 and citations.

30. One might even return here to Prospero's line regarding Caliban, "This thing of darkness I/Acknowledge mine" (V.i.275–276). Leslie Fiedler has argued that the placement of the line break ("This thing of darkness I") briefly suggests that the thing of darkness is "I," the speaker, Prospero (249). He goes on to argue that, even when the sentence is completed, there is at least a partial identification of the two (249–250).

31. Broadly similar points have been made by other critics. For example, Kiernan Ryan refers to "the renouncing of dominion and aggression in favor of empathy and concession" (149) with "closure in forgiveness, restitution and renewal" (155). From a rather different political perspective, Felperin argues that postcolonial critiques of the play have ignored Shakespeare's larger criticism of oppression. Although Felperin may overstate the cruelty ended by Prospero, he is, it seems, correct in recognizing that the political aim of the play is not to justify colonialism but to criticize something more encompassing.

4. Principles and Parameters of Storytelling

1. Of course, simulation may diverge extensively and radically from reality, as we see from fantasy literature. Indeed, this can occur even with a single change – as in the Miltonic idea of creatures that do not have fixed sex, but "when they please/Can either Sex assume, or both" (*Paradise Lost* I.423–424).

2. In mathematics, parameters are "those aspects of the function that are held constant when defining a particular function, but which can vary in a larger context so as to characterize a family of similar functions" (Baker "Parameters" 582). This entails a technical distinction between parameters (which vary across a family of functions) and variables (which vary for a particular function). With respect to the analysis of narrative idiolects, however, the distinction is rarely consequential; indeed, it rarely has clear correlates. Therefore, the terms *parameter* and *variable* will for the most part be used interchangeably in the following pages. On the other hand, as will become clear, some variables have far more extensive and significant consequences than others. For example, the parameter of a character's sex has consequences for many more local variables about that character.

3. For a lucid introduction to principles and parameters theory, see Baker *The Atoms of Language*.

4. As this suggests, the parameters in narrative idiolects are not generally innate. To take a very simple example, one set of variables in an author's idiolectal romantic prototype might be, roughly, "Hero has a [male] rival/hero does not have a [male] rival." Here "[male]" refers to an assumption that is not open to variation. However, the possible values might be readily changed to, "Hero has/does not have a male/female rival." Thus "male" may be parameterized, changed from constant to variable.

5. Some of the constancy and variability will be due to exempla as well. I leave these aside in part for clarity of exposition, but for other reasons as well. First, exempla are biographical and difficult to discern and apply outside a biographical study. Second, they are generally less germane to thematic interpretation or audience response. Finally, an author's exempla are random, a matter of what he or she happens to encounter at a particular time. In consequence, they are not part of a relatively systematic trajectory of development, which is the concern of the present chapter.

6. I will leave aside Racine's comedy, *Les Plaideurs*, and his two final plays. It seems clear that *Les Plaideurs* is generically unrelated and thus should not be included. As to the others, the nine plays from *La Thébaïd* through *Phèdre* were written over the course of about a dozen years and show clear continuities. The two final plays, however, were written after a hiatus of about a dozen years and are quite different from the preceding works. The division is recognized by Racine scholars (see, for example, Heyndels on the reasonableness of giving *Esther* and *Athalie* separate treatment from the rest of Racine's plays [157]; see also Berthelot on separating *Les Plaideurs* and the two late plays from the "profane tragedies" [11]).

7. The political power of women has been an important topic of analysis in Racine criticism. These studies do not seem to pay much attention to the sorts of cognitive concerns at issue here. Rather, they tend to be historically oriented, locating Racine in the context of broader political and social trends in the period (see, for example, Derval Conroy). A fuller treatment of Racine's tragedies would, of course, seek to integrate the two approaches. For instance, the operation of a gender parameter might be fruitfully integrated with Desnain's insights on the historical and cultural details of women's "struggle to find a place in a world order which continually works at keeping them down" (ix).

8. In keeping with the arguments of Chapter 2, the following analyses presuppose that character is, in general, singularly important in particularizing prototypes. Thus the following analyses focus on character variations. However, scene is far from insignificant, as some critical work suggests (see Barthes 3–5 and Maskell).

9. Blanc nicely summarizes a number of other attempts to explain the "coherence" of Racine's works. However insightful, they are largely limited in the same general ways. For example, Daniel Hubert sees each work as organized around "a fundamental image" (Blanc 586). Georges Poulet, treating the "time consciousness" of the works, finds a recurring desire to return to the beginning, a goal rendered impossible by the weight of evil from the past (Blanc 586).

10. *La Thébaïd* concerns the conflict between the brothers Étéocle and Polynice over the throne of Thebes. Their mother, Jocaste, and sister, Antigone, seek to reconcile

them. However, their uncle, Créon, plots for his own advancement. Antigone's lover, Hémon, is the son of Créon. Despite this, Créon has designs on Antigone as well. The brothers kill one another; Hémon is killed when trying to stop them. Antigone commits suicide, after which Créon commits suicide as well.

11. In the title of this chapter, I refer to Racine's various plays as "romantic" because they all include a romantic story; however, as this indicates, they are not confined to romance.

12. On the other hand, the conjunction is not surprising or unique. We find examples outside Racine's work – for instance, the character of Sabine in Pierre Corneille's *Horace*. Here, as elsewhere, we would expect the components of narrative idiolects – and even some configurations of components – to recur across different writers.

13. This is consistent with general critical views. As Tobin notes, "Most readers familiar with Racine's major plays conclude that *La Thébaïd* is not the equal of other Racinian tragedies" (33). However, see Blanc for a much more positive evaluation of that play (115).

14. *Alexandre le Grand* treats the invasion of India by Alexander the Great. Two Indian kings, Porus and Taxile, face him. In addition, both are in love with Axiane, who favors Porus. Porus remains loyal to India, while Taxile is convinced to collaborate with Alexandre, with whom his sister (Cléofile) is romantically involved. Porus kills Taxile in combat. Alexandre, although victorious, withdraws, leaving Porus his kingdom and allowing Porus and Axiane to be united.

15. The phrasing of this motif is likely to recall writers such as Propp. This is because such separable motifs are the sorts of element commonly isolated by folklorists – sometimes cross-culturally, sometimes for a particular tradition. Also, in keeping with Proppian analysis, this motif is not unique to Racine. There are, for example, two false reports of death in Pierre Corneille's *Le Cid*, and there is a false report of survival in his *Horace*.

16. The complexity of characterization in the play has been recognized by critics, although in a different theoretical context. For example, Forestier notes the integration of seemingly opposed character traits, often related to different dramatic traditions (18) – a valuable perspective that complements the one presented here.

17. *Andromaque* takes place in the aftermath of the Trojan War. Hector's widow, Andromaque, and her son, Astyanax, are prisoners of Pyrrhus. Formerly in love with Hermione, Pyrrhus has now shifted his feelings to Andromaque, leading to terrible jealousy on the part of Hermione. Oreste is in love with Hermione. He has been charged by the Greek leadership with taking Astyanax from Andromaque to be killed. Andromaque agrees to wed Pyrrhus in order to protect her son. To please Hermione, Oreste agrees to kill Pyrrhus. After the murder, however, Hermione rejects Oreste and commits suicide. Andromaque ascends the throne.

18. This is her "so true incoherence" pointed out by Blanc (147). It is worth noting here that Corneille's Chimène (in *Le Cid*) is almost certainly a significant influence on Racine's Hermione. However, Chimène's divided relation to D. Rodrigue is largely developed as a conflict between feeling and duty. In contrast, Hermione's response to Pyrrhus is much more clearly a matter of genuine emotional ambivalence.

19. Thus Desnain rightly notes that Andromaque's "power stems from the men she has married" (32), but it is important to stress that the power continues after Pyrrhus's death.

20. A good example of how mastery involves enhanced parameterization may be found in the production of oral poetry. Phillips points out that skilled bards of Minangkabau (West Sumatra) acquire "over the years, an ability to vary expression by substituting alternative words within the same grammatical framework" (168). This is a process of turning fixed components of expressions into variable or parametric components. Lord makes a similar point about Yugoslav bards (36–37).

21. *Britannicus* concerns the Roman emperor Néron; his brother, Britannicus, who should be emperor; and Junie, loved by both brothers but reciprocating only the love of Britannicus. Other characters include Agrippine, the mother of Néron and stepmother of Britannicus, as well as Burrhus and Narcisse, advisers to Néron and Britannicus respectively. Néron kills Britannicus, in part due to the machinations of Narcisse. Junie takes refuge in a shrine, while Narcisse is killed by the crowd protecting her.

22. Tobin points out that "there was no one like Junie in the history of Néron's reign" (70). An understanding of Racine's idiolectal generation of stories helps clarify why Racine introduced and how he developed this nonhistorical character.

23. Blanc rightly observes that it is part of "Racine's genius" to integrate the "love intrigue" with the "history" by "making Néron and Britannicus rivals" (167). In this case, that "genius" is precisely the idiolectal operation of his generation of narratives.

24. *Bérénice* concerns the reciprocal love between Bérénice, queen of Palestine, and the Roman emperor Titus, a love that comes into conflict with Roman society. It also treats the unrequited love of Antiochus – a Middle Eastern king and friend of Titus – for Bérénice. Eventually, all the lovers are separated.

25. *Bajazet* takes place in the sultan's court at Constantinople. While the sultan, Amurat, is away, Roxane – his "favorite" (II: 10) – rules. Roxane has fallen in love with Amurat's brother, Bajazet. However, Bajazet is in love with Atalide. The love triangle is complicated further by an order from Amurat to kill Bajazet. Eventually, Roxane, having learned of Bajazet's love for Atalide, has Bajazet killed. However, Amurat, learning of Roxane's relationship to Bajazet, has Roxane killed as well. Atalide commits suicide. The vizier, Acomat, who has contributed to the intrigues, leads an unsuccessful uprising that briefly interrupts the killings.

26. In *Mithridate*, King Mithridate has left his kingdom for battle, having named Monime as queen, though they are not yet married. Mithridate's two sons, Pharnace and Xipharès, have fallen in love with Monime, who in turn loves Xipharès. While Pharnace has traitorous tendencies, Xipharès is loyal to his father and his homeland against their enemy, the Romans. When the news arrives that Mithridate has died, the brothers both pursue Monime. However, it turns out that the news was false and Mithridate returns. He eventually learns about Xipharès's and Monime's shared love. Xipharès flees, and Mithridate condemns Monime to death. Meanwhile, Pharnace joins the Romans to attack Mithridate, who stabs himself when defeat seems inevitable. Unbeknownst to Mithridate, Xipharès has been fighting against the Romans. He eventually wins. Before he dies, Mithridate, realizing Xipharès's loyalty, reverses his condemnation of the lovers (barely in time to save Monime's life) and blesses their union.

27. Actually, the case of Créon is ambiguous between the two types. Nonetheless, as these cases suggest, suicide is closely interrelated with gender in Racine's idiolect,

with sacrificial suicide linked to men and despairing suicide strongly connected with women.

28. This was a "more or less" fixed value because of the ambiguity in Créon's suicide, which had elements of romantic despair. I have been speaking as if there is only parameterization following a fixed value. However, a more likely scenario in many cases is that there is, initially, no control of a particular property. The property may then become a fixed value. Finally, the fixed value may be parameterized. Thus, at the time of *La Thébaïd*, there may have been no gender/suicide connection in Racine's idiolect. This lack of connection changed to a fixed value with the plays that followed. That fixed value was disrupted by the large-scale gender parameterizations that occurred with the reconfiguration underlying *Bajazet*.

29. *Iphigénie* takes place when the Greek army is stranded, unable to leave to fight the Trojan War. The priest, Calchas, has divined that they will only be able to depart when Iphigénie is sacrificed. Agamemnon has therefore sent for his daughter, Iphigénie, to come to the camp, telling her she is to be married to Achille. Subsequently, Agamemnon changes his mind and sends a message that Iphigénie should not come as Achille has fallen in love with Ériphile, a captive of unknown origins. Iphigénie does not receive the letter and arrives with her mother Clytemnestre – and Ériphile, who wishes to learn about her parentage. In fact, Achille does love Iphigénie, although Ériphile loves Achille. Achille and Agamemnon try to save Iphigénie but are thwarted, in part due to their betrayal by Ériphile. Ultimately, it is discovered that Ériphile was formerly named *Iphigénie*. She then sacrifices herself.

30. Blanc makes a similar point (213).

31. This is not to say that the play is comic. However, this ambivalence does suggest some reasons why critics have on occasion argued that the play cannot really be classed as tragedy. For a nuanced discussion of this issue, in relation to concerns with the condition of women particularly, see Chapter 2 of Desnain.

32. Indeed, the masterpiece of the period (see Blanc 251).

33. *Phèdre* concerns the love of Phèdre for her stepson, Hippolyte. Hearing that her husband, King Thésée, has died while away, Phèdre confesses her love to Hippolyte. However, Hippolyte loves the disenfranchised princess, Aricie, who is forbidden to marry as she is the descendent of a rival household. It turns out that the king has not been killed and he returns. Phèdre's nurse, Oenone, seeking to protect Phèdre, misinforms Thésée about the events, claiming that Hippolyte pursued Phèdre. In a fury, Thésée curses Hippolyte. On his way to marry Aricie, Hippolyte is killed by a sea monster. Phèdre confesses her guilt and kills herself, having rejected Oenone, who also commits suicide.

34. The connection between a (false) report of death and the revelation of love is not unique to Racine. It is found, for example, in Corneille's *Le Cid*. In *Le Cid*, however, it appears in a form that is dramatically limited. There it serves as a device by which a brief misunderstanding enables the final union of the lovers.

35. This obvious parallel has been noted by critics (see, for example, Blanc 197).

36. This is in some ways analogous to the disruption of a stable system, when the "system is 'shocked' by briefly introducing a random element (noise)," after which the system "settles into a new configuration" (Ball 309). Of course, the change in an author's work is not random. But it is anomalous with respect to the previous configuration and in any case has the effect of "shocking" the system. For example, in

the case just given, this would be due to the extensive and strong connections of gender with other principles. In terms of PDP analysis, Goldblum points out that habitual associations form "'attractors' in our mental networks." In other words "some patterns of activity ... have become so greatly strengthened by repeated use that any new incoming information that sufficiently resembles our old knowledge is treated as if it were exactly the same as what we already know" (112). Gender divisions are undoubtedly primary "attractors." One "way of getting out of 'attractor' patterns is by a radical shift in perspective" (113). Goldblum mentions shifting parent and child roles. Shifting gender roles fits the point perfectly.

37. A shift in configuration may be viewed as a parameterization of a metaprinciple. However, speaking of reconfiguration emphasizes the underlying neural network, thus the broadly systemic – distributed and parallel – quality of the change.

5. Argument and Metaphor in Brecht and Kafka

1. The target is what one is characterizing through the use of the metaphor or more exactly the metaphorical source. For instance, in "Smith was a cornered rat," Smith is the target that we are characterizing by way of the metaphorical source, "cornered rat."

2. Perhaps unsurprisingly, there does not seem to be any criticism on either work treating simulation in the technical, cognitive sense. There is, however, some cognitively informed writing on other topics, treating different works from those considered here (see for example Gobert on Brecht's *The Caucasian Chalk Circle*).

3. This play is widely seen as Brecht's first fully Communist work. For a discussion of the play as it emerges from Brecht's earlier work, see Chapter 1 of Mittenzwei.

4. These facts suggest that Brecht would not merely have conjectured negative consequences to Stalin's China policy, as Horn indicates (50). The policies had already proven themselves to be a failure. This makes it even more implausible that Brecht "implicitly took Stalin's standpoint" on China (50).

5. On the topic of party discipline in the play and in relation to Stalin's emphases at the time, see Horn; see also Schumacher 364. For Brecht's own account of the play in terms of party discipline, see Steinweg *Das Lehrstück* 31.

6. The "teaching of the classics" that bears most directly on spontaneism is Lenin's *What Is to Be Done?* It is worth noting that Lenin connects spontaneist deviation with the "young" activists (38), which bears on the "young comrade" in an obvious way.

7. On voluntarism, see, for example, Lukács *History* 4, 124, 134, 191, 318, and 322.

8. These included the 1930 "increase in votes ... to 6½ million," making the Nazis "the second largest party in the Reichstag" (Noakes and Pridham 70). For an overview of this development, see Caplan.

9. In Horn's account, Brecht is criticizing Stalin's "destruction of internal party democracy." However, he is doing it in a "dialectical" manner.

10. For example, the word "*Maßnahme*" in the title of the play refers most obviously to the killing of the young comrade by the agitators, as signaled by the title of the eighth scene ("Die Maßnahme"), in which that killing occurs. But it refers also to "the measures of the Communist party," "die Maßnahmen der Kommunistischen Partei" (257).

11. See Hogan *Affective* 229–233.
12. Perhaps the best-known cases of this are the films of Sergei Eisenstein from the period just before Brecht wrote *Die Maßnahme*, a period when Eisenstein rejected "the individualist conception of the bourgeois hero" (16).
13. It is important that the version published in Soviet Union did not include a decision by the agitators. Rather, the young comrade devises the plan for his death and asks for the agreement of the agitators (Steinweg *Bertolt Brecht* 99). Presumably, this change reflects a feeling on the part of Soviet authorities that the decision of the agitators was treated at least equivocally, perhaps even critically, in Brecht's original play.
14. The point is developed by Esslin, who links the play with "the great confession trials of the Stalinist era" and characterizes the work as "the only great tragedy on the moral dilemma of Soviet Communism" (140). Esslin notes that this shows foresight on Brecht's part, but the point is not as surprising as it may seem. As long as Stalin's dictatorial tendencies were clear, it should have been easy to predict (or infer) Inquisition-like practices on his part. Indeed, Bertrand Russell saw this even before Stalin, in his 1920 treatment of Bolshevism. A parallel point holds for the development of a rigid bureaucracy – arguably what we find in the Control Chorus. Indeed, the development of such a rigid bureaucracy was identified and criticized at least as early as 1925 by Trotsky (see Mandel 137n.6). Other critics recognize the general connection, although they do not necessarily take Brecht as critical of coerced confession (see, for example, Fuegi 248).
15. Some critics have recognized at least an element of this. For example, Motoyama points out that "the Young Comrade may be viewed ... as a sacrificial scapegoat" (49). The analysis of Rienäcker suggests that the connection is enhanced by resonances of the play's music.
16. A sense of this may be what led Motoyama to point out a possible sacrificial view of the young comrade but simultaneously say that such a view would be "mistaken" (49).
17. To avoid misunderstanding, I should perhaps note that Brecht does not present in any way a compelling case that empathic feeling leads to a sense of inevitability. Indeed, this is a rather implausible claim.
18. As blending theorists have stressed, there are cases where we cannot really speak of one item as the source and one as the target. This is true and important. However, I would not count these as cases of modeling. For example, "If Brecht had debated Bertrand Russell, Russell would have won" does not have a source and a target. But it is also not a model. (On blending theory, see Fauconnier and Turner.)
19. Clearly, the treatment of metaphor in this chapter agrees with the "conceptual metaphor" account of Lakoff and others in viewing metaphor as having cognitive consequences (see, for example, Lakoff and Johnson). However, the full algorithmic account of models and metaphors suggested by this chapter is much closer to the work of Johnson-Laird and Ortony. On the account of metaphor assumed here, see Hogan "Metaphor" and citations.
20. In contrast with the view presented here, a number of critics take Gregor's transformation as a (usually unconscious) choice (see Gross 89, Fuchs 37, and Sokel 28). Although Gross draws on biographical information about Kafka's relation to work, most conclusions of this sort rely on a psychoanalytic model. As commonly

invoked, that model leads to interpreting unconscious contents in terms of wishes, leading to the otherwise strange view that in some sense Gregor wants to be an insect. Further psychoanalytic elaborations of the novella may be found in the highly influential study of Kafka by Deleuze and Guattari and in Thiher.

21. It is possible that the model came first. However, it seems more likely that the experience of simulated shame provoked the model. In other words, it seems unlikely that the model would initiate such a forceful simulation of shame and humiliation, as recognized by Breen.

22. There may be a connection between the sacrificial ending and allusive aspects of the insect model. Specifically, we may distinguish between the usual semantic operation of the model and a more extended use of the source – a use that incorporates cultural developments of the image of the dung beetle. Thus Norman Holland ("Realism") discusses Egyptian associations and Leadbeater treats Greek connections. There are also possible etymological resonances (see Weinberg 316–317). The sacrificial narrative is implicitly recognized by the writers who link Gregor with Jesus (e.g., Holland "Realism"). Part of the disagreement over this identification (see Corngold "Explanatory" 63 and citations) comes from overemphasizing the particular Christian story rather than recognizing the general prototypical pattern.

23. Alternatively, he may be viewed as disabled. This is consistent with the main Yiddish source for the novella, as discussed by Beck (38–39).

24. The text goes on to say "or a foreigner" (72). There are hints that one of the local models Kafka drew on was the treatment of Jews and others who were considered alien and disgusting by many in the majority population. There are, of course, critical analyses of the work in relation to anti-Semitism and related issues. Some of these take up the insect metaphor, although toward different ends and typically with a theoretical approach very different from that adopted here (see, for example, Simon Ryan).

25. Witt suggests that there is a model of imprisonment at work in the novella. Witt's points are well taken. However, it seems that this is more immediately a matter of hospitalization.

26. Greve develops a suggestive interpretation of the story in relation to "the *temptation* of [mind/body] dualism" (53). A difficulty with Greve's argument is that the mind/body interrelation in the story seems clearly premised on there being a mind/body distinction of some sort. Given the operation of the models, however, the distinction need not entail dualism. After all, a stroke can prevent speech and movement without destroying consciousness or thought.

27. The different meanings of the term have been noted by other critics; see, for example, Fuchs 37.

28. Contrary to this view of Gregor's fundamental innocence, some critics have argued that Gregor suffers guilt. Because it is difficult to ascertain any such guilt, they often turn to psychoanalytic principles (e.g., his "withdrawal from the exacting genital position" [Kaiser 150]). Recognition of the genre prototype – along with its commonly innocent sacrificial victim – may have made this inclination to find guilt less pressing.

29. Other critics have noted the relation to dreams (see, for example, Sokel 38). However, they have not taken this up as a cognitive model. Rather, they tend to

have seen this connection as supporting a psychoanalytic reading (e.g., in terms of wish fulfillment). There has been some disagreement on whether the story is a dream (see Corngold 68 and citations). In part, this disagreement can be resolved by understanding the operation of modeling.

6. Emplotment

1. *Hamlet* has obviously generated a vast amount of criticism. (For a brave attempt to overview this criticism, see Wofford.) However, I have not located work focusing on the discourse structure of the play. There is criticism that addresses "plot" in the Aristotelian sense of the action; however, in our terms, that is the story. For example, in his discussion of plot, Bowers addresses "what is the true turning-point of the action" (208), but he does not address what distinguishes the *telling* of that action. There is also work that treats narration embedded within the play (see, for example, Osborne; for broader treatments of embedded narration in Shakespeare's works, see McLuskie, Costigan, and Nünning and Sommer "Performative"). But that is a different topic from the narrational discourse of drama itself.

2. For a vigorous discussion of the details and subtleties of the mimetic/diegetic distinction, see Nünning and Sommer "Diegetic"; for further analysis of related points, see Fludernik "Narrative." I am grateful to Andrew Davis for drawing my attention to these essays.

3. On some of the complex ways in which a narrator or narrator-like elements enter drama, see Pfister 3–4 and 69–84.

4. See, for example, Richardson "Drama" and Jahn. In *Narrative Discourse*, I argue for conceptually distinguishing an encompassing, nonpersonified narrator as the source of the selected, organized, and construed information defining the plot. Clearly, this is not an argument that can be recapitulated here, in a chapter concerned with the particularization of plot. However, nothing in the following pages rests on that analysis. Readers who agree with Bordwell (*Narration*) in rejecting this idea of a narrator should feel free to follow Bordwell and substitute "narration" for "encompassing nonpersonified narrator." Readers who are simply uncomfortable with the term *narrator* may wish to follow Chatman or Bareis. Given that narrational functions are verbal in the case of prose fiction and partially nonverbal in the case of drama and film, Chatman proposes using the more general term *presenter*, rather than *narrator*, to cover both cases (115); similarly, Bareis proposes *mediator*.

5. Here, I am drawing on David Bordwell's phrase "intensified continuity," which he uses to characterize recent techniques in Hollywood filmmaking (see *The Way* 121–138).

6. Honigmann notes a similar phenomenon across plays, suggesting that this is an enduring property of Shakespeare's narrative idiolect. As Honigmann puts it, "Scenic development can be strangely similar" (176).

7. Both schemers and unobserved observers recur cross culturally. The former include Cāṇakya in Viśākhadatta's Sanskrit *Mudrārākṣasa* and Wang Yün in the Chinese Yüan drama *A Stratagem of Interlocking Rings*. Sanskrit works such as Bhāsa's *Svapnavāsavadattam* or Japanese works such as Chikamatsu's *Drum of the Waves of Horikawa* provide examples of unobserved observers.

8. The focus of the present chapter is discourse. However, an author's production of discourse is not entirely separate from his or her production of the story. Thus the discussion will necessarily make reference to the story from time to time (just as earlier chapters, which focused on story, necessarily made occasional reference to discourse).

9. On embedded narration, see Nelles.

10. As would be expected, the representation of espionage in the play points toward some historical considerations, which we will not be able to explore. For one suggestive discussion of relevant historical context, see Parker.

11. This occurs at the intersection of plot and narration in the sense that access to a character's inner thought is usually defined by the limits placed on the narrator's knowledge.

12. Plantinga suggests a more fine-grained set of distinctions (see the summary in *Moving* 69).

13. I use the phrase "story emotion," rather than "fiction emotion," since we have the same sort of emotional response to nonfictional stories.

14. See Vuust and Kringelbach, although they formulate the conclusion differently; for discussion, see Hogan "Stylistics."

15. Outside artifacts, we find this in facial beauty, as the most beautiful face is, roughly, the most average face (see Langlois and Roggman). In the case of artifacts, see Martindale and Moore and Whitfield and Slatter. The point is also suggested by Ramachandran's reflections on "peak shift" (in which an ordinary property or relation is enhanced, as in artistic representations of male or female bodies; recall that a prototype is a sort of weighted average).

16. This technique recurs elsewhere in Shakespeare's plays and in other works, as Brian Richardson has valuably discussed ("'Time'"). For a wide-ranging treatment of other aspects of time in drama, see chapter 7 of Pfister.

17. In cases such as this, we see an important, if somewhat obvious, emplotment device, not only in Shakespeare's works but almost everywhere else. This is the selective withholding of information crucial for understanding the story's main causal sequences. Following Sternberg, narratologists commonly refer to a narrator's provision or withholding of information as the narrator's *communicativeness*.

18. Technically, the play suggests that espionage is vitiated by confirmation bias, our tendency to take evidence in favor of our views as confirmatory while discounting evidence against our views as exceptions (see, for example, Nisbett and Ross 238–242).

19. More technically, he shows that he has not simulated the encompassing, nonpersonified narrator as limited to Hamlet in access to the internal states of characters.

20. Recall Levin's comment that "maintaining ... positive feelings for Hamlet is no simple task" (218).

21. As Frijda points out, "elicitation of emotion" is not only a function of current events but also of "the context of prevailing expectations" (280). The point is obvious in the very existence of emotions such as disappointment. One feels disappointed in, say, not winning the Nobel Peace Prize only if one had some anticipation or hope of winning. In the case of Ophelia, there is a stark contrast between her mentally disturbed state and our tacit expectations from previously seeing her. As to gradients of change, Ortony, Clore, and Collins refer to someone trying to make a

flight. In keeping with common intuitions, they explain that, if he "does not make his connection, the closer he gets to catching the plane the more intense will be his disappointment." Conversely, "if he does make it, the closer he thinks he came to missing it, the more intense the relief" (75; see also 64 and citations).

22. This section partially recapitulates points made in Chapter 3. It is important to recall them here in order to relate them to the play's emplotment, which of course was not treated in that chapter. As already noted, some of these interpretive claims have been urged by other critics. Thus, for example, Ferguson points out the parallel between Hamlet and Claudius (146), as do Westlund (246) and Kastan ("His Semblable" 199); Levin suggests the cultivation of ambivalence toward Hamlet (218), and so on. However, again, no one seems to have developed the points in relation to the play's discourse structure.

Afterword

1. Owing to reports of some confusion, acknowledged ("Dear Sir, I am painfully unable to make sense out of your gibberish. Recommending you to the good services of my literary namesake, I am, sincerely yours, H. Rumbold") and anonymous or pseudonymous ("To Professor Windbag," etc., etc., "Please return the purchase price," etc., etc., signed, "Bewildered in Dubuque"), the despairing author invited me to provide occasional scholarly commentary, highlighting and clarifying. Here, the reader needs to recall that "narration" refers to the other main component of discourse, along with plot (treated, as you recall, in Chapter 6). The burden of the present chapter is to maintain that narration too is a form of simulation with all the ordinary properties and purposes of said cognitive process. Signed, H. Windbag, Ph.D., F.R.C.S., L.H.O.O.Q.

2. In his queer and verbose fashion, the speaker is alluding to the fact that simulation mimics the neural activation of our actual perception but without external sensation – all explained perspicuously and perspicaciously in Chapter 1. The irony, of course, comes from the fact that, as a ghost, he has no brain at all and, as a simulation of a ghost, even less so. (H. Windbag, esq.)

3. The careful reader will note that this introduces the importance of prototypes for organizing narrational simulation in parallel with their importance for organizing story simulation (as treated in Chapter 1). (H. Windbag, Raja of Piplinagar)

4. The purpose of this elaboration is – I hardly need point it out, but the author has asked me to undertake just this sort of business – the purpose is to indicate that character and scene have the same particularizing role in narrational simulation as they do in story simulation (which you recall from Chapter 2). (H. Windbag, A.M., P.M.)

5. These last are, of course, the emotional and thematic purposes of literary simulation so emphasized by our pertinacious author and introduced, aptly, in the Introduction. (H. Windbag, Order of the Garter)

6. I take it that the obviousness of the continuity of narrational and story simulation here is, well, obvious. (H. Windbag, Apostolic Nuncio)

7. Here, we see the parallel between story and narrational simulation extended to argument (you recall that from Chapter 5). Can metaphorical modeling be far behind? (H. Windbag, B.C., A.D.)

8. What did I just tell you, about modeling? (H. Windbag, K.M.R.I.A.)
9. Unfortunately, Professor Windbag passed away before he could annotate the rela-
    tion of this to the earlier chapters. It seems to bear on Chapter 6 – but, to tell you
    the truth, I couldn't bring myself to read it. (I. Calvino)
10. 'Ere, I might draw your kind attention to wha' 'Erman says abou' apostrophe
    in second-person narratives in chapter 9 of *Story Logic*. As Abbott puts it, in
    "second-person narration … the narrating voice turn[s] its attention toward what
    is most likely the reader," thereby "extend[ing] the world of the narrative out into
    the world of the reader – i.e., incorporat[ing] the reader into the diegesis" (342).
    (H. Rumbold, master barber)
11. Our author here might be put in mind of Brian Richardson's comment that
    "Calvino's characteristic tone is … fully present even (or especially) in lines where
    he denies its existence. This is the Calvino we all recognize" (*Unnatural* 124). (I.
    Calvino, avid reader of Brian Richardson)
12. As Professor Windbag pointed out to me before his untimely and tragic demise (at
    the unsteady hands of some barber named Rumbold, who seems to have mistaken
    the poor fellow for yours truly), this is by no means to say Calvino never tried
    to narrate the resistance. There was *Il Sentiero dei Nidi di Ragno* (*The Path to the
    Spiders' Nests*). Critics even recognize a sort of unnarratability in that early book
    (see Markey 41). But this has only contributed to their sense that *Se una Notte* is
    a postmodern work that claims "reality" is something "fictitious" that "we con-
    trive ourselves" (117) and that literature has a "far-reaching role … in human lives
    … decidedly more substantive than daily events, political or otherwise" (25). Of
    course, Calvino does give literature importance, and the novel does address a num-
    ber of issues relating to the value of literature (for a useful discussion of these top-
    ics, see 122–128). But that doesn't mean that it is more important than the reality.
    (After all, the novel itself is part of reality. If it were fictitious, we'd never be able to
    read it. That would be no fun.) Anyway, the interpretive point is that critics recog-
    nize how I. and I are engaging in "sly parodies of popular fictional genres" such as
    "convoluted spy thrillers" (Markey 117), but they don't seem to see that the parody
    particularly touches Robbe-Grillet and the postmodern spy novel.

Works Cited

Abbott, H. Porter. "Narration." In Herman, Jahn, and Ryan, 339–344.

Abhinavagupta. *The Aesthetic Experience According to Abhinavagupta*. Ed. and trans. Raniero Gnoli. 2nd ed. Varanasi, India: Chokhamba Sanskrit Series, 1968.

Addis, Donna Rose, Ling Pan, Mai-Anh Vu, Noa Laiser, and Daniel L. Schacter. "Constructive Episodic Simulation of the Future and the Past: Distinct Subsystems of a Core Brain Network Mediate Imagining and Remembering." *Neuropsychologia* 47 (2009): 2222–2238.

Adelman, Janet. *Suffocating Mothers: Fantasies of Maternal Origin in Shakespeare's Plays, Hamlet to The Tempest*. New York: Routledge, 1992.

Aristotle. *Poetics: Aristotle's Theory of Poetry and Fine Art with a Critical Text and Translation of the Poetics*. Ed. and trans. S. H. Butcher. 4th ed. New York: Dover, 1951.

Austen, Jane. *Emma*. In *The Works of Jane Austen*. London: Allan Wingate, 1962.

Baddeley, Alan. "Episodic Memory: Organizing and Remembering." In *Memory*. By Alan Baddeley, Michael Eysenck, and Michael Anderson. New York: Psychology Press, 2009, 93–112.

"What Is Memory?" In *Memory*. By Alan Baddeley, Michael Eysenck, and Michael Anderson. New York: Psychology Press, 2009, 1–17.

Baker, Mark. *The Atoms of Language*. New York: Basic Books, 2001.

"Parameters." In Hogan, *Cambridge*, 582–584.

Ball, Philip. *Critical Mass: How One Thing Leads to Another*. New York: Farrar, Straus and Giroux, 2004.

Bareis, J. Alexander. *Fiktionales Erzählen: Zur Theorie der Literarischen Fiktion als Make-Believe*. Göteborg, Sweden: Acta Universitatis Gothoburgensis, 2008.

Barenghi, Mario and Bruno Falcetto. "Cronologia." In Calvino, xvii–xlvi.

Bargh, John. "Social Psychological Approaches to Consciousness." In *The Cambridge Handbook of Consciousness*. Ed. Philip David Zelazo, Morris Moscovitch, and Evan Thompson. Cambridge: Cambridge University Press, 2007, 555–569.

Barthes, Roland. *On Racine*. Trans. Richard Howard. New York: Octagon Books, 1977.

Baumeister, R. and E. Masicampo. "Conscious Thought Is for Facilitating Social and Cultural Interactions: How Mental Simulations Serve the Animal-Culture Interface." *Psychological Review* 117 (2010): 945–971.

Beck, Evelyn Torton. "Gender, Judaism, and Power: A Jewish Feminist Approach to Kafka." In Gray, 35–42.

Belletti, Adriana and Luigi Rizzi, eds. "Editors' Introduction: Some Concepts and Issues in Linguistic Theory." In *On Nature and Language*. By Noam Chomsky. Cambridge: Cambridge University Press, 2002.

Berthelot, Anne. *Andromaque: Racine*. N.p.: Éditions Nathan, 1992.

Blanc, André. *Racine: Trois Siècles de Théâtre*. N.p.: Fayard, 2003.

Bleikasten, André. "Caddy, or the Quest for Eurydice." In Bloom, 73–83.

Bloom, Harold, ed. *Caddy Compson*. New York: Chelsea House, 1990.

Bonheim, Helmut. "Shakespeare's Narremes." *Shakespeare Survey* 53 (2000): 1–11.

Bordwell, David. *Narration in the Fiction Film*. Madison: University of Wisconsin Press, 1985.

The Way Hollywood Tells It: Story and Style in Modern Movies. Berkeley: University of California Press, 2006.

Bowers, Fredson. "Dramatic Structure and Criticism: Plot in Hamlet." *Shakespeare Quarterly* 15 (1964): 207–218.

Brecht, Bertolt. *Die Stücke von Bertolt Brecht in Einem Band*. Frankfurt am Main, Germany: Suhrkamp Verlag, 1992.

Breen, Margaret. *Narratives of Queer Desire: Deserts of the Heart*. New York: Palgrave Macmillan, 2009.

Cacioppo, John, Penny Visser, and Cynthia Pickett, eds. *Social Neuroscience: People Thinking about Thinking People*. Cambridge, MA: MIT Press, 2006.

Caldicott, Edric and Derval Conroy, eds. *Racine: The Power and the Pleasure*. Dublin, Ireland: University College Dublin Press, 2001.

Calvino, Italo. *Se una Notte d'Inverno un Viaggiatore*. Milano, Italy: Oscar Mondadori, 2006.

Caplan, Jane. "The Rise of National Socialism, 1919–1933." In *Modern Germany Reconsidered, 1870–1945*. Ed. Gordon Martel. London: Routledge, 1992, 117–139.

Carroll, Noël. "Film, Emotion, and Genre." In Plantinga and Smith, 21–47.

Chai, Winberg, ed. *Essential Works of Chinese Communism*. New York: Bantam, 1969.

Chatman, Seymour. *Coming to Terms: The Rhetoric of Narrative and Film*. Ithaca, NY: Cornell University Press, 1990.

Clore, Gerald and Andrew Ortony. "Cognition in Emotion: Always, Sometimes, or Never?" In *Cognitive Neuroscience of Emotion*. Ed. Richard Land and Lynn Nadel with Geoffrey Ahern, John Allen, Alfred Kaszniak, Steven Rapcsak, and Gary Schwartz. Oxford: Oxford University Press, 2000, 24–61.

Codden, Karin. "'Such Strange Desygns': Madness, Subjectivity, and Treason in *Hamlet* and Elizabethan Culture." In *Hamlet*. By William Shakespeare. Ed. Susanne Wofford. Boston: Bedford Books, 1994, 380–402.

Conroy, Derval. "Gender, Power, and Authority in *Alexandre le Grand* and *Athalie*." In Caldicott and Conroy, 55–74.

Conroy, Jane. "Constructions of Identity: Mirrors of the 'Other' in Racine's Theatre." In Caldicott and Conroy, 75–99.

Corneille, Pierre. *Horace*. In Corneille, *Théâtre II*, 283–253.

Le Cid. In Corneille, *Théâtre II*, 195–281.

Théâtre II. Ed. Jacques Maurens. Paris: Garnier-Flammarion, 1980.

Corngold, Stanley. "Explanatory Notes to the Text." In Corngold, *Metamorphosis*, 61–101.

ed. *The Metamorphosis.* By Franz Kafka. New York: Bantam, 1972.

Costigan, Edward. "Aspects of Narrative in Some Plays by Shakespeare." *English Studies* 4 (1996): 323–342.

Crane, Mary Thomas. *Shakespeare's Brain: Reading with Cognitive Theory.* Princeton, NJ: Princeton University Press, 2001.

Culpeper, Jonathan and Dan McIntyre. "Activity Types and Characterisation in Dramatic Discourse." In *Characters in Fictional Worlds.* Ed. Jens Eder, Fotis Jannidis, and Ralf Schneider. Berlin: De Gruyter, 2010, 176–207.

Dawson, Michael. *Understanding Cognitive Science.* Oxford: Blackwell, 1998.

Decety Jean and Jennifer Stevens. "Action Representation and Its Role in Social Interaction." In Markman, Klein, and Suhr, 3–20.

Deleuze, Gilles and Félix Guattari. *Kafka: Toward a Minor Literature.* Trans. Dana Polan. Minneapolis: University of Minnesota Press, 1986.

Desnain, Véronique. *Hidden Tragedies: The Social Construction of Gender in Racine.* New Orleans, LA: University Press of the South, 2002.

Doherty, Martin. *Theory of Mind: How Children Understand Others' Thoughts and Feelings.* New York: Psychology Press, 2009.

Duckitt, John H. *The Social Psychology of Prejudice.* New York: Praeger, 1992.

Ebihara, Hiroshi. "Ambivalence in Shakespeare – Mainly on the Problem of Order and Tudor Political Doctrine." *Studies in English Literature* (Tokyo) 44 (1968): 123–134.

Edelman, Gerard. *Second Nature: Brain Science and Human Knowledge.* New Haven, CT: Yale University Press, 2006.

Eisenstein. Sergei. *Film Form: Essays in Film Theory.* Ed. Jay Leyda. New York: Harcourt, 1949.

Esslin, Martin. *Brecht, A Choice of Evils: A Critical Study of the Man, His Work, and His Opinions.* London: Heinemann, 1965.

Fauconnier, Gilles and Mark Turner. *The Way We Think: Conceptual Blending and the Mind's Hidden Complexities.* New York: Basic Books, 2002.

Faude-Koivisto, Tanya, Daniela Wuerz, and Peter Gollwitzer. "Implementation Intentions: The Mental Representations and Cognitive Procedures of If-Then Planning." In Markman, Klein, and Suhr, 69–86.

Faulkner, William. *As I Lay Dying.* New York: Random House, 1930.

　Light in August. New York: Random House, 1932.

　The Sound and the Fury. New York: Random House, 1929.

Felperin, Howard. "Political Criticism at the Crossroads: The Utopian Historicism of *The Tempest.*" In Wood, 29–66.

Ferguson, Margaret W. "*Hamlet*: Letters and Spirits." In Kastan, *Critical*, 139–155.

Fergusson, Francis. *Shakespeare: The Pattern in His Carpet.* New York: Delacorte Press, 1958.

Fiedler, Leslie. *The Stranger in Shakespeare.* New York: Stein and Day, 1972.

Fisher, Helen. "The Drive to Love: The Neural Mechanism for Mate Selection." In *The New Psychology of Love.* Ed Robert Sternberg and Karin Weis. New Haven, CT: Yale University Press, 2006, 87–115.

Fludernik, Monika. "Narrative and Drama." In Pier and García, 355–383.

　Towards a Natural Narratology. London: Routledge, 1996.

Foakes, R. A. "Hamlet's Neglect of Revenge." In Kinney, *Hamlet*, 85–99.

Fodor, Jerry. *The Language of Thought.* Cambridge, MA: Harvard University Press, 1979.

Forestier, Georges. "The Racinian Hero and the Classical Theory of Characterization." In Caldicott and Conroy, 14–26.

Fortin, René. "Julius Caesar: An Experiment in Point of View." *Shakespeare Quarterly* 19 (1968): 341–347.

Frijda, Nico. *The Emotions.* Cambridge: Cambridge University Press, 1986.

Frye, Northrop. *The Anatomy of Criticism: Four Essays.* Princeton, NJ: Princeton University Press, 1957.

Fuchs, Anne. "A Psychoanalytic Reading of *The Man Who Disappeared.*" In Preece, 25–41.

Fuegi, John. *Brecht and Company: Sex, Politics, and the Making of the Modern Drama.* New York: Grove Press, 1994.

Fulton, Helen, with Rosemary Huisman, Julian Murphet, and Anne Dunn. *Narrative and Media.* Cambridge: Cambridge University Press, 2005.

Gamboz, Nadia, Maria A. Brandimonte, and Stefania De Vito. "The Role of Past in the Simulation of Autobiographical Future Episodes." *Experimental Psychology* 57 (2010): 419–428.

Garber, Marjorie. *Shakespeare's Ghost Writers: Literature as Uncanny Causality.* New York: Methuen, 1987.

Gaut, Berys. "Identification and Emotion in Narrative Film." In Plantinga and Smith, 200–216.

Gazzaniga, Michael. *The Ethical Brain: The Science of Our Moral Dilemmas.* New York: Harper Perennial, 2005.

Gellert, Inge, Gerd Koch, and Florian Vaßen, eds. *Massnehmen: Bertolt Brecht/Hanns Eislers Lehrstück Die Massnahme, Kontroverse, Perspektive, Praxis.* Berlin: Theater der Zeit, 1998.

Girard, René. "Collective Violence and Sacrifice in *Julius Caesar.*" In Wilson, 108–126.

Gobert, R. Darren. "Cognitive Catharsis in *The Caucasian Chalk Circle.*" *Modern Drama* 49 (2006): 12–41.

Gogol, Nikolai. *Dead Souls.* Trans. D. J. Hogarth. Available at Project Gutenberg: www.gutenberg.org/ebooks/1081.

Goldblum, Naomi. *The Brain-Shaped Mind: What the Brain Can Tell Us about the Mind.* Cambridge: Cambridge University Press, 2001.

Goldmann, Lucien. *The Hidden God: A Study of Tragic Vision in the Pensées of Pascal and the Tragedies of Racine.* Trans. Philip Thody. New York: Humanities Press, 1964.

Gorman, David. "Fiction, Theories of." In Herman, Jahn, and Ryan, 163–167.

Graff, Gerald and James Phelan, eds. *William Shakespeare, The Tempest: A Case Study in Critical Controversy.* Boston: Bedford/St. Martin's, 2000.

Gray, Richard, ed. *Approaches to Teaching Kafka's Short Fiction.* New York: The Modern Language Association of America, 1995.

Green, Melanie and John Donahue. "Simulated Worlds: Transportation into Narratives." In Markman, Klein, and Suhr, 241–254.

Greenblatt, Stephen. *Hamlet in Purgatory.* Princeton, NJ: Princeton University Press, 2001.

Shakespeare's Freedom. Chicago: University of Chicago Press, 2010.

Will in the World: How Shakespeare Became Shakespeare. New York: W. W. Norton, 2004.

Greve, Anniken. "The Human Body and the Human Being in 'Die Verwandlung.'" In *Franz Kafka: Narration, Rhetoric, and Reading.* Ed. Jakob Lothe, Beatrice Sandberg, and Ronald Speirs. Columbus: Ohio State University Press, 40–57.

Gross, Ruth. "Kafka's Short Fiction." In Preece, 80–94.

Hanks, William. "Deixis." In Herman, Jahn, and Ryan, 99–100.

Hattaway, Michael. "Tragedy and Political Authority." In McEachern, 103–122.

Haug, Wolfgang Fritz. "Kritik ohne Mitleid? Notiz zu Brechts *Massnahme*." In Gellert, Koch, and Vaßen, 33–38.

Hawkes, Terence. "The Old Bill." In Kinney, *Hamlet*, 177–191.

Herman, David, ed. *The Cambridge Companion to Narrative*. Cambridge: Cambridge University Press, 2007.

Herman, David. *Story Logic: Problems and Possibilities of Narrative*. Lincoln: University of Nebraska Press, 2002.

Herman, David, Manfred Jahn, and Marie-Laure Ryan, eds. *Routledge Encyclopedia of Narrative Theory*. New York: Routledge, 2005.

Hernadi, Paul. "Literature and Evolution." *SubStance* 30 (2001): 55–71.

Heyndels, Ingrid. *Le Conflit Racinien: Esquisse d'un Systèm Tragique*. Bruxelles, Belgium: Editions de l'Université de Bruxelles, 1985.

Hill, Christine, ed. *Racine: Théâtre et Poésie*. Leeds, UK: Francis Cairns, 1987.

Hogan, Patrick Colm. *Affective Narratology: The Emotional Structure of Stories*. Lincoln: University of Nebraska Press, 2011.

Hogan, Patrick Colm, ed. *The Cambridge Encyclopedia of the Language Sciences*. Cambridge: Cambridge University Press, 2011.

Hogan, Patrick Colm. *Cognitive Science, Literature, and the Arts: A Guide for Humanists*. New York: Routledge, 2003.

Colonialism and Cultural Identity: Crises of Tradition in the Anglophone Literatures of India, Africa, and the Caribbean. Albany: State University of New York Press, 2000.

"Metaphor, Information Transfer in." In Hogan, *Cambridge*, 488–489.

The Mind and Its Stories: Narrative Universals and Human Emotion. Cambridge: Cambridge University Press, 2003.

Narrative Discourse: Authors and Narrators in Literature, Film, and Art. Columbus: Ohio State University Press, 2013.

On Interpretation: Meaning and Inference in Law, Psychoanalysis, and Literature. Athens: University of Georgia Press, 1996.

"Stylistics, Emotion, and Neuroscience." In *The Routledge Handbook of Stylistics*. Ed. Michael Burke. New York: Routledge, forthcoming.

Understanding Nationalism: Narrative, Identity, and Cognitive Science. Columbus: Ohio State University Press, 2009.

What Literature Teaches Us about Emotion. Cambridge: Cambridge University Press, 2011.

Hogan, Patrick Colm and Lalita Pandit. "Ancient Theories of Narrative (Non-Western)." In Herman, Jahn, and Ryan, 14–19.

Holland, John, Keith Holyoak, Richard Nisbett, and Paul Thagard. *Induction: Processes of Inference, Learning, and Discovery*. Cambridge, MA: MIT Press, 1986.

Holland, Norman. *The Dynamics of Literary Response*. New York: Oxford University Press, 1968.

Literature and the Brain. Gainesville, FL: The Psyart Foundation, 2009.

"Realism and Unrealism: Kafka's 'Metamorphosis.'" *Modern Fiction Studies* 4 (1958): 143–150.

Honigmann, E. A. J. "Shakespeare's Self-Repetitions and *King John*." *Shakespeare Survey* 53 (2000): 175–183.

Horn, Peter. "Die Wahrheit ist Konkret. Bertolt Brechts *Maßnahme* und die Frage der Parteidisziplin." *Brecht-Jahrbuch 1978* (1978): 39–65.

Hühn, Peter and Roy Sommer. "Narration in Poetry and Drama." *The Living Handbook of Narratology*. http://hup.sub.uni-hamburg.de/lhn/index.php/Main_Page (accessed June 1, 2011).

Huisman, Rosemary. "Magazine Genres." In Fulton, Huisman, Murphet, and Dunn, 271–284.

"Soap Operas and Sitcoms." In Fulton, Huisman, Murphet, and Dunn, 172–187.

Hume, Kathryn. *Calvino's Fictions: Cogito and Cosmos.* Oxford: Clarendon Press, 1992.

Ito, Tiffany and John Cacioppo. "Affect and Attitudes: A Social Neuroscience Approach." In *Handbook of Affect and Social Cognition.* Ed. Joseph Forgas. Mahwah NJ: Lawrence Erlbaum, 2001, 50–74.

Ito, Tiffany, Geoffrey Urland, Eve Willadsen-Jensen, and Joshua Correll. "The Social Neuroscience of Stereotyping and Prejudice: Using Event-Related Brain Potentials to Study Social Perception." In Cacioppo, Visser, and Pickett, 189–208.

Jahn, Manfred. "Narrative Voice and Agency in Drama: Aspects of a Narratology of Drama." *New Literary History* 32 (2001): 659–679.

James, Henry. *The Portrait of a Lady.* Old Saybrook, CT: Tantor Media, 2008.

Jeffries, Lesley. *Critical Stylistics: The Power of English.* New York: Palgrave Macmillan, 2010.

Jeffries, Lesley and Dan McIntyre. *Stylistics.* Cambridge: Cambridge University Press, 2010.

Johnson-Laird, P. N. "Mental Models and Language." In Hogan, *Cambridge,* 479–481.

Kafka, Franz. "Die Verwandlung." *Sämtliche Erzählungen.* Ed. Paul Raabe. Frankfurt am Main, Germany: Fischer Taschenbuch Verlag, 1984.

Kahneman, Daniel and Dale Miller. "Norm Theory: Comparing Reality to Its Alternatives." *Psychological Review* 93.2 (1986): 136–153.

Kaiser, Hellmuth. "Kafka's Fantasy of Punishment." In Corngold, *Metamorphosis,* 147–156.

Kandel, Eric. "Cellular Mechanisms of Learning and the Biological Basis of Individuality." In Kandel, Schwartz, and Jessell, 1247–1279.

Kandel, Eric, James Schwartz, and Thomas Jessell. *Principles of Neural Science.* 4th ed. New York: McGraw-Hill, 2000.

Kastan, David Scott. *Critical Essays on Shakespeare's Hamlet.* New York: G. K. Hall, 1995.

"'His Semblable Is His Mirror': *Hamlet* and the Imitation of Revenge." In Kastan *Critical,* 198–209.

Kazan, Alfred. "Introduction." *Uncle Tom's Cabin.* By Harriet Beecher Stowe. New York: Bantam, 1981.

Keen, Suzanne. *Empathy and the Novel.* New York: Oxford University Press, 2007.

Khan, M. H. "An Approach to Shakespeare's *Henry V.*" *The Aligarh Journal of English Studies* 1 (1976): 51–65.

Kiernan, Victor. *Eight Tragedies of Shakespeare.* New York: Verso, 1996.

Kim, Ji-Woong, S.-E. Kim, J.-J. Kim, B. Jeong, C.-H. Park, A. Son, J. Song, and S. Ki. "Compassionate Attitude toward Others' Suffering Activates the Mesolimbic Neural System." *Neuropsychologia* 47 (2009): 2073–2081.

Kinney, Arthur, ed. *Hamlet: New Critical Essays.* New York: Routledge, 2002.

Klinger, Eric. "Daydreaming and Fantasizing: Thought Flow and Motivation." In Markman, Klein, and Suhr, 225–240.

Kondo, Hirohito, Naoyuki Osaka, and Mariko Osaka. "Cooperation of the Anterior Cingulate Cortex and Dorsolateral Prefrontal Cortex for Attention Shifting." *NeuroImage* 23 (2004): 670–679.

Kosslyn, Stephen. *Image and Brain: The Resolution of the Imagery Debate.* Cambridge, MA: MIT Press, 1994.

Kunda, Ziva. *Social Cognition: Making Sense of People.* Cambridge, MA: MIT Press, 1999.

Kupfermann, Irving, Eric Kandel, and Susan Iversen. "Motivational and Addictive States." In Kandel, Schwartz, and Jessell, 998–1013.

Lakoff, George and Mark Johnson. *Metaphors We Live By.* 2nd ed. Chicago: University of Chicago Press, 2003.

Lamont, Rosette. "The Hamlet Myth." *Yale French Studies* 33 (1964): 80–91.

Langlois, J. H. and L. A. Roggman. "Attractive Faces Are Only Average." *Psychological Science* 1 (1990): 115–121.

Leadbeater, Lewis. "Aristophanes and Kafka: The Dung Beetle Connection." *Studies in Short Fiction* 23 (1986): 169–178.

LeDoux, Joseph. *Synaptic Self: How Our Brains Become Who We Are.* New York: Viking, 2002.

——— *The Emotional Brain.* New York: Touchstone, 1996.

Leki, Ilona. *Alain Robbe-Grillet.* Boston: Twayne, 1983.

Lenin, V. I. *What Is to Be Done? Burning Questions of Our Movement.* New York: International Publishers, 1969.

Levin, Richard. "Hamlet, Laertes, and the Dramatic Functions of Foils." In Kinney, *Hamlet,* 215–230.

Lévi-Strauss, Claude. *The Raw and the Cooked.* Vol. 1 of *Introduction to a Science of Mythology.* Trans. John and Doreen Weightman. New York: Harper Colophon, 1969.

Lewis, David. *Counterfactuals.* Cambridge, MA: Harvard University Press, 1973.

Lieberman, Matthew and Naomi Eisenberger. "A Pain by Any Other Name (Rejection, Exclusion, Ostracism) Still Hurts the Same: The Role of Dorsal Anterior Cingulate Cortex in Social and Physical Pain." In Cacioppo, Visser, and Pickett, 167–187.

Locher, Paul. "How Does a Visual Artist Create an Artwork?" In *The Cambridge Handbook of Creativity.* Ed. James Kaufman and Robert Sternberg. Cambridge: Cambridge University Press, 2010, 131–144.

Lord, Albert. *The Singer of Tales.* New York: Atheneum, 1960.

Lukács, Georg. *Essays on Realism.* Ed. Rodney Livingstone. Trans. David Fernbach. Cambridge, MA: MIT Press, 1980.

——— *History and Class Consciousness: Studies in Marxist Dialectics.* Trans. Rodney Livingstone. Cambridge, MA: MIT Press, 1983.

MacDonald, Angus, Jonathan Cohen, V. Stanger, and Cameron Carter. "Dissociating the Role of the Dorsolateral Prefrontal and Anterior Cingulate Cortex in Cognitive Control." *Science* 288.5472 (June 9, 2000): 1835–1838.

Machiavelli, Niccolo. *The Prince.* Trans. Daniel Donno. New York: Bantam, 1966.

Mandel, Ernest. *Trotsky: A Study in the Dynamic of His Thought.* London: NLB, 1979.

Markey, Constance. *Italo Calvino: A Journey Toward Postmodernism.* Gainesville: University Press of Florida, 1999.

Markman, Keith, William Klein, and Julie Suhr, eds. *Handbook of Imagination and Mental Simulation.* New York: Psychology Press, 2009.

Martindale, Colin and Kathleen Moore. "Priming, Prototypicality, and Preference." *Journal of Experimental Psychology: Human Perception and Performance* 14 (1988): 661–670.

Maskell, David. "La Précision du Lieu dans les Tragédies de Racine." In Hill, 151–171.

Mason, Pamela. "*Henry V*: 'The Quick Forge and Working House of Thought.'" In *The Cambridge Companion to Shakespeare's History Plays.* Ed. Michael Hattaway. Cambridge: Cambridge University Press, 2002, 177–192.

Matlock, Teenie. "Fictive Motion as Cognitive Simulation." *Memory and Cognition* 32 (2004): 1389–1400.

Mauron, Charles. *L'Inconscient dans l'Oeuvre et la Vie de Jean Racine.* N.p.: Centre National de la Recherche Scientifique, 1957.

McAlindon, Tom. "What Is a Shakespearean Tragedy?" In McEachern, 1–22.

McEachern, Claire, ed. *The Cambridge Companion to Shakespearean Tragedy.* Cambridge: Cambridge University Press, 2002.

McLuskie, Kate. "'Is All Well?': Shakespeare's Play with Narratives." *Shakespeare Jahrbuch* 142 (2006): 78–94.

McMahan, Alison. "Simulation and Narrative." In Herman, Jahn, and Ryan, 532–533.

Miles, Geoffrey. *Shakespeare and the Constant Romans.* Oxford: Clarendon Press, 1996.

Milton, John. *Paradise Lost.* In *John Milton: Complete Poems and Major Prose.* Ed. Merritt Hughes. Indianapolis, IN: Bobbs-Merrill, 1957, 207–469.

Minter, David, ed. *The Sound and the Fury.* By William Faulkner. New York: W. W. Norton, 1994.

Mitchell, Jason, Malia Mason, C. Macraw, and Mahzarin Banaji. "Thinking about Others: The Neural Substrates of Social Cognition." In Cacioppo, Visser, and Pickett, 63–82.

Mithen, Steven. "The Evolution of Imagination: An Archaeological Perspective." *SubStance* 30 (2001): 28–54.

Mittenzwei, Werner. *Bertolt Brecht: Von der "Maßnahme" zu "Leben des Galilei."* Berlin: Aufbau-Verlag, 1977.

Miyashita, Yayoi. "Interweaving the Love Plot and the Reunion Plot in *Twelfth Night.*" *Annual Report on Cultural Science* (Hokkaido University, Japan) 131 (2010): 41–72.

Morel, Jacques. "Le Personnage Sacrifié dans l'Oeuvre de Racine." In Hill, 83–91.

Morrissette, Bruce. *The Novels of Robbe-Grillet.* Ithaca, NY: Cornell University Press, 1975.

Motoyama, Kate. "*Mauser*: A Critique of *The Measures Taken.*" *Text and Performance Quarterly* 11 (1991): 46–55.

Myers, Michael and Sara Hodges. "Making It Up and Making Do: Simulation, Imagination, and Empathic Accuracy." In Markman, Klein, and Suhr, 281–294.

Nelles, William. "Embedding." In Herman, Jahn, and Ryan, 134–135.

Nelson, G. E. "The Birth of Tragedy out of Pedagogy: Brecht's 'Learning Play' *Die Maßnahme.*" *The German Quarterly* 46 (1973): 566–580.

Nisbett, Richard and Lee Ross. *Human Inference: Strategies and Shortcomings of Human Judgment.* Englewood Cliffs, NJ: Prentice-Hall, 1980.

Noakes, J. and G. Pridham, eds. *Nazism 1919–1945, Vol. I, The Rise to Power 1919–1934: A Documentary Reader.* Exeter, UK: University of Exeter, 1983.

Nünning, Ansgar and Roy Sommer. "Diegetic and Mimetic Narrative: Some Further Steps towards a Transgeneric Narratology of Drama." In Pier and García, 331–354.

"Die Performative Kraft des Erzählens: Formen und Functionen des Erzählens in Shakespeares Dramen." *Shakespeare Jahrbuch* 142 (2006): 124–141.

Oatley, Keith. "The Mind's Flight Simulator." *The Psychologist* 21 (2008): 1030–1032.

The Passionate Muse: Exploring Emotion in Stories. Oxford: Oxford University Press, 2012.

"Suggestion Structure." In Hogan, *Cambridge*, 819–820.

"Why Fiction May Be Twice as True as Fact: Fiction as Cognitive and Emotional Simulation." *Review of General Psychology* 3.2 (June 1999): 101–117.

Omesco, Ion. *Shakespeare, Son Art et Sa Tempête: Essai.* Paris: Presses Universitaires de France, 1993.

Ortony, Andrew. "Are Emotion Metaphors Conceptual or Lexical?" *Cognition and Emotion* 2 (1988): 95–104.

"The Role of Similarity in Similies and Metaphors." In *Metaphor and Thought.* 2nd ed. Ed. Andrew Ortony. New York: Cambridge University Press, 1993, 342–356.

Ortony, Andrew, Gerald Clore, and Allan Collins. *The Cognitive Structure of Emotions.* Cambridge: Cambridge University Press, 1988.

Osborne, Laurie. "Narration and Staging in *Hamlet* and Its Afternovels." In *The Cambridge Companion to Shakespeare and Popular Culture.* Ed. Robert Shaughnessy. Cambridge: Cambridge University Press, 2007, 114–133.

Parker, Patricia. "Othello and Hamlet: Dilation, Spying, and the 'Secret Place' of Woman." *Representations* 44 (1993): 60–95.

Pavel, Thomas. "Structure Profonde et Postulats Narratifs dans *Bajazet*." In Venesoen, 121–133.

Pearlman, E. "Shakespeare at Work: The Invention of the Ghost." In Kinney, *Hamlet*, 71–84.

Pfister, Manfred. *The Theory and Analysis of Drama.* Trans. John Halliday. Cambridge: Cambridge University Press, 1988.

Phelan, James. "Rhetoric/Ethics." In Herman, *Cambridge*, 203–216.

Phillips, Nigel. *Sijobang: Sung Narrative Poetry of West Sumatra.* Cambridge: Cambridge University Press, 1981.

Pier, John, and José Ángel García, eds. *Theorizing Narrativity.* Berlin: Walter de Gruyter, 2008.

Plantinga, Carl. *Moving Viewers: American Film and the Spectator's Experience.* Berkeley: University of California Press, 2009.

Plantinga, Carl and Greg Smith, eds. *Passionate Views: Film, Cognition, and Emotion.* Baltimore, MD: Johns Hopkins University Press, 1999.

Porter, Carolyn. *William Faulkner.* New York: Oxford University Press, 2007.

Preece, Julian, ed. *The Cambridge Companion to Kafka.* Cambridge: Cambridge University Press, 2002.

Propp, Vladimir. *The Morphology of the Folktale.* Trans. Laurence Scott. Austin: University of Texas Press, 1968.

Proust, Marcel. *À la Recherche du Temps Perdu (I): Du Côté de Chez Swann.* Paris: Gallimard, 1954.

Pyrhönen, Heta. "Suspense and Surprise." In Herman, Jahn, and Ryan, 578–580.

"Thematic Approaches to Narrative." In Herman, Jahn, and Ryan, 597–598.

Racine, Jean. *Théatre Complet*. 2 vols. Ed. André Stegmann. Paris: Flammarion, 1964, 1965.

Ramachandran, V. S. *The Tell-Tale Brain: A Neuroscientist's Quest for What Makes Us Human*. New York: W. W. Norton, 2011.

Rebhorn, Wayne. "The Crisis of the Aristocracy in *Julius Caesar*." In Wilson, 29–54.

Richardson, Brian. "Drama and Narrative." In Herman, *Cambridge*, 142–155.

———. "'Time Is Out of Joint': Narrative Models and the Temporality of the Drama." *Poetics Today* 8.2 (1987): 299–309.

———. *Unnatural Voices: Extreme Narration in Modern and Contemporary Fiction*. Columbus: Ohio State University Press, 2006.

Rienäcker, Gerd. "Musik als Agens: Beschreibungen und Thesen zur Musik des Lehrstückes *Die Massnahme* von Hanns Eisler." In Gellert, Koch, and Vaßen, 180–189.

Rimé, Bernard. *Le Partage Social des Émotions*. Paris: Presses Universitaires de France, 2005.

Roberts, J. A. G. *A Concise History of China*. Cambridge, MA: Harvard University Press, 1999.

Rosch, Eleanor. "Prototypes." In Hogan, *Cambridge*, 680–682.

Rosen, William. *Shakespeare and the Craft of Tragedy*. Cambridge, MA: Harvard University Press, 1960.

Rubin, David C. *Memory in Oral Traditions: The Cognitive Psychology of Epic, Ballads, and Counting-out Rhymes*. New York: Oxford University Press, 1995.

Russell, Bertrand. *The Practice and Theory of Bolshevism*. London: G. Allen and Unwin, 1921.

Ryan, Kiernan. *Shakespeare*. 3rd ed. New York: Palgrave, 2002.

Ryan, Marie-Laure. "Possible-Worlds Theory." In Herman, Jahn, and Ryan, 446–450.

Ryan, Simon. "Franz Kafka's *Die Verwandlung*: Transformation, Metaphor, and the Perils of Assimilation." *Seminar: A Journal of Germanic Studies* 43 (2007): 1–18.

Scarry, Elaine. *Dreaming by the Book*. New York: Farrar, Straus and Giroux, 1999.

Schacter, Daniel and Donna Rose Addis. "Remembering the Past to Imagine the Future: A Cognitive Neuroscience Perspective." *Military Psychology* 21 (2009): (Suppl. 1) S108–S112.

Schacter, Daniel, Donna Rose Addis, and Randy L. Buckner. "Remembering the Past to Imagine the Future: The Prospective Brain." *Nature Reviews: Neuroscience* 8 (2007): 657–661.

Schaeffer, Jean-Marie and Ioana Vultur. "Immersion." In Herman, Jahn, and Ryan, 237–239.

Schank, Roger. "Scripts." In Hogan, *Cambridge*, 727–728.

Scheff, Thomas and Suzanne Retzinger. *Emotions and Violence: Shame and Rage in Destructive Conflicts*. Lexington, MA: Lexington Books, 1991.

Schumacher, Ernst. *Die Dramatischen Versuche Bertolt Brechts, 1918–1933*. Berlin: Rütten & Loening, 1955.

Shakespeare, William. *Henry V*. Ed. John Russell Brown. New York: Signet, 1988.

———. *Julius Caesar*. Ed. William and Barbara Rosen. New York: Signet, 1987.

———. *King John and Henry VIII*. Ed. David Bevington. Assoc. eds. David Scott Kastan, James Hammersmith, and Robert Kean Turner. Toronto: Bantam, 1988.

The Tempest: A Case Study in Critical Controversy. Ed. Gerald Graff and James Phelan. Boston: Bedford, 2000.

The Tragedy of Hamlet Prince of Denmark. Ed. Sylvan Barnet. New York: New American Library, 1998.

Siemon, James R. *Word against Word: Shakespearean Utterance.* Amherst: University of Massachusetts Press, 2002.

Simons, Oliver. "Theater of Revolution and the Law of Genre – Bertolt Brecht's *The Measures Taken (Die Maßnahme)*." *The Germanic Review* 84 (2009): 327–352.

Smith, Murray. "Gangsters, Cannibals, Aesthetes, or Apparently Perverse Allegiances." In Plantinga and Smith, 217–238.

Sokel, Walter. "Kafka and Modernism." In Gray, 21–34.

Spencer, Theodore. *Shakespeare and the Nature of Man.* New York: Macmillan, 1949.

States, Bert. "The Persistence of the Archetype." *Critical Inquiry* 7 (1980): 333–344.

Stegmann, André. "Notice sur *Iphigénie*." In Racine vol. 2, 127–129.

Stein, Dan and Bavanisha Vythilingum. "Love and Attachment: The Psychobiology of Social Bonding." *CNS Spectrums* 14.5 (2009): 239–242.

Stein, Nancy and Valerie Kissel. "Story Schemata and Causal Structure." In Herman, Jahn, and Ryan, 568–569.

Steinweg, Reiner. *Bertolt Brecht Die Maßnahme: Kritische Ausgabe mit einer Spielanleitung.* Frankfurt am Main, Germany: Suhrkamp Verlag, 1972.

Das Lehrstück: Brechts Theorie einer Politisch-Ästhetischen Erziehung. Stuttgart, Germany: J. B. Metzlersche Verlagsbuchhandlung, 1972.

Sternberg, Meir. *Expositional Modes and Temporal Ordering in Fiction.* Baltimore, MD: Johns Hopkins University Press, 1978.

Stockwell, Peter. *Cognitive Poetics: An Introduction.* London: Routledge, 2002.

Stowe, Harriet Beecher. *Uncle Tom's Cabin.* New York: Bantam, 2003.

Szpunar, Karl and Kathleen McDermott. "Episodic Future Thought: Remembering the Past to Imagine the Future." In Markman, Klein, and Suhr, 119–130.

Tagore, Rabindranath. "Exercise-Book." In *Selected Short Stories.* By Rabindranath Tagore. Ed. and trans. William Radice. New York: Penguin, 2005, 140–145.

My Reminiscences. New York: Macmillan, 1917.

Tan, Ed. *Emotion and the Structure of Narrative Film: Film as an Emotion Machine.* Trans. Barbara Fasting. Mahwah, NJ: Lawrence Erlbaum Associates, 1996.

Taylor, M., A. Shawber, and A. Mannering. "Children's imaginary companions: What is it like to have an invisible friend?" In Markman, Klein, and Suhr, 211–224.

Thiher, Allen. *Franz Kafka: A Study of the Short Fiction.* Boston: Twayne, 1990.

Tobin, Ronald. *Jean Racine Revisited.* New York: Twayne, 1999.

Tooby, John and Leda Cosmides. "Does Beauty Build Adapted Minds? Toward an Evolutionary Theory of Aesthetics, Fiction, and the Arts." *SubStance* 30 (2001): 6–27.

Van Boven, Leaf, Joanne Kane, and A. Peter McGraw. "Temporally Asymmetric Constraints on Mental Simulation: Retrospection Is More Constrained Than Prospection." In Markman, Klein, and Suhr, 131–147.

Venesoen, Constant, ed. *Racine: Mythes et Réalités.* N.p.: Société d'Étude du XVIIe Siècle et Université de Western Ontario, 1976.

Von Wiese, Benno. *Die deutsche Novelle von Goethe bis Kafka.* Vol. 2. Düsseldorf: Bagel, 1962.

Vuust, Peter and Morten Kringelbach. "The Pleasure of Music." In *Pleasures of the Brain*. Ed. Morten Kringelbach and Kent Berridge. Oxford: Oxford University Press, 2010, 255–269.

Watson, Robert N. "Tragedies of Revenge and Ambition." In McEachern, 160–181.

Watts, Cedric. "Where Is the Ghost From? Is He Stupid? and: Is Hamlet Really Hamleth?" In *Henry V, War Criminal? and Other Shakespeare Puzzles*. By John Sutherland and Cedric Watts. Oxford: Oxford University Press, 2000, 17–30.

"Who Killed Woodstock?" In *Henry V, War Criminal? and Other Shakespeare Puzzles*. By John Sutherland and Watts. Oxford: Oxford University Press, 2000, 92–98.

Weinberg, Kurt. *Kafkas Dichtungen: Die Travestien des Mythos*. Bern-Munich: Franke, 1963.

Weis, René, ed. *King Lear: A Parallel Text Edition*. London: Longman, 1993.

Westlund, Joseph. "Ambivalence in the Player's Speech in *Hamlet*." *Studies in English Literature* 18 (1978): 245–256.

Wheeler, Richard P. "Fantasy and History in *The Tempest*." In Wood, 127–164.

Whitfield, T. and P. Slatter. "The Effect of Categorization and Prototypicality on Aesthetic Choice in a Furniture Selection Task." *British Journal of Psychology* 70 (1979): 67–75.

Wilson, Richard, ed. *Julius Caesar: Contemporary Critical Essays*. New York: Palgrave, 2002.

Witt, Mary Ann. "Confinement in *Die Verwandlung* and *Les Séquestrés d'Altona*." *Comparative Literature* 23 (1971): 32–44.

Wofford, Susanne. "A Critical History of *Hamlet*." In *Hamlet*. Ed. Susanne Wofford. Boston: Bedford Books, 1994, 181–207.

Wojciehowski, Hannah Chapelle and Vittorio Gallese. "How Stories Make Us Feel: Toward an Embodied Narratology." *California Italian Studies* 2 (2011). http://www.escholarship.org/uc/ismrg_cisj.

Wong, Elaine, Adam Galinsky, and Laura Kray. "The Counterfactual Mind-Set: A Decade of Research." In Markman, Klein, and Suhr, 161–174.

Wood, Nigel, ed. *The Tempest*. Buckingham, UK: Open University Press, 1995.

Woolf, Virginia. *A Room of One's Own*. New York: Harcourt, 1981 (1929).

Würzbach, Natascha. "Motif." In Herman, Jahn, and Ryan, 322–323.

Young, Kay. *Imagining Minds: The Neuro-Aesthetics of Austen, Eliot, and Hardy*. Columbus: Ohio State University Press, 2010.

Zarrow, Peter. *China in War and Revolution, 1895–1949*. New York: Routledge, 2005.

Zunshine, Lisa. *Why We Read Fiction: Theory of Mind and the Novel*. Columbus: Ohio State University Press, 2006.

Zwaan, Rolf A. "Situation Model." In Herman, Jahn, and Ryan, 534–535.

Index

Abbott, H. Porter, 202
Abhijñānaśākuntalam (Kālidāsa), xii, 35–6
action trajectories, xiii, 13, 14, 77, 191
activation, 18–19, *See also* character activation
Affective Narratology (Hogan), xii
agents, 13
Alexandre le Grand (Racine)
   antagonizer, reconciler, and rival doubling
      in, 84
   canon continuity with, 84–5, 86–7, 89–90,
      92, 94–5, 97–8, 99
   description of, 84–7, 193
   narrative idiolect in, 84
   parametric shifts in, 84, 85–7
alignment, 50, 52–3, 54, 59, 72, 189
alteration principles
   characters affected by, 36
   defined, 33
   for discourse, 33–4
   example impact of, 33
   motifs as part of, 34–5
   prototype affected by, 33, 34–5, 76
   summary of, 45, 110
   types of, 34, 35
ambiguity
   Brecht's work displaying, 120–1, 122–3, 124,
      196, 197
   Shakespeare's work evincing, 54–5, 60, 62–7,
      69–71, 142, 148–50, 151–2, 153, 154–6, 189,
      190, 191
ambivalence, 54
   in character simulation, 41, 87, 193
   emotion containing, 40–1, 42
   in Racine's work, 87, 90, 91, 95–6, 97, 98, 102,
      107, 193

   in Shakespeare's plays, 56, 58, 59–61, 63–4,
      67, 72, 73, 189, 190, 191
Andromaque (Racine), 104
   ambivalence in, 98
   canon continuity with, 88, 89–90, 91, 92, 94,
      95–6, 98, 100, 102, 106, 107
   character ambivalence in, 87, 193
   character emotion shifts in, 88, 105, 193
   contradictory properties and relations in, 91
   description of, 87–9, 193
   female protagonist growth in, 193
   motivation treatment in, 91–2
   narrative idiolect in, 87, 89, 91
   narrative trajectory in, 98–9
   parametric shifts in, 87, 90, 91–2, 194
   reconciliation after war in, 87
argument, 181, *See also specific topics*
   authorial continuities in, 115
   cross-cultural patterns and motifs for, 115,
      122
   narrative compared to, 113, 171, 201
   particularization and, xviii, 116, 117, 118, 127
   simulation of, xviii–xix, 111–12, 196
argumentative simulation
   in Brecht's work, 116–21, 123–4, 125, 126
   for critics, 126
   exploratory simulation in relation to, 123–4
   implemental simulation compared to,
      111–12, 135–6
   of narration, 165
   narrative particularization with, 112
   summary of, 135–6
artifice
   in Calvino's work, 172–3, 174–5, 177–8
   concealed, 166, 175, 176, 181

215

variation of, 80
particularization, *See also* narrative
  particularization; *specific topics*
  argument or reasoning and, xviii, 116, 117,
    118, 127
  emplotment for, xix–xx
  of experience, 185
  narrative cognitive theory ignoring author,
    xi–xii
  of narrative prototype, xvi
  narrative voice for, xix–xx
  patterns, nature of, xx–xxi
  of plot, 103, 138, 140, 159–60
  simulation as central to, xiii, 43
patterns, 47–50, 51–2, 75, 81–2, 191,
    See also cross-cultural patterns and
    motifs; narrative idiolect
Pavel, Thomas, 80
PDP. *See* parallel distributed processing
people. *See* real people
Phèdre (Racine), 79
  ambivalence in, 107
  canon continuity of, 105, 107, 192
  character development in, 108
  description of, 195
  emotional response in, 106
  female protagonist growth in, 105, 106
  narrative idiolect in, 106–7
  narrative trajectory on display in, 105, 107–8
  parametric shifts in, 106
  rival protagonists in, 105
  story genres on display in, 107
  usurpation in, 105–6
plot, *See also* emplotment; emplotment, of
    Hamlet; heroic prototype; sacrificial
    prototype
  construction, 52–3, 143
  discourse containing, xix, 138, 142, 161,
    200, 201
  emplotment as formation of, xix–xx
  interest, 142, 143
  nature of, xix
  particularization, 103
  prototypes, 30–2
  revenge, 32, 107, 141, 147, 149
  romantic, 31, 83, 86, 96, 100, 102, 107, 141–2,
    148, 150–1
  seduction, 31–2, 142, 148, 150–1, 156
plural formation, xiv
political function, *See also* socialist activism
  in Brecht's work, 115, 116–17, 118, 119–22,
    196, 197

in Shakespeare's work, 53–4, 61, 69, 189
Porter, Carolyn, 167
possible world's ontology, 1–2
postmodern self-consciousness, 178–9
Poulet, Georges, 192
primed, xii, xiii, 22
priming, 18, 23–4
principles, *See also* alteration principles;
    development principles; evaluation
    principles; linguistic principles and
    parameters theory; metaprinciples;
    specification principles; storytelling,
    principles and parameters of
  metaprinciples governing, 78
  narrative idiolect and clusters of, 109–10
  storytelling functioning of, 78–9
prototypes, *See also* heroic prototype;
    sacrificial prototype
  action trajectories defined by, 14
  alteration principles influencing, 33,
    34–5, 76
  author's mind containing, 27
  character and character functions through,
    27, 35, 36, 75, 79, 187, 192
  cognitive approach treatment of, 46, 188
  combination of, 34–5
  criminal investigation, 32, 121–2
  cross-cultural, xi, xiii, xix, 29–33, 75, 130, 184
  defined, 27
  in *Emma*, 23
  familial separation, xiii, 31, 100, 187
  goal achievement obstacles from, 14, 186
  for guided simulation, 10, 11–12
  as idiolectal, 27
  individual works relation to, xii, 183
  in literary creation, xv
  in literary simulation, 27, 28–9, 187
  material conditions impact on, 14
  motifs and, 29, 33, 187
  narration/story simulation organized by,
    162, 201
  neural networks providing, 78
  particularization of, xvi
  revenge plot, 32, 107, 141, 147, 149
  romantic plot, 31, 83, 86, 96, 100, 102, 107,
    141–2, 148, 150–1
  seduction, 31–2, 142, 148, 150–1, 156
  Shakespeare's use of, 50, 51, 64
  storytelling parameters and, 78
  summary of, 44–5
  variants, 14
Proust, Marcel, 188

theory of mind
  defined, xiv, 13
  Emma exploring capacities of, xv, 17, 21,
      23, 186
  for narrative imagination, i
  opposing views of, 13
  other people understood through, 13, 36
  PDP and, 21
  simulation, 13, 21-2
  simulation and, 13, 186
  task conflict and, 13, 186
time, conflated, 145-6, 150, 154, 156, 200
timing, 138, 145-6, 150, 153, 154, 156
Titus Andronicus (Shakespeare), 69-70
Tobin, Ronald, 80, 193, 194
tragicomedy, 47, 52-3, 69, 72-3, 124, 157, 158
trajectory interruption, 139-40, 144
typological categorization, 37-9

Ulysses (Joyce), xviii, 1-2, 39, 40
Uncle Tom's Cabin (Stowe), xxi, 114

united front tactics, 119-20, 196
universal narrative genres, 29-33, 47-8
usurpation
  as heroic story component, 48, 52-3
  in Racine's plays, 82, 84, 93, 96, 100-1, 104,
      105-6
  in Shakespeare's heroic plays, 54, 56, 58, 62,
      64, 65-7, 69-73, 154

verbal art, 5, 8, 41, 113

Waiting for the Barbarians (Coetzee), 43
war, 54, 56-9
Watson, Robert, 190
Watts, Cedric, 190
Witt, Mary Ann, 198
Woolf, Virginia, xi
Wuerz, Daniela, 111

Zunshine, Lisa, xv, 186
Zwaan, Rolf A., 7

Lightning Source UK Ltd.
Milton Keynes UK
UKHW041421151220
374876UK00009B/83